W9-ATH-161

Shame in Context

Susan B. Miller

THE ANALYTIC PRESS

1996   Hillsdale, NJ   London

Published by
The Analytic Press, Inc.
  Editorial Offices:
  101 West Street
  Hillsdale, NJ 07642

Library of Congress Cataloging-in-Publication Data

Miller, Susan B. (Susan Beth)
    Shame in context / Susan B. Miller.
      p.   cm.
    Includes bibliographical references and index.
    ISBN 0-88163-209-0
    1. Shame.   I. Title.
  BF575.S45M57   1996
  152.4—dc20   96-28331
                                                           CIP

Printed in the United States of America
10 9 8 7 6 5 4 3 2 1

Contents

for my father

Acknowledgments

I came to the study of shame indirectly, through an earlier study of disgust. An advisor, Dick Hertel, thought that research on shame might be a better choice than further exploration of disgust, given the then-burgeoning literature on narcissism. His advice ushered me into an area of study that has sustained my interest for quite a number of years and it directed me to the writing of many colleagues working in the same or related areas. This book is to a considerable extent an analysis and critique of the work of those colleagues and an application of their thinking and my own to clinical data. Thus I am especially grateful to those who have worked to create that body of literature, many of whose names and ideas will be found in the pages that follow. I would especially like to thank Frank Broucek, with whom I corresponded regarding questions raised for me by his 1991 book. He was also kind enough to allow me to discuss a chapter to be published in an upcoming volume edited by Andy Morrison. Thanks, too, to Andy Morrison for generously giving his permission for that discussion and to Léon Wurmser and, again, Frank Broucek, for their willingness to invest their time in writing prepublication reviews of this book.

Writing a book is for the most part a lonely occupation. Concrete help in the drafting of this book came primarily from my cat, Grace, who could not be restrained from some amount of daily typing at my keyboard and from the occasional deletion, when my prose did not suit her. Another form of help a writer needs is a supportive milieu of friends, family, and colleagues who see the work of writing a book as a worthwhile undertaking. In that I have been fortunate in my friends in Ann Arbor and elsewhere, a number of whom are also colleagues. I would like to thank friends and colleagues Irv Leon, Ann Hinton, Maria Sylvester, Jack Novick, Cecily Legg, Teresa Hunt, and Deb and Michael Jackson, as well as Nancy Leon, Amous Maue, Carol Furtado, Amie Casson, and Judith Saltzman, all of whom were willing to listen to many tellings of my progress and reversals with this project.

The primary impetus for this book was my wish to explore how looking at shame in a variety of clinical contexts might provide an opportunity for a critique of some of the current theories of shame. I was particularly interested in bringing to this exploration the idea, shared by many, that while painful emotions such as shame are crucial to early personality structuralization, psychotherapists must look not only at those early instances of shame but also at the role painful emotions play in the ongoing functioning of the adult personality. Though these ideas had long interested me, for a number of years I resisted the impulse to write this book because a previous book had left me well aware of the industry a book required and of the periods of confusion and frustration through which one must persevere. When I approached The Analytic Press with a query, I was quite ready to be dissuaded from proceeding, but Paul Stepansky's early interest in the project I outlined and his confidence in my ability to complete it moved me to attempt a proposal, and from that proposal a draft soon emerged. Through the three drafts that led to the book's completion, Paul provided steady encouragement and a supply of informed and useful questions and observations that nudged me toward fuller development of my thinking. I count myself lucky in having such a capable and congenial editor. The work of Nancy Liguori, Joan Riegel, and others at The Analytic Press was also essential to the publication of this work.

I am especially grateful to my patients, both those discussed and the many others whose treatments helped me to better understand shame as it occurs in the context of individual lives. I hope I have rendered their experiences in ways that are essentially accurate, but with adequate regard for their privacy. I would like finally to thank the many members of my family who have lent support during this project, especially my father, Albert Miller, who has been a fine friend to me and my writing and to whom this book is dedicated, and my sisters Lisa and Laura, whom I cherish. I would like also to remember my aunt, Rose M. Wovell, a source of support during the early phases of this project whose death saddened its later months.

CHAPTER 1

Foundations

It is a cramped little state with no foreign policy,
Save to be thought inoffensive. The grammar of the language
Has never been fathomed, owing to the national habit
Of allowing each sentence to trail off in confusion. . . .
And it must be said of the citizens (muttering by
In their ratty sheepskins, shying at cracks in the sidewalk)
That they lack the peace of mind of the truly humble.
                              —Richard Wilbur ("Shame")

Following a long fallow period, the shame literature entered a season of proliferation. What we have harvested from that span of rapid growth is now sufficient that it seems wise to pause and survey the yield in order to consider which beginnings merit future investment. Therein lies the broad incentive for the present work. A more specific impetus has been a personal impression that the recent explosion of shame literature in psychology, psychoanalysis, and the popular culture has begun to exert a reductionistic effect on clinical thinking. Among shame theorists, the centrality of shame as an acknowledged motive force threatens to skew clinical thinking so that shame is recognized to the exclusion of other emotions, and full regard for the complex clinical phenomena with which it interacts is lost. One sometimes gets the sense that shame is the only emotion that drives human behavior, in which case we are headed toward an overcorrection of the emotion's longstanding neglect.

It would be regrettable if increased sensitivity to one important aspect of life were to dull our perception of others, including some that once were quite apparent, such as the role shame plays in individuals' attempts to circumvent areas of conflict or difficulty or to maintain highly invested fantasies. Guilt, which often shows itself in action and symptom formation more than in feeling, has been an early casualty. In my 1985 book, I argued that shame is not fundamentally a defense but is an expression of narcissistic distress that can be used defensively. I continue to hold that view but am concerned now that the study of defensive, self-protective, and homeostatic functions that shame fulfills

1

has been overshadowed by our valid interest in shame as a primary emotional response, one that is especially implicated in narcissistic disorders.

Expanded interest in shame has led writers to lift it from its varied natural settings in order to hold it up to the light of study. With some notable exceptions, when shame has been studied *in context,* it has been viewed only in the context of narcissism, since its importance there is so conspicuous. While it is necessary and important to think about shame as an entity that preserves certain of its aspects regardless of setting, isolating shame as a subject for study has led to certain distortions in our thinking. These distortions are akin to those that arise when a living thing is removed from the field to the laboratory and examined in isolation from its ecosystem.

In the field of wildlife management, attention is shifting from single-species management to ecosystem management as understanding of the interdependence of living systems grows. Within the mental health sciences, we have concepts such as family systems or intersubjectivity; these ideas emphasize interacting parts of a system, rather than individual components. The present study is an effort to consider shame as a dynamic element within the overall ecology of mental functioning. It is an element that has a place both in sickness and in health and one that cannot be well understood apart from other emotions or from the dynamic dimensions of psychic life, which include conflicts, defenses, adaptations, fantasies and self-protective mechanisms. I begin the present exploration from the point of view that an emotion such as shame is a structure that has multiple functions—or multiple ecological niches, to extend the metaphor—within the individual personality and for communities of individuals as well.

Inquiry is complicated by the fact that shame, like all emotion labels, represents an indistinctly bounded category of feeling and behavior. Wurmser (1981) states and I concur, "This means that shame in its typical features is complex and variable, a range of closely related affects rather than one simple, clearly delimited one. It shades into moods on one side, into attitudes on the other" (p. 17). Though shame has a range of meanings, it always refers to a moment of felt experience or at least to the potential for such experience; thus, it is a level of concept different from those often used in discussions of psychopathology. Frequently, in considering psychological dynamics, we refer to the patient's circumstances in broad terms, saying, for example, that his self-esteem is deficient or that she behaves narcissistically. Emotions may be implied, but they are not stated. The study of shame or of any specified emotion is an attempt to consider actual moments of experience, which we characterize as precisely as possible.

One can question whether some of the emotional experiences writers tend to assemble under "shame"—embarrassment, for example, or humiliation—belong within the same tent at all. Different writers have idiosyncratic ways of dividing the whole. Lewis (1992) tentatively suggests that shame and embarrassment might be considered separate, distinguishable states, but many others (Broucek, 1991) feel that these clearly are variations on a theme. Wurmser (1981) refers to "shame or its cognate feelings of embarrassment and put down, of slight and humiliation, or of shyness, bashfulness, and modesty" (p. 17). The various efforts at categorization have value not because of any likelihood they will yield a final set of categories, but because they represent careful efforts at highlighting the features that characterize particular states and link them with, or differentiate them from, other states.

A recent statistical study by Hibbard (1994) lends support to an inclusive shame category (that subsumes, among other states, disgrace, mortification, shyness, and embarrassment) as one that is meaningful to the average, English-speaking person on the street but is also meaningfully subdividable into factors. It is a similarly inclusive category that I wish to consider in the pages to follow. The decision to explore a comprehensive and imprecise category makes for many difficulties. Accordingly, some writers have narrowed their definitions of shame to focus attention on the particular shame variety related to their area of theoretical interest. For example, Kohut, who was interested in infantile exhibitionism and its relationship to narcissism, looked at the form of shame that occurs when the grandiosity of the narcissistic adult is stimulated. I will attempt to consider shame that develops in diverse clinical and nonclinical contexts and for individuals at different stages of the life cycle, though I do so with some trepidation because the incorporation of so many variables can be treacherous.

Achieving a definition of this indistinct category humans call shame is no easy matter. One feels a bit like a preschooler, in pursuit of a circle, who must repeat his effort over and over, finding that each pass of the crayon inscribes a different form: all one can hope for are decent areas of overlap. Throughout the remainder of this book, I will use *shame* in two ways. First, along with Wurmser, Nathanson, Hibbard, and many others, I use it to designate a family of related emotions. Each member of the family is characterized by an experience of the self as inadequate, or at least in disarray, thus not comfortably exposable to others; also present is the urge to hide, silence, vacate, or instantly reform the disturbed self. The reference to disarray, as opposed to inadequacy, is added to extend the shame category so as to include embarrassment, which is one of the more distinct of the shame subtypes. By *disarray*, I mean a state of disorganization that leaves the person feeling not presentable to others: he may be thinking unclearly, or be half dressed, half asleep, or overexcited. As indicated earlier, some would sever embarrassment from shame altogether, but most treat it as within the shame family because it holds thematic and physiognomic common ground with the other shame group emotions. The shame group of emotions as I define it would include embarrassment, humiliation, self-consciousness, disgrace, and a number of other states, some of which I considered in more detail in my earlier book than I will do here. "Feeling *bad*" fits within the shame group only when the state includes some representation of viewing the bad self and feeling deficient as a consequence of what one perceives.

The inadequate or diminished self of shame is in some instances primarily experienced through a regressive alteration of the behavioral self, for example, slouching, blushing, mumbling, or loss of intellectual acuity. At other times, functional disorder combines with painfully negative *ideas* about the self to produce a composite that is shame. Painful ideas alone may constitute the shame experience; no broad influence on the person's behavioral state need occur. The thread through all varieties of shame experience, including those as divergent as moral shame (i.e., shame over immoral behavior), deep humiliation, and passing embarrassment, is the diminished or disordered self and the self one would wish to hide from others (though one may maintain concurrent wishes to display it). Whenever I do not specify my intended usage, I am using this first, broader meaning of shame as a family of emotions.

The second way in which I will use *shame* will be as the designation for one particular member of the larger group. I think of this type of shame as "shame proper." I hope I will not be accused of generating multiple referents for shame to promote complexity or confusion; I am trying to reflect as accurately as possible the usage of the word shame in our language and literature, which is unfortunately varied and confusing and, to make matters worse, shifts over time (W. Miller, 1993). Shame, in its more restricted usage, is distinct from embarrassment, mortification, humiliation, and other shame variants because of the distinctly reflexive character of the experience. Shame proper is the experience that generates the phrase, to be ashamed *of oneself*. Such a construction is not present for other shame group words. One is not bashful of oneself or humiliated of oneself or shy of oneself or embarrassed of oneself. These other states do, in fact, involve looking at the self or listening to the self and sensing the self as a social being perceivable by others, but used in its narrower sense, shame stands apart in its clearer emphasis on viewing the self and subjecting the self to one's own negative feeling or judgment.

This more restricted version of shame is worth isolating because it calls attention to important human experiences in which a person, in public or in private, considers and judges his own actions and finds them lacking, concluding in the end, "I feel ashamed of myself." My description of shame proper is not likely to call to mind the shame states Kohut and others primarily interested in failed exhibitionism describe. Their shame profiles emphasize the red-faced, overstimulated, socially discomforted state of the person, not the inner experience of self-appraisal. Speaking metapsychologically, Kohut (1972) spoke of "this disorganized mixture of massive discharge (tension decrease) and blockage (tension increase) in the area of exhibitionistic libido which is experienced as shame" (p. 395).

Descriptions of a person suffused both with sensation and emotion, and standing visible to others, make many people, myself included, think of the descriptor *embarrassment,* but others would balk at using that term to refer to Kohut's intended subject matter because, for them, embarrassment connotes a trivial disturbance of equanimity. My own inclination is to say that embarrassment can be trivial or agonizing but is distinguishable from shame proper in the lesser attention to abiding defects of the self. In embarrassment, one is primarily concerned with the visible self, not with a lasting sense of being flawed. So if red-faced, hyperstimulated states of failed exhibitionism bring a judgment of inner defect, however inarticulate in form, then I would classify them as shame proper. If they primarily focus one's attention on the other's watching eyes and on one's current state of psychic disarray, then I am content to call them embarrassment, which in its intensity may be slight or stunning.

Embarrassment is always an excited state of social visibility, and shame proper may be at times, as long as the element of self-judgment is present. Such excited states frequently betray an element of pleasure. Hibbard (1994) groups embarrassment under "libidinous shame." He feels that libido, or pleasure, is implicated in selective shame states, such as embarrassment, because they represent benign, perhaps loving, superego activity through which the conscience gently restricts behavior. But libido is operative in the excited forms of shame in a second way: pleasurable impulses to display the self are alive in the moment. Embarrassment often is accompanied by a blush or laugh that exposes pleasure in the revelation of thoughts, feelings, or body. An example is the young child dashing naked through a room full of adults, in a state of squealing, excited embarrassment. In embarrassment, a person often holds to some sense of pleasure in his activity, while simultaneously responding to social cues (from outside or within) that the performance is questionable in its acceptability. Those cues may lead to shame proper or only to the mix of display and inhibition that constitutes embarrassment. In his observations of young children, Lewis (1992) noted the link between embarrassment and pleasure:

> At the same time they averted their gaze, the children smiled broadly. This smile seems to differentiate embarrassment from shame. Finally, some children nervously touched their bodies with their hands, although they did not cover their faces with their hands. . . . It does appear that embarrassment can be differentiated from shame, at least in some situations [p. 26].

Lewis differentiated two types of embarrassment. One type, akin to shyness, is a discomforted response to exposure but implies no enduring negative self-evaluation. Another type, which Lewis sees as a low intensity form of shame, does involve negative self-judgment.

Unlike the metapsychological definition quoted from Kohut, the working definitions I have offered are phenomenological ones that aim to help us recognize shame as a group of felt experiences. Other definitions might be offered that would emphasize shame's functions: for example, the function of reducing one's interest in engaging with forbidden or dangerous activities or that of encouraging behavior in line with the conduct of the group. In looking at shame in its various contexts, it will be useful to consider both what shame feels like and how it operates and useful to consider as well its functioning at a number of different levels, including, for example, its operation within an economy of emotions, its operation as a species-wide occurrence with adaptive functions, and its operation as an experience that contributes to the individual's sense of self.

Returning now to the broader definition of shame as a family of feelings, we can conceive of the shame emotions as operating within a dynamic personality organization as a school of fish exists within the sea: there is some fluidity of shape and movement within the subject that is our primary focus and within the larger subject that is its context. In order to understand the operation of our subject, we must examine its internal structures and its relations to a variety of contexts.

Because shame is a label writers and researchers attach to a loosely bounded category of experiences and because this set of experiences fills a variety of functions in the individual personality and the social group, writers attempting to define too narrowly the function of shame or the single set of rules for its operation often excite into voice other writers who illuminate alternate functions or exceptions to the rule. For example, Broucek (1991) reflects on the incomplete explanatory power of Kaufman's concept of "the interpersonal bridge" and says, "This is an example of a recurrent problem in existing theories of shame; no theory about the causes, sources, or mechanisms of shame adequately accounts for all characteristics of the shame experience" (p. 22). Broucek goes on to develop a theory of "objectification" that has admirable clarity and organizes much shame data but not all of it. In overgeneralizing the applicability of this concept, he tends to exclude certain important findings regarding shame. His more recent writing on the topic (unpublished chapter) strives to correct this situation.

Many shame theories have been added to the literature in recent years. Like Broucek's, some have come in response to, and refutation of, others. Ways in which the previous theory failed to account for certain shame data are cited as support for the new theory. It has been my impression that quite a number of rather divergent-sounding theories have validity in that they well describe some piece of the whole that is shame, and they astutely examine how such shame operates in one of its various settings. But writers often fail to acknowledge that shame, like any emotion, is the proverbial elephant and that others may have well defined a trunk or tail or torso, whereas one's own exploration has uncovered a tusk; so what may be needed now is something closer to an overall anatomy.

I think of this book then as an integrative effort. I will draw on my own previous work and even more heavily on the work of others, especially those more recent writers whose work synthesizes what has preceded it. The number of writers examined will be limited in order to maintain some focus to the presentation; thus, I will give short shrift to many, especially the earlier writers whose contributions have been well-reviewed elsewhere. My overall aim is to place abstractions up against clinical data and the data of everyday life or life as portrayed within literature, in order to look at how the theories "play" in living contexts. Of course, the various abstractions grew from the soil of such everyday experience, but each writer has brought his own limited experience to his abstracting activity, so here will be an opportunity to hold various writers' abstractions against my own experiential base.

A second aim of this work is to extract points of difference and points of correspondence among important current ideas about shame, again using clinical material to illuminate the discussion. I will also examine shame as it operates within certain groups of individuals outside the consulting room, in the larger context of society, though that topic could support a much more complete treatment than I will give it here. In the last chapter, I will range further from the book's central concern with pathology and personality dynamics and make use of some concepts from allied disciplines in order to consider shame and the affiliated emotion, pride, as elements in the gift commerce that is basic to human relationships, including that of psychotherapy. That final chapter will also concern itself with creativity as it relates to the notion of "giftedness," which, in turn, bears on the concept of wealth as a source of pride and honor.

Instead of utilizing the generic "he" throughout the book, as has been customary until recent years but slights the female half of the population, I will alternate chapters, using "he" in the present chapter when referring to an unspecified therapist or patient, "she" in the next, and so on.

EARLIEST SHAME-RELEVANT EXPERIENCES

We can begin in this first chapter by laying out and discussing a number of writers' ideas, especially those propositions concerned with shame's inborn (hard-wired) aspects or with its early development. In many points of this discussion, I will be sounding a keynote to be further developed in one or more of the clinical contexts, the discussion of which will comprise the bulk of later chapters.

It may be helpful first to clarify some general assumptions I make about personality. I assume that human actions are motivated by strong inclinations to use inherent, unfolding capabilities, both privately and in engaging with the environment. These innate capabilities are reflected in behavior that is motor, intellectual, sensory, and expressive. The effective use of basic capabilities contributes to experiencing a sense of meaning in life.

If allowed reasonably free use of his repertoire of capabilities, the maturing child develops a highly valued and complex sense of self that is both a direct experience of that child's own being-in-action (including inner action such as thinking, action in relation to things, and interaction with other human beings) and a set of concepts about "my self." Included among those self-concepts are images of the person interacting with others and images of the person as seen by others. In employing inclinations to engage the environment, the growing child also comes to value the objects in his surround, especially the other human beings, who provide a wealth of stimulation and in most cases comfort, as well as supplying feedback that continues to define the self and its qualities and value.

Each of the many unfolding capabilities to which I refer is narrower in scope and more behaviorally specific than the broad sexual and aggressive impulses that Freud and others have posited. I would see aggression not as a primary, discrete impulse, but as a derivative of the inclination to use an array of more circumscribed motor, communicative, and other endowments, both for the pleasure in their employ and to engage and influence the environment. Aggression might arise from a wish to experience one's fullest impact on something outside the self (and so a baby bangs a pot as loudly as he can) or from frustration of an effort at making an impression (Mother removes the pot and Baby protests), so that one must intensify one's efforts. Aggression also follows from incurring hurt, which leads to energetic protection of the self. I am comfortable with Wurmser's (1981) "partial instincts," delophilia and theatophilia, because they are fairly behaviorally specific and concern interactions between subject and environment: they are, respectively, the instinct to show the self and the instinct to look attentively in order to absorb what is outside.

The reference to incurring hurt introduces another assumption about the human organism, which is the supposition that human beings are endowed not only with action inclinations, but also with an array of fairly predictable response tendencies that are stimulated by action initiated outside the person, in relation to him. Emotional expressions, such as shame, have obvious aspects that categorize them as response inclinations, but as development proceeds, they evolve elements that place them with action tendencies as well.

When I refer in subsequent discussion to a person striving toward a whole or true or genuine self (or when I adopt Broucek's [1991] term "indwelling self"), I am not assuming a fixed, biologically determined, invariable core self (though certain givens of temperament and capability undoubtedly exist as limiting factors); I mean, instead, to designate the state of freedom to respond to situations with awareness of one's feelings and opinions, which, in turn, implies the absense of high levels of anxiety that might interfere with such contact. This notion of a genuine self assumes that the self changes over time so that the same situation may elicit very different responses on different occasions; each response constitutes "the genuine self" given the present state of the person. The genuine self is an amalgamation of endowment and experience. I recognize that the concept advanced here is not without theoretical problems, but I am striving only for a working concept, not an airtight definition. It may be of help here to recall a few of Winnicott's (1965) words describing the "true self":

> If the mothering is not good enough then the infant becomes a collection of reactions to impingements, and the true self of the

infant fails to form or becomes hidden behind a false self. . . . It is the well-cared-for babies who quickly establish themselves as persons, each different from any other infant that ever was, whereas the babies who received inadequate or pathological ego support tend to be alike in patterns of behaviour [p. 17].

The notion of self associated with concepts such as true self and false self is different from certain other uses of "self" I will employ. For example, when I refer to the "diminished sense of self" associated with shame, the emphasis is on the self as a group of images to which positive and negative evaluation attaches and on the self constructed from proprioception of one's physical and postural states and states of mental coherence or disarray. So a diminished sense of self might be the experience of suddenly seeing oneself as cowardly, while also feeling one's slumped posture and confused thoughts. The self is diminished in the value one assigns to it and in the organization of its activities.

I return now to the task of tracking shame's developmental course in order to help us understand the breadth of experiences that come to cluster under a single heading. As a child moves from the first months of life through stages of cognitive and social development, more complex forms of shame become possible, and the ideational elements of shame proliferate. It is my sense that, while the connecting threads of self-consciousness and self-in-disarray continue to be traceable, shame experience significantly changes by assuming new complexity in its construction and operation.

The "basic affects" theorists, exemplified by Tomkins (1963, 1987), Izard (1971), and Nathanson (1987, 1992), would disagree with my assessment that shame *changes* through development and with the idea that the shame concept covers a variety of experiences; these writers see shame as a well-boundaried, core "affect" that, at any given moment, is either occurring or not occurring, switched on or switched off (Nathanson, 1992, p. 61). The core affect appears in early childhood and remains unaltered throughout life. All of shame's variance is explained as differences in "intensity" of the affect or through the various ideas that associate with the affect as it is triggered over and over in different settings. Representing this group, Nathanson (1987) states:

Each of these innate affects has its own subcortical "address," or location in the brain, that contains the affect "program." Each is triggered by discrete activators of affect. Tomkins' theory is brain-centered, not mind-centered; thus he postulates that the seven affect-pairs named above are triggered by the way information enters a central assembly system through neural pathways [p. 13].

Tomkins (1987) himself says:

> Discouragement, shyness, shame, and guilt are identical as affects, though not so experienced because of differential coassembly of perceived causes and consequences. Shyness is about strangeness of the other; guilt is about moral transgression; shame is about inferiority; discouragement is about temporary defeat; but the core affect in all four is identical, although the coassembled perceptions, cognitions, and intentions may be vastly different [p. 143].

The complex cognitive elements of many shame experiences are understood by affect theorists to be *add-on's* to the hypothetical "core affect"; they are not integral to it. And the multiple shame words found in many languages (e.g., in English, shame, humiliation, embarrassment, mortification, self-consciousness, feeling ridiculous or pathetic) are often seen as obscuring the essential common ground, the basic affect—shame. Within this theory, cognitive and affective aspects of experience are quite separable. Representing this point of view, Kaufman (1989) states:

> Having so many different names for its various manifestations has hindered recognition of the underlying *affect* of shame present in each of these disturbing inner states. . . . A variety of inner states have been distinguished, given different labels, and so mistakenly conceived as distinctly different: *discouragement, self-consciousness, embarrassment, shyness, shame, and guilt* [p. 22].

While the notion of a discrete number of basic affects, each with its own subcortical address, is respectable as a theory, and while some inherited, affect-related structures surely do exist and do influence our categorization of feeling, I have not seen much persuasive data or analysis suggesting that hard-wired brain organization *fully establishes a set number of affect categories.* Michael Lewis (1992) has researched emotional expression in early life. He notes that "emotional expressions rarely bear a one-to-one correspondence to internal states" [p. 20]. This observation suggests that there is more flux and variability in the emotion system than the affect theorists imply. If there were nine basic affects, invariable in form, that are either switched on or switched off, one would expect that a switched-on emotion regularly would bring a switched-on expression, especially given that affect theorists often list facial expressions as among the defining characteristics of affects. It also seems reasonable to argue that, if a set number of basic affects were the primary organizers of our emotional experience, it should be less difficult than it is to agree on their number and characteristics.

Looking at the data of ordinary emotional life, I have difficulty with the basic emotions viewpoint for a number of reasons. First, I believe the various shame-related words designate significant differences in experience that are not well explained through a structure composed of a core affect plus accumulated ideas. I refer the reader to William Miller's book *Humiliation* (1993) for a sample analysis of the differences among humiliation, embarrassment, and shame proper, or to my own 1985 book. There is common ground among the shame family emotions, no doubt, and it is on that terrain that many studies of generic shame are built, but I am thus far not persuaded that the shared ground is best represented by the notion of a core affect.

A second objection to the basic affects theory derives from the observation that the emotion words available in various languages fail to map the entire terrain of emotional experience; for precision in expressing feelings, we often have need of a specific metaphor that defines a feeling by describing a situation that would, for most people, elicit it. If all affect experiences fell neatly into one of nine classifications, one would think that designating the appropriate label for a feeling would go farther than it does in conveying the essentials of an experience. W. Miller (1993) joins others before him, including William James (1890), who have talked about those experiences not well described by labels. During many subtle moments of feeling, none of the basic affects announces its presence.

W. Miller (1993) also talks about emotion words as summary terms that misleadingly can group somewhat dissimilar experiences and offer the illusion of sameness where there is, in fact, much difference:

> But surely having a word or a ready-made concept must affect our emotional life. Convenient easy simplex emotion terms or phrases,

it seems, tend to act as evaluative magnets. The existence of the concept and term, say, of anger might cause us to ignore the differences between closely related hostile feelings and lump them together. Such terms also save us the work of having to think all that precisely about how we feel. They tend to make us subsume our emotional states, or at least our understanding of our emotional states, into the ready-made category the word provides. Emotion terms, like words, generalize and in the process fuzz over a lot of individual variation [p. 101].

The basic affects theorist would say that neglect of core affects means missing the forest for the trees. But one could argue as well that the unproven notion of basic affects encourages the kind of "fuzzing over" to which Miller refers, which leads us to miss the trees.

When basic affects theorists attempt to use the dual concepts of intensity and cognitive add-on's to explain experiential differences between states presumptively sharing a core affect, their arguments often contradict an intuitive grasp of emotional reality. For example, Tomkins's (1963) nine basic affects are expressed as affect pairs (e.g., interest/excitement forms a pair, as does enjoyment/joy), with one term in the pair representing the weaker expression of the affect, the other the stronger. His shame pairing is shame/humiliation, but careful investigations of humiliation (S. Miller, 1988; W. Miller, 1993) suggest that differing intensity does not best characterize the relationship between humiliation and shame. In fact, to describe the difference between the two using the terms of affect theory, we would fare better invoking the notion of different "coassembled perceptions, cognitions, and intentions" (Tomkins, 1987, p. 143).

Guilt, incidentally, represents a problem for the basic affects theories. Guilt does not appear in Tomkins's list, which is accepted by Nathanson; thus, it would have to derive from another basic affect, through cognitive elaboration or shift in intensity. Nathanson (1992) recognized the problem and determined that guilt is a coassembly of shame and fear (p. 144). Yet it has neither the physiology nor the physiognomy of either and to my knowledge, has no distinct physical features of its own. Lewis (1992) agrees that shame and guilt differ significantly, but he assigns guilt some unique physical characteristics, which I have not personally noted. He says, "Whereas in shame we see the body hunched over itself in an attempt to hide and disappear, in guilt we see individuals moving in space as if trying to repair their action. The postural differences that accompany shame and guilt are marked" (p. 176).

Guilt presumes an understanding that one's behavior can harm another or can do damage through violation of a valued standard. If such recognition brings only a concern about the self—that is, a concern about what kind of person I am to have done such a thing—then we are talking about the variety of shame I call moral shame, not about guilt. But if the concern is for doing "wrong" in violating a valued standard or for the injury to another, which implies empathy for the other's suffering, then guilt is the appropriate term. Empathy is an underexplored foundation of guilt. Guilt and shame are distinct thematically as well as physically.

Another major problem with the basic affects approach is its division of experience into affect plus cognition. W. Miller (1993) addresses this age-old question of whether affect can be separated from cognition when he states:

> Universalists on this issue might argue that the internal feeling of fear is uniform across cultures, and that culture affects only how we will act and think when we are fearful. But how can we get at this feeling ridded of its cultural and cognitive baggage to know? . . . If consciousness of a feeling changes that feeling, then cross-cultural variations in how emotions are conceptualized, or in whether certain emotions are conceptualized at all in language, should affect the way people feel [p. 99].

My objection to the basic affects theorists is less with their innate affects hypothesis than with the notion that such a hypothesis has great explanatory power with regard to adult emotional experience. Efforts to bridge the gap between nine hypothetical, core affects and the complexities of later experience often do violence to the reality of that later experience, especially when they render insignificant the variability of experience that ordinary language, or metaphor, strives to express. The spirit of my criticism of the "additive" theories of emotion is captured in the following passage by Hyde (1979):

> When we say that "the whole is greater than the sum of its parts," we are usually speaking of things that "come alive" when their elements are integrated into one another. We describe such things

by way of organic metaphors because living organisms are the prime example. There is a difference in kind between a viable organism and its constituent parts, and when the parts become the whole we experience the difference as an increase, as "the whole is greater" [p. 150].

It is possible that the basic affects theory is partially correct but is too simplistic a brain model to account for the full range of human emotional experience. What might be needed is an affect theory allowing for interaction among several systems. One system might generate simple, stereotyped, largely facial and gestural responses—which we share to some extent with other species—while a second system, equally tied to the nervous system, would allow us to experience a great variety of internally and externally stimulated sense impressions, thoughts, and feelings. Also entering the mix of contributions to emotional life would be inherent, human category-forming activities that lead us to divide experience into pairings such as good and bad, self and nonself, weak and strong. The stereotyped, inherited aspects of emotion experience and emotion expression (e.g., blushing and gaze aversion in shame) would represent only one of a number of contributions to our categorizing of emotional life. The systems would operate simultaneously so that felt experience would be shaped by the interactions between them.

Anthropologists Kirkpatrick and White (1985) share their doubts about overvaluing of emotion categories that are based on facial displays, as follows:

Some analysts treat emotion words as labels for physiological states or related facial expressions. They can find, in different cultures, highly replicable human abilities to typify certain behavioral displays (Ekman, 1973). . . . The recognition of a behavioral display as meaningful depends on inferential processes that mediate perception and categorization. The cultural meaning and behavioral implications of emotions depend, we submit, far more on such reasoning about social contexts of emotion than on classification of a few displays (cf. Averill, 1980) [p. 17].

Having aired some objections to the notion of hard-wired basic emotions that emerge fully formed at specifiable points in development and remain unchanged, I return to the hypothesis that shame is presently best conceived as a category of experiences that evolves as development proceeds. The capacity to experience shame presumably originates with whatever wiring of brain and body underlies the range of self-diminishing physical responses (lowering the head, covering the face, slouching, garbling one's speech, clouding one's thoughts), and it begins as well with the potential for feeling incompetent as an agent or "I." Individual behaviors, sensations, or thoughts ultimately organized under the heading "shame" may be experienced earlier in development than are the various shame gestalts, by which I mean the fuller experiences that adults are willing to label shame (or one of its cognates).

Broucek (1991) does a good job of getting at some of the earliest manifestations of shame-related experience when he talks about the alterations in the *sense of self* that may occur when an infant is ineffective in its actions. We can resume the discussion of the developmental history of shame with consideration of his observations.

Broucek argues, as have others, that the sense of self long antedates the *concept* of self. He states:

> [T]he earliest sense of self grows out of the experience of efficacy, fulfilled intentionality, and the joy and excitement attendant on that experience. The sense of self at the bodily level is grounded in patterns of kinesthetic "flows" that flesh out volitional activity [p. 27].

Here and elsewhere, Broucek suggests that the earliest sense of self consists only of positive experience, but an inquiry to him on this point (personal communication) led him to clarify his view that painful experience, too, contributes to the sense of self.

Broucek's views on infancy raise a number of questions that, in my estimation, remain open issues about an infant's early experience. He argues that infants experience inefficacy mainly in the interpersonal sphere (e.g., a baby fails to elicit a smile or other signs of engagement from a caregiver). The infant may generalize from the interpersonal sphere to other areas of endeavor, such as motor performance, but it is the emotional exchange between human beings that awakens the sense of failure and shame. One can join Broucek in arguing that failure, for the baby, is limited to interpersonal exchange; therefore, so is shame. Or one can hold that only those failures that occur in the interpersonal sphere initially elicit shamelike emotion because of inborn differences in meaning between interpersonal and noninterpersonal experience. I find the latter argument more persuasive, since observation suggests that early failures at motor tasks bring emotional response, such as frustration and distress, once the baby is able to conceive of a motor intention.

There is ongoing debate within the literature as to whether the incipient forms of shame do refer exclusively to interpersonal failure, as Broucek supposes, or whether they may refer to failure that occurs without reference to the interpersonal. Nathanson, following Sylvan Tomkins, insists that shame is not fundamentally social, but responds instead to any frustration of the positive emotions of engagement, which Tomkins labels "interest-excitement" and "contentment-joy." Nathanson (1992) states unequivocally, "[M]any sober investigators have assumed that shame is at core a social emotion. It is not" (p. 170). He offers the following as an example of shame unrelated to social exchange:

> In order to anticipate the performance of a task the child must conceptualize it as a pattern. Inability to perform in accordance with this pattern forms a new, non-matching pattern. To the extent that the child remains interested in or excited by the task, the disparity between the internalized, hoped-for pattern and the actual pattern created by its behavior now acts as an impediment to interest and triggers shame affect. Painfully, for shame is an extremely uncomfortable affective experience, interest is reduced and the child thus encouraged to focus on other activities [p. 169].

There are a number of points to question in Nathanson's exposition, including the core idea that shame incurred around one task encourages refocusing onto another (and is designed by nature expressly for that purpose), but let me limit the present consideration to the question of whether shame is fundamentally social in nature. Nathanson, echoing Tomkins, says no. In contrast, Broucek (1991) says, "It seems indisputable that shame is about the self and its social context and is reflective of a disturbance in the sense of self as well as a disturbance in the nature of the relationship with the other" (p. 21).

It is my own best guess that while some diminishing of the confident sense of self would accompany a baby's failures and frustrations at motor or cognitive tasks, the feeling of being suddenly and personally diminished and wanting to hide (i.e., shame) depends on our sense of existing for another as a center of initiative who is seen and judged. Our love for others and longing for their warmth and communion stand apart from other loves and longings that characterize human life. The parts of the self that awaken only in the embrace of others surely contribute mightily to the texture of shame feeling. Failure may remain frustration in an asocial context but may become unmistakable as shame in a social context.

Alternatively, it might be hypothesized that ongoing interpersonal experience must awaken an investment in "myself" before shame will be possible but that, once such development has occurred, shame may be sparked whenever the valued self fails, whether interpersonally or in other endeavors. Therefore, the young child whose exchanges with caregivers have stirred in him the pride of eliciting desired responses will be capable of a shame-like diminishing of confidence when he cannot open a gate behind which his favorite toy sits. Whether they occur in response to other humans or to failed interactions with the nonhuman environment, I will call those shame experiences that depend on a proximal environmental stimulus *reactive shame*. The term is intended to highlight the environmental event that precedes and precipitates the shame feeling. I assume that all early shame feelings belong within this category, as do some later shame experiences. A boy embarrassed when a friend says, "You run like a girl," experiences reactive shame, as does an adult shamed when an instructor says, "You cheated on your last test."

We can state without doubt that, later in development, shame appears in response to all kinds of failed efforts, social and otherwise, but those later, nonsocial forms of shame do not weigh on the present argument about the origins of shame because later shame experiences build on the child's ability to take himself as an object, which would not exist during the early months. Since the bifurcated self of later development *internalizes relatedness*, a social aspect of shame may be present even in apparently nonsocial shame experiences. Once self relates to self as to another, shame over a failed effort to fix a faucet may not be at its root the shame of task failure; it may be the shame of the person saying to himself, "What is the matter with you that you cannot fix a faucet?" The critical, shaming other is speaking from within.

As a comparison and contrast with Nathanson's theory, we can consider Schore (1994), who, like Nathanson and Tomkins, sees shame as a response designed by nature to reduce interest in a highly interesting object. Schore's thinking seems consistent with Kohut's but is more specific about the developmental setting for the earliest instances of shame. Schore states:

> In contrast to affect attunement that promotes omnipotence and grandiosity (Stern, 1985), the visually transmitted misattunement of shame during reunions after early separation events uniquely and specifically acts as a brake on the developing child's narcissistic desire to be constantly at the center of his parents' attention [p. 208].

Considering internalization, Schore goes on to say, "[T]he mental image of the misattuned face of the mother engenders a rapid brake of arousal and the onset of an inhibitory state" (p. 210).

Schore differs from Nathanson and Tomkins and comes closer to Broucek in tying shame specifically to frustration with the caregiver. According to his schema, shame is stimulated when a practicing-period baby (Mahler, Pine, and Bergman, 1975), having ventured away from Mother, returns to Mother in a state of high excitement, desiring a mirroring response. If the mother's response does not mirror the baby's "hyperaroused grandiosity and exhibitionism," but is "misattuned," the child is imagined to feel shame, which is a painful disruption of interest and excitement and a state of "hypoarousal." Schore sees this inevitable toddler–mother sequence as adaptively valuable if handled well by the mother. The sensitive mother recognizes the baby's distress, comforts the ashamed baby, and rekindles his interest, but at a less excited and omnipotent, and therefore more adaptive, level. Schore's theory contrasts with Nathanson's and Tomkins's in associating the pain of shame with reduced sympathetic nervous system activity, whereas Nathanson (1987, pp. 13–14), incorporating Tomkins's theory, talks of decreased "stimulus density" as pleasurable. I believe Nathanson is less specific than Schore about the particular brain systems aroused or quieted.

Schore's theory is wedded to Kohut's concepts of normal infantile omnipotence and hyperaroused exhibitionism. Schore's theory also depends on the tight linkage between a specific infantile state (exhibitionism) and a particular set of maternal responses (misattunement). Though Schore is clear in his view that the practicing period represents the height of infantile exhibitionism, I share Broucek's uncertainty (unpublished chapter) as to why

Schore is convinced of the crucial association between shame and the mother–child reunions of that era. In articulating his critique, Broucek cites personal communication with Michael Lewis in which Lewis "has failed to elicit shame reactions through interruptions of activities of joyful or excited children." The relevance of that data to Schore's hypothesis would depend on the age of the children and the manner of interruption, that is, whether or not it was the mother who interrupted the child's activity.

In looking at shame as part of our earliest social experience, Broucek (1991) sees the infant's sense of inefficacy as primarily a response to being met with what he calls the still-face adult, the adult from whom a responsive gaze cannot be elicited. He states that, "The still-face gaze is the prototype of what will become the objectifying gaze, the gaze that denies or ignores one as a subject or self and recognizes only one's surface behavior or material aspects" (p. 36). An example of a developmentally later form of shaming objectification is the parent who relates to a child solely in terms of his grades or looks, never his inner experience, or the worker who knows his colleague only as someone who produces X amount of product per day, not as a person with thoughts and feelings.

In language more dramatic than Broucek's, Wurmser (1981) comments on infant experience that would seem at least to approximate Broucek's notion of developmentally early shame elicited by the still-face gaze. Wurmser asks, "What are the basic and archaic fears in shame?" (p. 83). He answers:

> Provisionally it can be said they are loss of the object and, with it, loss of the self. The other person turns away in contempt. Contempt removes the right of presence and even of existence. He who is not loved stops loving himself; he feels he is "a nothing," "empty," "frozen"—"like a stone." The basic fear to be feared is this total object loss and self-loss [p. 83].

Wurmer's description of early, reactive shame experience is based on psychoanalytic reconstruction and tends to be more particularized than Broucek's. It focuses on the sense of void created by loss of the other, not only on the disturbed sense of self. Wurmser also makes clear that he imagines such early shame experience to have, at times, a catastrophically painful or traumatic impact, whereas Broucek is not so explicit about the reverberations of the experience. One does learn from Broucek that repeated early experience of shame leads to alienation from the subjective self, which he calls the "indwelling self," a descriptor I find useful as long as we attend to the usage provisos mentioned earlier.

Broucek talks of the still-face adult; Wurmser considers the other turned away in "contempt." One must also think of the caregiver showing disgust or a scowling face. A friend reported her first observation of shame in her baby when she shouted at him angrily after he bit her arm, at age 17 months. Somewhat different alterations in the early sense of self might follow from each kind of disjunctive interaction with another. The emotional response presumably would reflect whether rejection took the form of disgust, contempt, indifference, or anger, but a baby likely would respond to each of these interpersonal situations with some disruption of the confident sense of self. All such reductive alterations in the sense of self would be early experiences relevant to shame.

Nathanson (1992) comments, "I suspect that shame produces a *sense of an incompetent self,* that there is a part of the self created by shame" (p. 210). Nathanson is arguing that the experience of the shame affect precedes and generates the sense of incompetence and not vice-versa, as some might contend, and not that the two are inextricable, as I might argue, but the comment nevertheless returns us to the general notion of task failure linked with shame. The word *incompetent* implies a task one is unable to perform, as does Broucek's (1991) emphasis on "failed intent or inefficacy" (p. 30). In Broucek's schema, early shame would include representation of an ineffectual self, paired with an unengageable other.

It is interesting that, while Broucek (1979, 1982,1991) emphasizes "inefficacy" as the source of early shame, he strongly disputes Basch's (1988) view that "the standard by which one judges one's own competence or incompetence is always internal, not external" (p. 59). It seems to me that efficacy would be judged by internal standards in the way that Nathanson (1992) articulates: one compares the actual outcome of a situation with an internally conceived, desired outcome. Thus, if the problem with the mother's still face gaze is that one intended to produce a smile but was ineffective in that effort and got this other face instead, the criterion for failure and shame is internal. If on the other hand, the problem with the still face gaze or the scowling or disgusted face is not primarily its conflict with one's intent but is, instead or additionally, its own, independent communication about what the child means to its mother, then we might say that the criterion for shame sometimes is external.

The clearest example of the notion of externally stimulated shame would be the image of a mother scowling at a child, who instantly drops his eyes in shame. No intention to produce a smile was present, and no specific failure has occurred; all that has happened is that the child read in his parent's expression a statement of his own worth. The internal–external distinction actually breaks down and loses meaning insofar as external judgments, such as a mother's angry face, are meaningful only if they encounter some internal life that finds them disturbing.

What remains meaningful is the idea of intent. Broucek's infant actively seeks a facial response he is not getting. Were Broucek to consider an infant at play surprised by an obviously punishing gaze (e.g., disgusted or contemptuous), there would be less need for the idea of intent. While I believe that intentionality, which ushers in the experiences of success and failure, sets up a greater likelihood of shame, a broadly conceived shame theory would allow for shame without antecedent intent on the part of the child.

Also relevant to the intentional infant is Wurmser's (1981) work on the earliest experiences of what he calls "unlovability," a complex concept that is meant to have as its experiential root the infant's sense of being rebuffed in its active use of its eyes to take in the world with great curiosity and in its proud display of face, voice, and body. Wurmser's work differs from Broucek's in a number of regards, including the major emphasis on the infant's looking and showing. Broucek is more general about infant behavior and refers only to the child's "intention" of engaging the other. Wurmser emphasizes the complex conflicts that can develop over the use of looking and showing if these activities become increasingly invested with aggression due to the frustration of their aims. He also describes a range of infantile emotional states that constitute the responses to punishment of drive activity; these states include withdrawal and freezing-type responses that Wurmser sees as part of the earliest shame phenomenology. He places them under the heading, "shame anxiety."

In Wurmser's formulation about unlovability, the child is imagined to draw the conclusion he is "unlovable," which means that his core activities (especially looking and showing), which are designed to give him power in relation to others, instead bring helplessness and rejection. The choice of the word *unlovability* may be an unfortunate one to describe such early experience in that it is a broadly implicative summary term better suited to later development, but Wurmser's more specific notions about what happens in infancy are plausible. I will further consider the concept of unlovability in Chapter Six.

Another way to get at some of what Wurmser approaches is to say that shame is about being and also about not being. Certain ways of being bring rejecting responses from others, which create shame. But if one shrinks or withdraws or freezes the self in order not to offend the other, that anticipatory diminishing of the self, that nonbeing, is also experienced as shame. So shame has a dual nature and pertains both to flawed expression and to inhibition of expression, to being wrong and to not being. The two experiences converge if one sees the shame that is responsive to being wrong as an effort not to be (in order not to be wrong). I will further explore this area in connection with obsessive-compulsive contexts for shame and, in Chapter Six, in conjunction with Kinston's (1980, 1982, 1983, 1987) ideas about shame and the abandonment of self.

Other theories of shame as a response to early developmental events have been put forward, for example, Spero's (1984) conceptualization of defensive splitting of self-representations and object representations, to be considered in Chapter Six.

THE SELF-STOPPING FUNCTIONS OF SHAME

In his pioneering work on affect theory, Tomkins (1963) argued that shame counters the affects of engagement by allowing a person to reduce emotional involvement with a person or other stimulus when the interaction ceases to satisfy. Many theorists arrive at one or another version of this conclusion; however, we need to be careful in applying the idea universally because the disrupted, weakened self of shame can lead, at times, to a highly engaged and aggressive protest response against a shaming other, which may link experiences of impeded engagement with narcissistic rage. Nevertheless, Tomkins is getting at something important, something that represents one of the warp threads that bind a number of shame theories.

As we enter the realm of adaptive and defensive functions of shame, we should note that the idea of shame as inhibitory to engagement fits within a long tradition. Freud (1908) saw shame as a reaction-formation against the sexual instinct, stating, for example, "Even before puberty, extremely energetic repressions of certain instincts have been effected under the influence of education, and mental forces such as shame, disgust and morality have been set up, which, like watchmen, maintain these repressions" (p. 45). For Freud, shame stopped the internal experience of certain mental contents and presumably stopped as well any behavior that might follow from unfettered sexual thoughts. Shame was understood to counter promiscuity and incest, which could erode the cohesion of a community. Kohut (1972) saw shame as a response to flooding exhibitionism and grandiosity. He recognized in shame both a discharge element and an inhibitory or self-stopping element. Knapp (1967) talked about shame "curbing" the sexual instinct. More recently, Schore (1994) has portrayed shame interrupting the infant's excited attempts to engage the mother.

Though there is common ground among them, it is important to note that the stopping of activity to which Tomkins, Schore, Freud, Kohut, Knapp, and others refer varies considerably with regard to the maturity of the child, the nature of the impediment to ongoing activity, and the type of behavior that is moderated. For example, Freud's stopping is an activity of the latency child's superego, one that depends largely on identifications made with the controlling functions of parents. Freud is imagining a relatively mature human being trying to maintain good human relations and stay on acceptable terms with his conscience by damming problematic instincts through emotions such as shame, disgust, and piety. In contrast, Kohut sees shame as an automatic mechanism that intervenes when the ego senses danger from unmirrored and unmodified exhibitionism and grandiosity. The shame Schore examines originates in the mother–child dyad during the separation-individuation phase (practicing period subphase, 12–18 months). He argues that, by restricting the child's exhibitionism, shame accommodates the child to caregiver responses that are different from those sought or imagined; shame requires the child to confront the limits of his power. Because Tomkins conceives of shame as a hard-wired, invariant affect designed by nature to reduce many forms of interest and excitement, he sees shame occurring in various developmental phases, with many different concerns at issue for the child.

Kinston (1987) also considers a self-stopping aspect of shame. Following Lichtenstein, he believes that human beings struggle to varying degrees with regressive and destructive urges to "abandon psychic life altogether." He conjectures that shame "developed as a signal that such an urge is about to be given in to" (p. 243). There is an implication here that the availability of shame as a signal of such imminent regression can be utilized by the individual as a spur to behaviors that arrest the destructive response, though this line of thinking is not well developed by Kinston, who tends to portray shame as signaling a decompensatory event that occurs ineluctably. We shall later see that Kinston differs from other theorists in conceptualizing shame as a transitional state located on the border between two distinct types of self-organization.

In considering not just the adaptive and defensive functions of shame, but the felt experience and all that follows from that variety of consciousness (including further, complex efforts at adaptation and defense), we need to add that shame stops not just the behaviors of confident interaction, but curtails as well the internal experience of confidence. So shame can be thought of both as a stopping of the self and as the proprioception of that stopping. One is stopped, behaviorally, and one feels oneself unable to think clearly or move decisively or act confidently.

Returning now to Tomkins's basic affects theory as one of the many self-stopping theories of shame, we note that Broucek (1991) is critical of Tomkins's highly inclusive notion that *any* impediment to positive affect brings shame as a means of discouraging unrewarding engagement. Broucek comments that one does not feel ashamed if the electrical power fails in the house when one is avidly following a sports event (p. 21). My own impression is that shame only occurs if events are experienced as reflecting on the value of the self. The average adult has no expectation that he should be able to control the electrical power supply to his television, so he feels only frustration, not shame, if the power goes out. But a person who believes that to exercise less than perfect control over his environment signifies personal deficiency might indeed feel shame if his electrical power failed during a televised basketball game. The friend whose 17-month-old baby showed shame when she shouted at him for biting her explained his behavior by saying that her son knew he shouldn't bite her (she had told him "no" many times), and he felt he had "hurt our relationship." In other words, the baby had a sense that his mother's anger reflected on him, on what he had done. Her anger signified something about his active being.

The notion that shamelike feeling can occur in infancy rests, I believe, on the assumption that certain events in the infant's purview speak to the worth of the self and that an impression of being valuable or devalued can be gained by the infant well before an abstract concept of self matures. This notion intersects Broucek's discussion (unpublished) of intentionality in that intention implies some expectation of influence on one's self or one's surround; there is an associated notion that the failure vis-à-vis such expectation would diminish the self. As stated earlier, I would argue that the self can feel diminished even in the absence of a specific intention, but the child must feel that the self is implicated in the events, either through failed intention or because the caregiver's emotion (for example, disgust) evokes a sense that the self is somehow in the wrong, even if doing nothing and seeking nothing.

LATER DEVELOPMENTS

A crucial development in the movement toward the *adult range* of shame reactions is the establishment of a concept of "me" or "myself" as a boundaried center of thoughts, feelings, and actions, which can be seen, characterized in words and ideas, and judged. Broucek (1991) and others call this developmental achievement "objective self-awareness (OSA)," which means "an awareness of oneself as an object for others and, through the mirroring of the observing others, taking oneself as an object of reflection (objectifying oneself)" (p. 37). Broucek's definitional statement contains the interesting, if debatable, assumption that the child takes itself as an object of reflection only secondary to recognizing such objectifying activity in the other and not as a partially independent function of maturation, but I will not further explore this set of ideas here.

Broucek (1991) probes the experience of objective self-awareness and its shame significance. He believes that the child's awareness that it exists as a definable, visible object for others represents a normative shame crisis. Even without negative judgments from others, the recognition that I am an object, that I exist for others as an object exists, may constitute a shameful diminishing of self. Broucek states:

Objective self-awareness has a derealizing and a depersonalizing function in that it turns the child away from what he immediately is, in order to direct him toward what he sees and imagines himself to be, or could be. The individual is thus transformed from an effective, centered being to a being entranced by an imaginal self or an ideal self; there is a primary dissociation here [p. 42].

Paired with the notion of primary dissociation, Broucek introduces the notion of "primary communion," the state preceding objective self-awareness, during which self and other are apprehended directly, through the life of feelings, thoughts, and senses, rather than being known through comparison with images and standards. Though his term is somewhat reminiscent of Mahler's notion of symbiosis, Broucek does not refer to Mahler's disputed developmental concepts and, in fact, seems to be thinking along different lines, since his emphasis is less on the early fusion of self and other and more on the initial absence of an objective sense of the self. According to Broucek, the loss of primary communion is experienced as a "fault," a term he explores for its reference both to a breach in continuity (within the self-experience and the self–other relationship) and its suggestion of defect. Learning that we exist as objects for others is experienced as deficiency or shamefulness (p. 44), and "to repair that fault then becomes the life project" (p. 45).

One can debate the notion that loss of primary communion is invariably experienced as a defect. Whether the child's newfound status as an object brings shame or pride or whether it is experienced as jarring or as so natural it occurs imperceptibly, may depend in large part on the caregiving environment, which supports a primarily positive or negative experience of looking at the self through another's eyes. The lifelong quest for states of primary communion that most people seem to undertake, to one degree or another, may depend less on the inherent shame of objecthood, as Broucek supposes, and more on certain lost, missed affect states of infancy that stand in contrast with the ego states prevalent in the experience of most adults. These losses might correspond to Broucek's first meaning of "fault," that of loss of continuity.

Though Broucek's emphasis on the primacy of shame aspects of objective self-awareness can be questioned, it seems indisputable that, once a concept of a definable, summarizable self exists, there also come to exist powerful evaluative notions such as good self and bad self, weak self and strong self, all of which make reference to the possibility of defect. In this new era, if one has an immediate sense of being disorganized or ineffective or rejected, which *feels* bad, along with that direct experience likely will come an emerging concept of such experiences as negative *traits* representing the self. So now if I have a reactive shame experience of feeling helpless and ineffectual and red in the face, on top of that immediate experience I may layer a second, more ideational experience, which is a negative thought that abstracts from direct experience some concept about myself: I *am* helpless; I *am* ineffectual. Or perhaps, if the infant's feeling of helplessness is more complex, that is, if it contains representation of an object and feels more like, "I am helpless in getting her to smile; she turns away and I feel bad," then the second layer of experience would also contain this object reference and would feel more like Wurmser's construction, "I am unlovable and alone and empty of warmth."

How does one go from an infant experience of shrinking or shriveling (or from an even more powerful Wurmseresque variant, an intolerable, wordless infant experience of feeling turned to stone by an adult's gaze) to a self-reflective self-concept that says, "I am small," or "I am inferior," a concept that, in turn, generates an additional feeling of smallness or worthlessness? This seems to me a crucial transition in shame development, but one little explored in the literature. Perhaps that which is painful (e.g., feeling helpless, feeling disorganized) automatically classifies as bad (i.e., as representing deficiency) according to an innate human logic. And that which affects the sense of self with painful diminishing or disorder automatically infects the idea of self, once that develops. Thus, there is a natural equivalence between the baby's, "I feel shriveled up," or "I can't do it" (and that *feels* bad) and the young child's, "I am no good." The equivalence rests on the association between feeling bad and being no-good, as a trait, and on the continuity between the afflicted sense of self and the negative concept of self. An alternative concept is that one must *learn* that feeling helpless is not just a discomfort but is to be regarded as a defining characteristic of the self. If so, culture must transmit that lesson.

Some would argue that shame cannot exist before the development of objective self-awareness, that shame depends on a concept of *myself*, without which there is no possibility for defined negative ideas about the self. A theory such as Morrison's (1989), which derives shame from the ideal self (which is a set of ideas about one's self and other selves), presumably would require objective self-awareness before shame feeling can occur, unless one construes the ideal self as established and active when consisting only of simple images of one's intentions. For example, the baby intends to grasp the counter and pull himself up, so his ideal self (which he cannot achieve) is the image of the standing self.

If one does not adhere to a basic affects theory, the boundaries around shame represent an act of decision, and it is possible to make arguments for various ways of drawing those boundaries. Writers have taken differing positions on this question. Michael Lewis (1992) is an example of one who appears to see shame as entirely dependent on self-concepts. He believes that shame occurs when the self falls short in relation to standards, rules, and goals (SRG's) regarding its functioning: "I present a cognitive attribution model of shame, guilt, hubris, and pride. The model is based on the general proposition that shame and guilt are the consequences of the self's failure in regard to a standard, goal, or rule" (p. 9).

Differing from Lewis, I have come, over time, to prefer a concept of shame as an evolving set of experiences that originates with early lapses in the confident sense of self and comes, after objective self-awareness, to include and prominently feature defined, negative ideas about the self, which exist in relation to standards, rules, and goals; for example, one says, "I am not as brave as I would like to be, and I feel shame over that failing." The earliest experiences of shame would require only a sense of self as a center of feelings and wishes and not a fully developed concept of existing in an "objective" form that others can see and judge. As already indicated, conceptual bridges need to be built between (a) the immediate feeling (presumably possible in early infancy) of being small, impaired, and diminished and (b) feelings of being small, impaired, or diminished created through the power of negative ideas or concepts about the self (possible only after objective self-awareness).

The overall trajectory of shame development would seem to predict an increasing percentage of shame experiences originating from one's own mentation. Early in life, the shame stimulus is apt to be another's face or voice. Later, it more often is the inner representation of that shaming face or voice or some combination of inner representation and outer stimulus. As internal structure becomes more complex, actual shaming by another may in some instances fail to elicit a shame feeling because the internal representation of the shaming other is not activated. Even if I am wrong in the implied notion that human interactions (e.g., another's face or voice) are the likeliest stimuli for early shame, it would remain true that, as we mature, our shame responses become more dependent on a stable set of inner standards and less dependent on the moment's stimulus.

Once the capacity for self-reflection develops, most shame experience will involve some amount of conceptualizing about the self. Shame that occurs as an immediate, relatively concept-free response to others' expressions and comment still may exist but will be hard to discern. That variety of shame might be detectable in the patient's careful attunement of his responses to a therapist's tone of voice or rhythms of speech and silence. Broucek (1991) states, "Whether the content of what is exposed is or is not shameful in the eyes of the patient, the response of the other (or absence of response), rather than the content of what is revealed is most often the primary source of shame" (p. 81). I would shift the balance somewhat and say that the other's response is one source of shame, but internalized sources—which may include complex *motivations* to feel ashamed—also are highly influential.

As language becomes important to a child, shame increasingly will occur in reaction to negative concepts others direct at the self, not just negative facial expression or body posture. Additionally, negative self-definitions may be collected as the child begins actively to divide up the world into the strong and the weak, the good and the bad, and as the child attunes to his culture's values and applies them to the self.

A fertile area for inquiry concerns the interactions between the individual's earliest shame history and his shame experience after objective self-awareness. The child much stressed by very early neglect or abuse, once becoming aware of the self as object, may now conceptualize the earlier feeling states (Mother turns away; I am angry, I am alone) in relation to the more abstractable self. The child thus feels, "I am unlovable" or "I am bad" or "I am nothing." Negative self-assessments that are less global may develop as well and interact with the global assessments. So we have, "I am lazy, I am dumb, I have big feet," which may feel like further refinements of the broader, "I am bad," or they may feel like the essence of badness. Contrasted with the child who is uneasy in his earliest relationships, another child may feel secure in his interpersonal world before objective self-awareness but may find that OSA brings a new, more negative set of communications from caretakers; that child may long for a return to the safer, more loving preconceptual world.

Let me briefly detail a few additional post-OSA shame developments to be discussed further in later chapters. With the advent of objective self-awareness, the sense of the self as literally visible becomes elaborated, because now there is a notion of a specific self behind or within one's eyes, and increasingly, there are notions that one can shut out shame by restricting the visibility of that self. The availability of the inner self through vision may have more psychological weight than other forms of access but should not be emphasized to the exclusion of other sensory channels for knowing, as the following brief passage by Maxine Hong Kingston (1977) helps us see. Kingston describes a Chinese-American girl whose frenum has been cut by her mother. Speech has become knotted by shame; thus, others are refused entree to the self through hearing:

> When I went to kindergarten and had to speak English for the first time, I became silent. A dumbness—a shame—still cracks my voice in two, even when I want to say "hello" casually, or ask an easy question in front of the check-out counter, or ask directions of a bus driver. I stand frozen, or I hold up the line with the complete, grammatical sentence that comes squeaking out at impossible length. "What did you say?" says the cab driver, or "Speak up," so I have to perform again, only weaker the second time. A telephone call makes my throat bleed and takes up that day's courage. It spoils my day with self-disgust to hear my broken voice come skittering out into the open [p. 191].

As the child becomes a more complex, independent center of action and thought, he becomes a fuller partner for the adult because he is able to relate to more of the adult's spheres of functioning. The adult no longer finds in the child the restoration of his own infantile, primary communion. The child offers new gratifications, but he also may become threatening to the adult, because he can see and know and judge in ways that can discomfort. Here is another link to vision, but the vision now belongs to the child, who increasingly can see behind others' appearances and may cause others shame through penetration with eyes linked now to a more discriminating mind. Thus, as it becomes possible to open new doors of communication, other doors may begin to close, and walls go up. Adults will actively use shaming to stop the child from being himself (that is, from looking, judging, and so forth) when such activities disquiet the adult.

SHAME AND CONSCIENCE

As a child begins to establish memory for situations that have elicited shame and to attach language to self-aspects that evoke shame, that child becomes capable of his own shame-generating activity. He may characterize himself in shame-laden fashion, saying, for example, "You are boring" (because you don't interest Mother) or "You are slow" (because Dad always says, "Can't you hurry up?"). At this point, where the self is bifurcated into an agent looking at an object, shame can be described as *internalized*. Internalized shame, which requires standards, rules, and goals, contrasts with reactive shame that depends on an immediate interpersonal stimulus or at least on a current interaction with the environment.

The question arises as to whether shame proper, defined earlier in this chapter as requiring a distinctive negative feeling or judgment about the self, requires internalization of the shaming function or whether it is a legitimate subcategory of reactive shame. I would tend to argue that shame proper can occur in the context of reactive shame, since the very young child, prior to objective self-awareness, may not judge the self with words and concepts, but that child would be able to focus negative, judgmental emotion on the self as agent, which should suffice to support the "shame proper" categorization.

The question next arises as to whether internalized shame, through which the self negatively appraises the self, is synonymous with superego shame or the shame of conscience. Definitions of these terms vary. My own preference is to restrict the terms "superego" and "conscience" to those experiences that make reference to a person's stable values, which generally are based in part on internalization of parental or societal values, not just parental emotions. Thus, if a child who has been much chastized for wrong answers on spelling tests tells himself he is "stupid," that experience is not superego shame. But if he cheats on a spelling test when he believes that cheating is wrong, the shame over being a cheater is appropriately called superego shame. The two situations are distinguished by the reference to a stable belief system in one, which is absent in the other. The nature of the belief system is immaterial. It may be Christianity or a skinhead view of right and wrong. Superego shame is a subcategory of internalized shame.

Early in development, Mother's face stops a child's self-expressions directly and produces a shame experience. That level of stopping and shame induction still may occur later in life, but now, in addition, there are internal versions of that process, some of which constitute superego activity. Wurmser elaborates on shame as a superego component and stands out among writers in seeing all shame (except early "shame anxiety") as punitive superego activity.

Wurmser also sees shame within the superego as invariably harsh and condemning, another area of debate. One can argue that superego activity also has benign, guiding aspects, which temper impulses through shame and guilt (see Schafer, 1960) rather than condemning them. A more loving superego may use shame to say to the offending self, "You can do better than that, so try harder." A harsher superego says, "You are worthless because you have broken this rule," and there the case is closed, without option of self-amendment.

Schore's (1994) notions of shame have at least an oblique bearing on the question of superego harshness and shame. Schore's idea of shame as a painful, but in moderation, valuable, emotion induced when a mother is misattuned with an infant's exuberant emotion positions shame between two distinct representations of Mother: one of Mother as nonresponsive to the exhibitionistic self and the second of Mother as highly responsive to the ashamed self. This schema for normal development actually supposes shame to be the specific prelude to loving attention from Mother. Such a scaffolding for early shame might make shame's later, internalized voice more benign, since the early experience is sandwiched between images of the unmirroring mother and the comforting mother.

Hibbard (1994) sees shame as a superego function. He believes that shame has more "libidinous" forms, such as embarrassment, blushing, and bashfulness, and more "aggressive" forms, such as humiliation and disgrace. He associates psychological health with a "predominance of more libidinally determined, inhibitory, and

self-esteem attenuating components over more aggressively determined, persecutory components" (p. 452). Hibbard's definition of
superego functioning is broader than the one I have proposed
and would include experiences I classify as internalized,
nonsuperego shame, as well as instances of reactive shame.

SHAME AND THE DYNAMICS OF CONFLICT

As the personality becomes more complex, experiences that once
simply befell us can be reproduced actively as ways to manage
relationships and inner life. This statement applies to emotions
as well as to other events in a person's psychological space. Shame
comes to be recognized as an experience with a particular profile:
shame creates a feeling of smallness and unworthiness; it causes
a person to retreat from social situations; it leaves a person with
images of himself as impaired and valueless; it may leave him
feeling in need of rescue from others, or so small he is incapable
of significant aggression. Paradoxically, these distressing features
of shame give it utility in a variety of psychological settings.
Shame has become an experience that the developing personality
may utilize when something can be gained by feeling small or
weak or in need of rescue.

Though the "choice" to feel a particular emotion generally is
made with negligible conscious sense of selecting, it remains helpful
in theories of personality and in therapy to think of the volitional
elements in the experiencing of emotion. However unconsciously,
we may begin to use shame as a tool as we manage our own
personalities and our relationships with others. A person may
have learned that, if he is insulted by a coworker and he reacts
with shame, his relationship to the insulting coworker will proceed
in a way that is different from the way it will continue if he reacts
with anger. If a man is sexually aroused and responds with embarrassment, the interaction with his date will unfold differently
than if he were to feel and appear proud. The particular ways in
which people use shame can become deeply carved channels of
response and defining characteristics of their personalities.

Some of the more specific uses to which shame can be put
have given rise to theories of shame dynamics; these theories are
extremely valuable if recognized as addressing one application of
shame, not its full range. Many theorists miss not the complexity,
but the plasticity or multiple functions of shame.

As is often the case when a phenomenon comes under increased scrutiny, the explosion of attention to shame has led in some quarters to an overvaluing of shame experience as the root of almost all psychic pain and dysfunction. As indicated at the outset of this chapter, particularly problematic is the removal of shame from the more complex fabrics of psychological organization (thus, my emphasis on contexts) and its positioning, instead, as the "underlying" cause of most psychopathology. Lost is the understanding of shame's interweaving with other emotions, except insofar as shame, as the supposed root cause, has generated other emotions for defensive cover. A clear exception here is Wurmser (1981), whose book, in his words, "is riveted to the premise of conflict" (p. 15). Wurmser retains in his presentation a keen awareness of the dangers of fashionable, "rubber" concepts "overextended, excessively applied and imbued with more and more meaning" (p. 4). It is my own view that shame is a highly important emotion with profound motivational muscle but that it seldom exists on its own as the sole cause of psychopathology. Inevitably, it is one of a constellation of problematic emotions that derive from past strain and trauma, present conflict, and attempts at defense and adaptation. It generally is counterproductive in a psychotherapy to single out any single painful feeling as the key to self-understanding; invariably, that emphasis will be used as an exclusionary defense, in order to restrict consideration of the dauntingly complex and mercurial psyche.

Some of the main arguments of this chapter are summarized as follows: (1) Shame represents the combined influence of inherited structures and human category formation; stereotyped responses such as gaze aversion contribute to our category-forming activity but are not the sole influence on it. (2) Earliest shame requires a sense of the self as an agent who experiences his own intentions and actions and experiences his impact on others, but it does not require descriptive concepts of the self, such as, "I am tall, I am smart, I am slow," which can be compared against standards, rules, or goals. (3) Once such concept formation occurs, shame increasingly is organized around ideas about personal deficiency; "internalized" shame then is possible, though "reactive" shame still may occur. (4) Ideas about the deficient self come to operate within the superego as ways to restrict behavior that is judged, by stable internal values, to be "wrong"; superego shame is a subset of internalized shame. (5) As personality organization becomes more complex, shame can be called into service whenever self-stopping or self-diminution might serve an overall need of the personality. Such calls to service are generally unconscious, but can be made conscious through self-examination.

The chapters to follow explore shame in a number of clinical and nonclinical contexts. Certain of the cases considered have features of more than one diagnostic category; therefore, I may introduce a particular individual in multiple contexts, in order to attend to various aspects of the person's dynamics. The therapies discussed all fit Gill's (1994) definition of "psychoanalytic therapy," by which he means therapy that establishes a "psychoanalytic situation" (p. 63). Essential to psychoanalytic therapy or the psychoanalytic situation is the "two-person situation" and the utilization of the transference. Gill states that "the *decisive* criterion of psychoanalysis, one intrinsic to that therapy as against its extrinsic features, is that the transference—the patient's experience of the interaction—is analyzed as much as is possible, whereas in psychotherapy it is to a greater or lesser degree *wittingly* left unanalyzed" (p. 62). Psychoanalytic therapy is any therapy that meets the intrinsic criteria for psychoanalysis, even though it may not meet external criteria such as use of the couch or frequent visits.

CHAPTER 2

Shame in Obsessive-Compulsive Contexts

Meanwhile the marriage was appointed to be solemnized in eight weeks' time, and Mr. Bounderby went every evening to Stone Lodge, as an accepted wooer. Love was made on these occasions in the form of bracelets; and, on all occasions during the period of betrothal, took a manufacturing aspect. Dresses were made, jewellery was made, cakes and gloves were made, settlements were made, and an extensive assortments of Facts did appropriate honour to the contract. The business was all Facts, from first to last. The Hours did not go through any of those rose performances which foolish poets have ascribed to them at such times; neither did the clocks go any faster, or any slower, than at other seasons. The deadly statistical recorder in the Gradgrind observatory knocked every second on the head as it was born, and buried it with his accustomed regularity.

—Charles Dickens *(Hard Times)*

NOSOLOGICAL CONSIDERATIONS

In the clinical chapters to follow, I have chosen to concentrate on three patient groups in which shame dynamics can be examined: obsessive-compulsive personality disorders, narcissistic personality disorders, and masochistic personality disorders. Other diagnostic groups could have been chosen as easily; in fact, any group of people would serve since shame concerns are widely distributed. Attempts to define and make use of the particular categories selected and to place individuals within them brought, at times, a dismaying sense of the classifications as highly overlapping, with respect to membership and to dynamics. As descriptions of readily observable stylistic or behavioral features of individuals, the categories are a bit more separable, yet even so, two or even all three of the classifications occasionally describe features of one person.

The sharing of psychological dynamics among diagnostic groups surely should not surprise us, though it troubles efforts at organizational clarity. Certain features are, in fact, common to *all* psychopathology, and some of these shared characteristics have relevance to shame. David Shapiro (1981) states that "Some impairment of autonomy . . . is intrinsic to all psychopathology. Every condition of psychopathology is characterized by modes of action that in one way or another compromise or distort normal volitional processes" (p. 5). If one accepts the association Broucek and others make between shame and inefficacy, such impairment of autonomy is surely pertinent to shame, across all diagnostic groupings.

Neither should it surprise us that people fail to fall nicely into our diagnostic groupings. Many individuals have more than one approach to managing conflict or to achieving feelings of personal power; the more varied their approaches to handling their lives' problems, the less likely they make an easy match for a single diagnostic category.

I retain the nosological categories despite their inherent limitations and my own imperfect use of them. I do so as an attempt to focus attention on particular features or dynamics that are prominent in the category under discussion. At times, I will discuss under a particular heading, such as masochistic personality disorder, individuals whose use of masochistic mechanisms is circumscribed, but nonetheless instructive.

Those I have placed in the obsessive-compulsive category display a pervasive effort at utilizing repetitive activity, including mental activity, magically to control dangers associated with a host of feelings and wishes that are seen as perilous to the self, to others, or to both. Awareness of those dangerous feelings and wishes is carefully restricted, often by the same repetitive activity meant to control the fundamental hazards. A sense of momentary security and power is achieved through elaborate controls over one's own activity and mentation. One becomes a master of self-restriction or of self-coercion.

Those I have classified as narcissistically disturbed flaunt or secretly protect images of the perfect self. They maintain a constant concern with elevating the self and are made uneasy by anything short of flawlessness. Their efforts are anxiety-laden and are attuned to omnipresent dangers to self-regard. Often, aspects of the physical and human environment are experienced as extensions of the self over which perfect control must be established. Failure to maintain such control signifies personal weakness and insignificance; it brings rage and shame. Many people have both narcissistic and obsessive-compulsive features. Perfectionistic and controlling behavior can signify either pattern; thus, the behavior must be analyzed in context.

Those I have considered to be masochistically organized demonstrate: (a) a primary preoccupation with controlling a central relationship between self and caregiver and (b) a persistent conviction that painful experience is a tool in that management task. Here, I draw on Novick and Novick's (1991) statement about the childhood experiences of masochistic adults, "For these children, the gap was not between the real and the ideal self, but between the real and the ideal mother–child relationship" (p. 317).

Returning now to the obsessive-compulsive individual, let me further explain my thinking by saying that "obsessive-compulsive" describes a way of being in which thoughts, feelings, and actions, the manifestations of selfhood, are seen as requiring strict oversight. The free and playful movement entailed in such self-aspects is not permitted. Constant effort is exerted toward the maintenance of self-control, and lapses of control are anxiously noted. The ideal of functioning is the well regulated, predictable machine, not because the machine is a symbol of perfection, as it might be for the narcissistic individual, but because it is controlled and not subject to the influence of emotion. Within the obsessive-compulsive group, there is much room for variation, and the two cases I will discuss (in addition to one fictional individual) describe only a portion of the range of possibilities.

Shapiro (1981) takes as a central defining characteristic of obsessive-compulsive conditions the severe distortion of normal autonomy or of the experience of "will." The cases I will discuss both show this characteristic, though in many ways their surface presentations are opposite. Though Shapiro's chapter heading is "obsessive-compulsive rigidity," he regularly refers to "the compulsive person," as in the following description:

> We know, for example, that compulsive people are typically characterized by extraordinary determination, tenacity, and stubbornness.

> Yet these strong, determined individuals may be thrown into a
> state of anxiety and confusion by what would be, to anyone else,
> a trivial decision. . . . It is exactly in the nature of rigidity to be
> undeviating from an established course, yet incapable of estab-
> lishing a new one [p. 78].

Questions have been raised in the literature regarding the relationship between "obsessive-compulsive disorders," which are
characterized by highly irrational rituals or obsessions, and obsessive-compulsive characters or personalities, marked by general
rigidity but often lacking clearcut symptoms. Esman (1989) states,
"At least, these recent findings raise serious questions about the
conflictual origins of the obsessional character, whatever its relation to the obsessive-compulsive disorder" (p. 331). I will be
concentrating on people who are broadly obsessional or compulsive, whose character rigidity has pronounced, detrimental effects
on their relationships with people and their endeavors, while it
may also contribute to areas of special effectiveness. I am working
from the assumption, different from Esman's, that while inborn
tendencies may predispose a person to one or another character
organization, extreme characterological stances that reduce
adaptability likely are born to a significant degree out of developmental difficulties. The patients I discuss also have specific
obsessional or compulsive symptoms such as checking, ruminating,
or irrational, repetitive behavior.

Regarding the "obsessive" personality organization, Salzman
(1980) offers the following sketch, which can be juxtaposed with
Shapiro's remarks to fill out the picture of obsessive-compulsive
individuals:

> Obsessive character structures were described by Freud as orderly,
> stubborn, and parsimonious; others have described them as being
> obstinate, orderly, perfectionistic, punctual, meticulous, parsimo-
> nious, frugal, and inclined to intellectualism and hair-splitting
> discussion. Pierre Janet described such people as being rigid, inflex-
> ible, lacking in adaptability, overly conscientious, loving order and
> discipline, and persistent even in the face of undue obstacles. They
> are generally dependable and reliable and have high standards and
> ethical values. They are practical, precise, and scrupulous in their
> moral requirements. Under conditions of stress or extreme demands,
> these personality characteristics may congeal into symptomatic
> behavior that will then be ritualized.
>
> When present, the rituals are dramatic and pathognomonic [p. 10].

SHAME OCCURRENCES IN
TWO OBSESSIVE-COMPULSIVE INDIVIDUALS

Annette and Sidney both have prominent obsessive-compulsive features. Annette shows much obsessiveness, as well as some masochistic dynamics to be addressed in a later chapter. Sidney shows more compulsiveness, juxtaposed with narcissistic features. I will describe the appearance of shame and shame avoidance in their adult personalities and then consider how the shame that is experienced, or circumvented, relates to the characteristically obsessive-compulsive aspects of their personality organizations.

Sidney is a bright young professional who holds extremely high standards for his own and others' functioning. To others, he appears intimidatingly precise and demanding and, occasionally, smug and uncompromising. He is stubborn, persistent, and at times argumentative. Efficiency and order are guiding principles for Sidney. Anything that is ill-defined, untidy, or effusive disturbs him, as do things that resist counting and measuring. He has great trouble making sense of therapy, since it involves commerce with feelings that are impossible to measure, at times even hard to know. Sidney's fantasy life is restricted; that restriction corresponds to an ego-syntonic disdain for indulgence. At one point in time, his generalized compulsiveness was joined by a compulsive symptom characterized by a need to engage in a behavior he saw as irrational and unhealthful.

Sidney's shame experience was carefully circumscribed by defenses, but when shame did occur, it usually took the form of "shame proper," discussed in the introductory section, and the shame was internalized, meaning that a self-critical voice spoke, generally with reference to superego standards, telling him his behavior deviated from inner expectations. Sidney also seemed to experience some embarrassment, though he never used that term to describe his experience but used words both idiosyncratic and vague as if to obscure the implications his experience had for his self-regard.

The shame Sidney occasionally allowed focused on imperfect performance. The shame could be accepted due to a prevailing assumption that the deficient performance was a temporary aberration he soon would amend. If Sidney was surprised in therapy by my use of a word that had implications for pride and shame, such as "identity" or "self-esteem," he generally protested the use of the word as not related to him or as too general or too pigeonholing in its nature. Sidney was highly avoidant of dependency, and there were myriad indications that he saw needs for other people as shameful, but that statement represents an *inference* about his values, rather than something to which he could attest.

Annette's major similarity to Sidney was her ongoing effort at self-control and self-restriction. She was perfectionistic about performance and intolerant of her own failings, but not to the extent Sidney was. Her most vigorous efforts at control were directed against sexual and aggressive feelings and fantasy. These brought great anxiety, which took the form of obsessional doubting and checking, and also generated physical complaints and overwhelming fatigue. While Sidney's compulsiveness and perfectionism led to excellent independent work and difficulty with collaboration, Annette's obsessional indecision and enervation interfered with independent action. Where Sidney tolerated only direct, apparently linear, and powerful action from himself, Annette was inclined to inaction or to paired, countervailing actions that had the character of doing and undoing. She grounded herself in quotidian routines to the point of boring others and feeling bored. Intellectual curiosity was inhibited.

Annette's shame experiences were divided between shame proper and embarrassment. She felt shame that had two major foci, both of which set her experience apart from Sidney's. Often, she felt inept and foolish, or like a "dummy," an experience that sometimes had the quality of embarrassment, sometimes of shame proper. She also felt shame over strong emotion that defined her as an individual, particularly if the emotion involved sexual or aggressive wishes. For a long time, she was extremely inhibited in talking about sexual matters or in revealing aggressive fantasies. Her more vigorous emotions represented evidence that she was separate from and, at times, discomforting to others, especially her mother. She associated such feelings with willfulness and badness.

Because the vulnerable aspects of humanness were a primary trigger for Sidney's shame, experiencing shame, a very human emotion, was itself highly shameful; thus, we encounter in his personality organization a fierce set of anti-shame structures. One result was that when shame was experienced, for example, around his irrational, symptomatic behavior, it was often intense since the very experience of shame signified deficiency and led to more shame. Another result was that emotions more consistent with his values were favored, for example, cool or haughty anger. Compared with Sidney, Annette was less ashamed of shame itself; thus, she was able to exploit shame experiences for certain protections she found in them.

OBSESSIVE-COMPULSIVE DYNAMICS
AND THEIR RELATIONSHIP TO SHAME

If we take self-control as the central feature of the obsessive-compulsive organization, two somewhat different developmental hypotheses, one relevant to Annette and the other to Sidney, account for an emphasis on self-control and provide some understanding of shame's role in the personality. According to this way of thinking, hypertrophied self-control is a final common path for a number of developmental sequences, all of which create anxiety about the person's ability freely to be herself. Symptomatic behavior reflects both the wish to express one's wishes and one's identity and the wish to restrict such self-expression. Ironically, forceful self-restriction can become a primary means of self-expression.

One meaning of the obsessive-compulsive's self-control is to state, "I restrict myself to show I can do it. My self-control demonstrates my power." This, I believe, was the primary communication of Sidney's obsessive-compulsive presentation. It is a communication that becomes important to children who have felt defeated, either by coercive parenting or, in some cases, parenting that disregarded the child's will and wishes.

The second meaning of the obsessive-compulsive's self-control is to establish: "I restrict myself because I *am* powerful, and I must limit my power because some of its potentials are bad." Annette's self-control sought to make this point.

With each of the two meanings of self-control, certain similar experiences flow from the primary statement. Someone who must prove her power through self-control will also feel she has surrendered something of her indwelling self by overcontrolling herself. She is in a state of confusion over whether she has gained power through self-control or lost it by constraining herself. She may swing back and forth between self-restriction and rebellious self-indulgence. The person like Annette who controls herself in order to limit her dangerous power also will feel she has compromised herself, and she will want to rebel.

Where then does shame enter the picture in each of these two developmental scenarios? For those like Annette, whose self-control aims at disarming a self experienced as dangerously sexual or aggressive, shame enters as a straightforward reflection on the ineffective state of the disabled self, which may be halting, indecisive, obtuse, and otherwise stymied. This shame is internalized, and it is superego-generated to the extent that it follows from the person's values, which insist on more activity and effectiveness.

Shame may also be called into action as part of the effort to hobble the lively self. So, in Annette's case, she utilizes memories of Father's shaming to hold herself back from social activity and assertiveness; echoing Father, she tells herself she is a dummy or a weirdo who should just stay home and hide. Shame works in tandem with typical obsessive-compulsive devices in that both restrict free activity. The simple experience of recalling with pain Father's humiliating comments is not pathognomonic of obsessive-compulsive disorder or any other pathology. What speaks to an obsessive-compulsive organization is the utilization of such shaming self-imagery to hinder the impassioned aspects of the self and the use of such self-imagery as a component of rumination.

We also can conjecture that, in Annette's case, her overconcern about her impulse life and her sense of its dangerousness followed in part from *wishes* to be very strong and powerful—indeed, powerfully destructive—which, in turn, followed from earlier childhood experiences of reactive shame occasioned by Father's overt disparagement, by Mother's unreliable engagement with her daughter, and by intense sibling rivalry. Thus, the shame Annette experiences as an adult results from a two-part process, one part being the earliest experiences of reactive shame and the second the character developments that followed from them.

Early wishes for heightened power might have followed either from reactive shame or from other painful, nonshame emotions associated with helplessness. Wishes to wield destructive power would have led to anxiety, given that neither of Annette's parents provided adequate, firm limits: Mother was too depressed and characterologically passive, and Father was alcoholic and erratic. Early experiences of helplessness (whether due to shaming or other occurrences) would explain the coexistence, for Annette, of self-control that says, "I stop my destructive power," and the second type of self-control, akin to Sidney's, that says, "I control myself to manifest my power.'

In Sidney's case, we see less anxiety over impulses than Annette showed, but much determination to demonstrate control over the self and to assert independence from others. Shame in Sidney's early life likely was associated with wanting and needing one or both parents. Pride depended on the ability to renounce dependency, to show that "I can do it myself." Compulsive behaviors developing under such circumstances would prove one independent, perhaps by using a metaphor for independence such as being clean or empty or being as flawless as a diamond that needs no setting. The anorexic's state of needing nothing would be an example of utilizing emptiness and freedom from appetite as a metaphor for perfect independence. When compulsive behaviors assume a drivenness that is evident to the person herself, they may represent simultaneously both her pride and her humiliation. She feels powerful in her capacity for determined self-control, but also out-of-control and buffeted by impulses, because she no longer can cease controlling herself.

Though not clearly in evidence in Annette's history or Sidney's, an equally likely basis for early shame and later obsessive-compulsive determination to control the self would be early experiences of being defeated by a caregiver determined to impose her will on the child, a form of interaction Erikson (1963) explored that has been undervalued in the recent literature that seeks to locate shame's deepest roots in "oral" phase interactions. Though I believe that children in the "oral" phase of development do have experiences that contribute to later life shame (both ordinary shame and pathological), many instances of serious adult shame difficulty appear to be anticipated by toddler-age or later childhood experiences of being overpowered in the exercise of one's will. In such instances, we see obsessive-compulsive adults dead set on controlling the self as an emblem of their effective will and as a counter to shame. Since achieving such self-control signifies rebellion and self-assertion, the self-control feels aggressive and brings superego conflict.

SHAME AS A RESPONSE TO OBJECTIFICATION

It is noteworthy that the obsessive-compulsive person relates to herself in a way that, recalling Broucek's (1991) term, might be characterized as "objectifying." The self is viewed as a collection of functions that are adequately or improperly executed and is viewed without regard for inner life as something to be recognized and valued. This pattern suggests some failure of those parenting functions that enable a child to integrate her emotions into the daily life of the self, but one cannot leap to the conclusion that such an objectified view of the self necessarily implies objectifying parenting.

Of the two cases I have presented, Sidney seems the better candidate for the objectification theory of shame. His complaints about significant others often focused on the person's failure to treat him as an individual, with due acknowledgment of his assets and his difficulties. However, even in Sidney's case, other hypotheses with regard to shame-generating parent–child interactions suggest themselves. Often, he talked of both childhood and present-day experiences of being grossly misunderstood, as if his communications traveled through a distorting filter and emerged bent and unintelligible. There seemed to be some shame in that experience in that he felt unable to decipher the cause for the miscommunication. Was he deficient in communicating? Did people not want to understand? His shame seemed a result of the experience of beating his head against the wall trying to be heard but getting little response. He felt helpless to understand and helpless to make himself understood.

Is a child's experience of being unable to get through to a parent who distorts communication a form of objectification? It is certainly in the ballpark. In defining objectification, Broucek (1991) states that shame follows as "a response to having one's status as a subject ignored, disregarded, denied, or negated" (p. 8), which is an extension of the infant's experience of being gazed at unresponsively, with a "still face." Broucek says, "It is when one is trying to relate to the other as a subject but feels objectified that one is apt to experience shame" (p. 47). He gives as an example the kind of maternal attention that Kohut (1971) described as "fragmenting," in which a mother, faced with a child eager to tell of a recent experience, responds to the child by telling her some detail of her grooming has been unattended. Perhaps Sidney's parents were not overfocused on his objective traits or fully ignoring his subjectivity, but certainly they failed to engage effectively with the inner life he felt to be "myself."

What about Annette? How does the concept of objectification pertain to her world? It seems a less apt descriptor of her circumstances, which appeared to include a significant amount of active undermining by one parent and selective withdrawal by the other. The active undermining by Father would be better described as a "scowling face" or a "deriding face" than as the "still face gaze" of objectification. Mother's withdrawal might be conceived of as objectification, with respect to certain, livelier areas of Annette's subjective self. If Annette tried to tell her mother a story of two dogs fighting on the road or mating, she likely was met with a maternal yawn or with Mother's retreat into the bedroom for a nap. But it was not clear that Mother's withdrawal regularly evoked *shame* in Annette. When she occasionally suggested that Mother's behavior brought shame, Annette's emphasis was not on Mother's simple disengagement, but on her actively punitive, cold, shunning rejection.

The notion of early shame elicited by a *defeating* caregiver also departs from the idea of an objectifying attitude toward the child as the primary generator of shame. The parent intent on overpowering the child likely sees that child as an unruly part of the self or as a hated other from the past and, thus, approaches the child with aggression and a determination to control her.

In distinguishing such an aggressive encounter from an objectifying one, I must add as a complicating factor the observation that objectification is, to some extent, a behavioral descriptor, and the behavior addressed may, in fact, carry a variety of subtle but detectable psychological messages. Ignoring another's subjectivity may be a disguised statement of envious hostility toward that person's indwelling self, or it may signify anxiety about her vitality and perhaps one's own vitality as well, or it may be an outgrowth of narcissistically skewed values that overstress externals such as physical beauty. Broucek tends to talk about objectification as a unitary set of behaviors (those of unresponsiveness), but distinctions of motivation and meaning, which a child likely would sense, might for a young child contain a world of significance. Thus, the unresponsiveness that communicates a wish to annihilate the child's inner life may have more in common with overt abusiveness or hostile authoritarianism than meets the eye. In discussing a man whose transient insistence that he had been sexually abused (though he recalled no abuse) seemed to defend against a more frightening acknowledgment of persistent neglect, a colleague recently commented that neglect sometimes signifies such profoundly annihilating sentiment toward a child that recognition of the neglect becomes intolerable. The unresponsiveness of such a parent would be psychologically different from the unresponsiveness of a narcissistic parent, whose attention was captured only by her adolescent son's acne as the boy tried to relate his exhilaration during a track meet.

Objectification can be seen as one of a *number* of shame-inducing aspects of problematic parenting. As Broucek (1991) argues, a child may indeed feel ashamed (and hurt, angry, or saddened) because the parent does not wish to know the child's inner self and refuses to relate to her on the basis of her subjectivity. It is not hard to imagine a child trying to tell a parent about her day, about her feelings and thoughts, adventures and trials, but the parent does not listen and wants only to know what homework needs to be done or what clothes must be ironed for the next day's activities, and so the child feels that her self as she presents it elicits no spark of interest or enjoyment in the parent. The child's fantasy of showing herself to the parent and being met with delight collides with an actual experience in which the parent remains remote from the child's experience; shame may result.

The child may also feel shame that is somewhat differently conceived. She may feel the parent has seen (i.e., known) what is inside of her and has hostilely rejected it by requiring that it be contained or denied. An example would be Annette's second shame concern, "feeling dumb," which she associates with her father's demeaning characterization of her actions. The alternative to shame in such a situation is to refuse the other's assessment of oneself. Such refusal spares one shame but requires a disruption of the tie to the loved one. In Chapter Seven, I consider whether shame may, in some cases, result from a parent's idealization of a child.

Other nuances of objectification require attention when considering its shaming import. A parent may objectify a child by focusing on traits that characterize that child accurately; these are traits that can be agreed upon by many people, including the child herself. In fact, it is inevitable that this type of objectification occurs and must be integrated by the child into her self-concept. The notions, "I am smart" or "I am messy" or "I have wavy, black hair," become features of the self that must be amalgamated with the indwelling-self features, which include experiences such as, "I want to hug Mother when she smiles" or "I feel clever telling a joke" or "I feel mad when there is nothing good to eat." Parental objectification that focuses on verifiable traits of the child will be easier for the child to integrate than parental objectification that focuses on a parent's distorted fantasy of a child's traits.

Also at issue is the positive or negative tone of the objectification. Some positively colored objectifications offer a delightful sense of the self extending through time and space, influencing and being seen by others. Consider, for example, the child of four studying a baby book Mother lovingly completed during the child's infancy. She sees that she made people laugh saying, "snowsnoot" instead of "snowsuit." "Our young comedian," Mother has labeled the photo of the baby in her snowsuit. "I did that?" the girl asks, finding delight in the image of the self in another time and place. In contrast, another four-year-old, forced in daily life to endure objectifications both distorted and demeaning, may look with chagrin at a baby book photo of himself, spaghetti smearing his face, annotated by Mother, "the little piglet." Somewhere between the experience of these two children is that of the careless youngster whose parent accurately identifies the child's heedlessness as a trait, even a fault, but does so without undue harshness.

Perhaps of greatest importance is the timing and tone of objectifying communication; differences in these features will separate intrusive and demeaning parenting from sensitive parenting. The parent who focuses on some detail of a child's presentation just at the moment when the child is consumed with desire for her inner experience to be known and admired is the parent most likely to evoke shame, as well as anger. There are other times when such a scrutinizing focus is acceptable to a child; indeed, it may be loving and necessary. The mother who fails to tell her son his shirttails are untucked before they enter a synogogue may be as destructive to the child's self-esteem as the parent, portrayed by Broucek, who focuses on the child's billowing shirt when the child is impatient to relate a recent adventure.

EGO IDEAL AND IDEAL SELF

An obsessive-compulsive fictional character (with narcissistic features) demonstrates a character structure organized to discourage affiliative human feelings such as dependency and sexual love, which create vulnerability to the shame of rejection. As with

Sidney, the character, Mr. Stevens, actually experiences little shame; thus, we do not see him using moments of "feeling dumb," or some other explicit shame experience, to enforce his compulsive efforts to do things properly. The compulsiveness is sustained primarily by the prideful investment he has made in it and not by episodes of fullblown shame.

Mr. Stevens is head butler in the house of a prominent English lord in the days anticipating World War I. The highly compulsive and somewhat obsessional Mr. Stevens is the creation of Kazuo Ishiguro (1989) in his justly celebrated novel, *The Remains of the Day*. Though fictional characters do not always operate according to usual principles of personality organization, this character's veridicality provides a basis for consideration of a number of questions about obsessive-compulsive organization as it relates to shame dynamics.

In looking at Mr. Stevens, we will see a not uncommon convergence of obsessive-compulsive and narcissistic features, something that was present with Sidney as well. My own working definition of these terms links obsessive-compulsive mechanisms primarily to the determination to maintain control (whether of aggression, sexual feeling, dependent wishes, or other emotion), whereas the narcissistic concern is for self-regard. The two readily intertwine; for example, a fear of losing control of dependent wishes may derive in part from a fear of the loss of self-regard such dependency signifies. But the emphasis for the obsessive-compulsive person remains with one aspect of the experience, whereas for the narcissistically disturbed person, it lies with the other. With Sidney, we saw some of each concern as he focused both on self-control and on pride; the same will be true with Mr. Stevens.

Mr. Stevens has a job that requires meticulous attention to detail and devotion to professionalism. But Stevens is not just a man who does his job well; he is a man whose job performance is a metaphor for his emotional life. Even in his most private moments, Stevens's attention is fully absorbed by details of management. He watches his inner house as closely as his employer's house, in part by renouncing all personal life, so that work *is* life for Mr. Stevens, and butlering is being. Salzman's (1980) comments describe Stevens well:

> Freud saw the obsessive-compulsive mechanism as a device for dealing with unacceptable hostile or sexual impulses. . . . However,

not only sexual or hostile impulses need to be controlled but also the tender, friendly, or stupid and unworthy thoughts and feelings. In my view, the obsessive-compulsive dynamism is a device for preventing any feeling or thought that might produce shame, loss of pride or status, or a feeling of weakness or deficiency—whether such feelings are hostile, sexual, or otherwise. I see the obsessional maneuver as an adaptive technique to protect the person from the exposure of any thought or feeling that will endanger his physical or psychological existence [p. 13].

Mr. Stevens's robotic functioning is both an avoidance and a pursuit. Through his perfectionism, he asserts that he is a well tooled machine, under tight control, and he avoids the shame (and other dangers) inherent in humanness. At the same time, he pursues a number of satisfying ideals that do more than defeat shame. They generate self-satisfaction as well. In acquainting ourselves with Mr. Stevens's inner life, through his first-person narrative, we know of his shame potential mostly by inference, since he never speaks of shame, but his life of ideals we know explicitly.

A look at Mr. Stevens brings us to the concepts of ego ideal and ideal self, both of which have been introduced into many discussions of shame. Ideal self-images have strong organizing and integrating effects within the personality. Feeling identified with one's ideal self-image brings pride, and departing from it under some circumstances generates shame.

Mr. Stevens's views on "dignity" in the execution of his profession speak to an ideal self-image. Stevens often ruminates about "dignity" as an earmark of greatness in a butler. This matter is of utmost concern to him, and he is given to philosophizing about it throughout the book. The following discourse on dignity begins to define his relationship to shame:

And let me now posit this: "dignity" has to do crucially with a butler's ability not to abandon the professional being he inhabits. Lesser butlers will abandon their professional being for the private one at the least provocation. For such persons, being a butler is like playing some pantomime role; a small push, a slight stumble, and the facade will drop off to reveal the actor underneath. The great butlers are great by virtue of their ability to inhabit their professional role and inhabit it to the utmost; they will not be shaken out by external events, however surprising, alarming or vexing. They wear their professionalism as a decent gentleman will wear his suit: he will not let ruffians or circumstance tear it off him in the public gaze; he will discard it when, and only when, he wills to do so, and this will invariably be when he is entirely alone [Ishiguro, 1989, pp. 42–43].

Mr. Stevens's comments describe his ideal self, not his shame experience. Indeed, he is well insulated from shame by his proud belief that he comes close to meeting his own ideals. Potential for shame is nevertheless implied by the nature of his ideal self (dignity is by definition shame's opposite), by the rigor of his pursuit of that ideal self, and by the particular images that embellish his exposition, for example, the image of having one's suit torn off in the public gaze, which is a classic shame image.

Reading the above material, one could conclude that the discussion of Mr. Stevens better fits a discussion of narcissism than one of obsessive-compulsive organization. As suggested earlier, it might fit under either heading. I include it here because Mr. Stevens's efforts to achieve self-control through manipulating the minutiae of his environment (with special emphasis on cleanliness and order) and adhering to fixed notions of correct behavior struck me as characteristically obsessive-compulsive. They recall Shapiro's (1981) description of obsessive-compulsive rigidity or dogmatism as "behavior that is determined by prior internal requirements, requirements of duty, responsibility, or fidelity to authoritative rules, principles, or theories that make further judgment unnecessary" (p. 79).

One of the features in the obsessive-compulsive personality is the need to maintain alienation from the emotional or impulsive self. The obsessive-compulsive is constantly broadcasting, "I do not know those feelings, those impulses. They are not me." For the obsessive-compulsive, one role of the ego ideal and ideal self is to help maintain the alienation, or not-me quality, of the self-aspects that are viewed as dangerously out of control. The ego ideal instructs, "That is not good; reject it. This over here is good; make it part of yourself." It operates to sort experience and attributes into those that can be embraced and those that must be denied. The ideal self says, "I am aiming for this beacon over here, which is bright and shining and has nothing to do with shame."

A bit of terminological clarification is needed regarding the terms *ego ideal* and *ideal self.* Schafer (1967) considers the various treatments of ego ideal and ideal self and concludes that "ego ideal" is best understood as a function or set of functions (within the superego) through which some aspect of the person's being is held up against inner standards and judged. In other words, "ego ideal," though grammatically a noun, is to be understood as a set of judging and comparing activities. In contrast, "the ideal self" refers to an idealized fantasy of what the self might be. It operates as a reference point toward which one can aim. In Schafer's words:

> Some of the metapsychological hard times on which the concept ego ideal has fallen (for which, see below) are the result of confusing a structure or function (systemic terms) with the mental representation or idea of that structure or function (content or phenomenological terms). It is speaking phenomenologically to say that it is an ideal self toward which one aspires. It is speaking systemically to say that the ego ideal is the superego function of holding up moral ideals or standards and that it plays an important though not exclusive part in determining the content of ideal selves. An ideal self may be to be altruistic, utilitarian, brutal, sybaritic, or, in certain masochistic instances, to be a complete and total failure. Ideal self is therefore not just another name for ego ideal; it differs from ego ideal in conceptual level and it pertains to a greater variety of content. It seems to be closer to, though not synonymous with, what Jacobson called the "wishful concept of the self" (1953a, p. 59; 1954b, p. 123) [p. 154].

I will attempt to maintain Schafer's useful distinctions in my discussion, while at the same time recognizing that there are many instances where ego ideal and ideal self work so closely in concert that the choice of terms is difficult and somewhat arbitrary. The two concepts overlap when the self-assessing activity called ego ideal utilizes an ideal-self image as a standard, while concurrently using less personified standards.

It is, of course, always too simple to talk of "the ideal self" as if it were a unitary image. We all have multiple versions of our ideal self, and often those versions contradict each other in ways that have great significance in the organization of the personality. An example of conflict between ideal selves would be one man's paired ideals of winning all competitions while at the same time being an easy-going, fairminded, "nice guy." Another example would be a woman's ideal of perfect and precise adherence to rules, which conflicts with her ideal of intellectual independence.

With regard to the obsessive-compulsive personality, we can say that the measuring activity of the ego ideal goes on constantly and that the ideal self used as a standard of success (or one of multiple ideal selves) features strict control of important areas of emotion and impulse. Here we can recall Mr. Stevens's comment that, for an inferior butler, "being a butler is like playing some pantomime role." For Mr. Stevens, taking what, for most people, would be a role and defining it proudly as his genuine self makes of his whole life a pantomime, yet he sees the person who maintains some private space as the greater pretender, whom he holds in contempt. Stevens wants the butler's obligatory control to characterize his entire self; he sees such pervasive self-governance as a masterful achievement.

It may also be of use to point out here that some individuals who have many obsessional and compulsive features make constant use of ideal self-images for envisioning personal goals, evaluating others, and generating pride, whereas other such individuals seem primarily concentrated on using the ego ideal to constrain dangerous self-aspects. The second group is less concerned with reaching for ideals represented through admirable self-images. Sidney is an example of the former, Annette of the latter. Those for whom ideal self-images are prominent are more likely to attract the label "narcissistic" than are those, like Annette, who seem content to sidestep danger with respect to superego condemnation. In Annette's case, the picture is complicated by the fact that exhibitionism, and the associated pride, is one of the aspects of living most vigilantly scrutinized by her conscience. Thus, to flaunt an ideal self, whatever its particulars, would bring superego denunciation. She needs to monitor images of superiority more carefully than Sidney, who shamelessly exhibits his.

SHAME OVER ABANDONING THE INDWELLING SELF

Thus far, we have considered the shame that derives, in reactive fashion, from early experiences of objectification or other narcissistic stresses. We also have considered circumstances, such as Annette's, in which shame first experienced when a child is narcissistically taxed is used by the more complex personality of later years to warn the person away from areas of conflict, for example, conflict over the expression of lively aggressive or loving feelings. Similar deterrence is achieved through obsessive-compulsive behavior, such as checking and doubting.

Another variety of shame in obsessive-compulsive contexts works opposite the shame that enforces the rejection of the indwelling self. The opposition of these two shame-types contributes to the states of conflict between compliance and self-assertion that are so characteristic of people with obsessive-compulsive personality organizations. The second source of shame is the abandoning of the indwelling self. Such desertion of self is felt as a kind of cowardice, in part because the indwelling self may be experienced as surrendered in the face of overpowering external pressure, but probably also because the valuing of self-expression is natural to humans.

We can again take Annette as an example. Convinced that her lively self elicited depression and rejection from her mother and fluctuations between ridicule and overstimulating interest from her father, Annette held fast to her memories of shaming responses from her parents, and she used that painful shame to help herself steer clear of spirited self-expression and fantasy. In disowning much of her own vitality, she felt identified with her parents, who had rejected energetic aspects of her personality or, in her father's case, alternately rejected them and dressed them in conflict. Thus, Annette became a "good girl," compliant with parental authority. She was determined to be polite and agreeable at all times and lovable to all, which led to willingness always to be last in line, lowest priority, and least considered, all of which protected her from shame that would follow were she to display prideful exhibitionism, assertiveness, or acquisitiveness. At times, she could derive pleasure from her meek behavior by telling herself she was exceptional in her goodness or her self-control, but such timidity led as well to shaming images of herself as a wimp or coward. This self-criticism, which grew in part from societal values incorporated into her superego, would lead to bursts of assertiveness, even to stubbornness or circumscribed belligerence. Another patient swung back and forth between impulses to conserve money as an act of self-denial and impulses to spend freely. For Annette and this second woman, ego ideal standards prescribed both the compliant, dutiful, "good girl" behavior and the more expressive, unfettered behavior, but the two sets of standards could not be reconciled.

To understand the rebelliousness that can attach to a person's sudden jettisoning of restrictive ego ideal standards, it is useful to examine the contribution parental identifications make to the more oppressive ideal selves. Mr. Stevens will again serve as a model, because the ideal, dignified self that protected him from vulnerability was clearly fashioned after his father. There is little doubt that Stevens's culture promoted his values, but his father, also a butler to whom Stevens, in his youth, was apprenticed, mediated the broader culture for his son and represented a specific model for self-control. In one of his ruminations on what constitutes a "great" butler, Mr. Stevens talks of his father's impressive dignity and his high regard for dignity in others. In the passage to follow (Ishiguro, 1989), Stevens reflects on his father and recounts a story Father liked to tell:

> [Y]ou may think me merely biased if I say that my own father could in many ways be considered to rank with such [great] men, and that his career is the one I have always scrutinized for a definition of "dignity." Yet it is my firm conviction that at the peak of his career at Loughborough House, my father was indeed the embodiment of "dignity" . . . [p. 34].

> I believe the telling and retelling of this story was as close as my father ever came to reflecting critically on the profession he practised. As such, it gives a vital clue to his thinking.

> The story was an apparently true one concerning a certain butler who had travelled with his employer to India and served there for many years maintaining amongst the native staff the same high standards he had commanded in England. One afternoon, evidently, this butler had entered the dining room to make sure all was well for dinner, when he noticed a tiger languishing beneath the dining table. The butler had left the dining room quietly, taking care to close the doors behind him, and proceeded calmly to the drawing room where his employer was taking tea with a number of visitors. There he attracted his employer's attention with a polite cough, then whispered in the latter's ear: "I'm very sorry, sir, but there appears to be a tiger in the dining room. Perhaps you will permit the twelve-bores to be used?"

> And according to legend, a few minutes later, the employer and his guests heard three gun shots. When the butler reappeared in the drawing room some time afterwards to refresh the teapots, the employer had inquired if all was perfectly well.

> "Perfectly fine, thank you, sir," had come the reply. "Dinner will be served at the usual time and I am pleased to say there will be no discernible traces left of the recent occurrence by that time" [p. 36].

Mr. Stevens tells a second admiring story concerning his father's ability to cater graciously to a general for whom his true feelings were "utmost loathing" (p. 41) because this general was responsible for an older son's death in a misguided, irresponsibly commanded engagement in the Southern African War. The younger Mr. Stevens prizes his father's adamantine refusal of his personal feelings. He commends his readiness to conceal every vestige of personal feeling and to deem such emotion irrelevant to his professional dealings with the general. Ironically, Stevens's adherence to his father's code of impassive professionalism finds its "finest moment" when Stevens declines to cease from work in order to spend a few moments with his father on his deathbed or to bow to sadness when the news of his father's death later finds him.

Stevens's ego ideal derives in good measure from his father, but no one operates according to simple, unified ego ideal standards that are carbon copies of a parent's expectations. So the child whose ego ideal says, "It is wrong to be emotional, but grand to be dignified," likely also makes the judgment, "It is wrong to be untrue to your own feelings and ideas." Counterideals may be formed in opposition to another's touted values, or they may have their source in the broader culture. They may even be present and influential when no one in the child's environment has strongly argued for or against them. Certain values seem inherent in human nature. Here I concur with Schafer (1967) who states:

> [M]orality also develops endogenously in some respects—it is not all acquired by identification, a point particularly emphasized by Melanie Klein and her followers. Indeed, Freud's basic theory of superego formation cannot stand without including spontaneous tendencies toward the development of morality [p. 143].

When Schafer talks of the endogenous aspects of morality, he may be referring primarily to standards governing behavior toward others, but the argument for inherent standards likely would apply as well to relations with the self. As we have seen with Mr. Stevens and earlier with Sidney, ideals are also heavily influenced by self-protective exigencies. In further consideration of Sidney's overvaluing of independence, we should ask whether his choice of self-protective ideal was modeled after a parental standard of independence, in which case the standard would be regarded with great ambivalence as both a protection against shame and a link to something once oppressively imposed. His ideal self then would contain an important element of identification with the aggressor.

Given that shame attends both one's humanness and its negation through rigid control, the obsessional person finds herself in a quagmire of conflict. She feels confusion and ambivalence over what in the self is good; thus, she experiences a profound uneasiness about where lies pride, where lies shame. For example, Sidney complained of feeling stiff and wary in his therapy hours and indicated that such an experience felt unnatural and shamed him, but when he relaxed a bit and the therapist acknowledged as a forward step his increased human comfort, he felt, "You're mocking me." He believed the therapist had a patronizing attitude toward Sidney's freer self, as if such spontaneity was good enough for the patient but wouldn't be something the therapist truly valued or would accept in her own behavior. He was like the child who senses that the restricted self that elicits her parent's respect (or at least a cessation of rebuke) represents a profound capitulation and a shameful treachery against her own feelings, and she wants to assert her independence of such tyrannical forces. Yet she has formed an ego ideal based on her parent's values and other compelling motives, and that ego ideal operates to reward her overcontrolled behavior, even to applaud her as superior to ordinary others, who are hobbled still by their passions.

Returning to the tiger story, one might think of the tiger under the table as the disavowed tendencies of the self, which ideally are to be disposed of without leaving a trace. Mr. Stevens seems to ward off incipient shame related to his readiness to betray aspects of his own nature and inclinations. Only near the end of his story, in one painful moment, does he admit to his shame. He is discussing his blind loyalty to his employer, Lord Darlington, a man revealed to be morally and politically misguided and a Nazi sympathizer. Stevens compares himself negatively to Lord Darlington who, despite his egregious failings, at least was true to himself. Stevens concludes that his own behavior actually *lacked dignity* compared with Lord Darlington's, which is an immense admission of shortcoming, given the dominant current in Stevens's values (Ishiguro, 1989):

Lord Darlington wasn't a bad man. He wasn't a bad man at all. And at least he had the privilege of being able to say at the end of his life that he made his own mistakes. His lordship was a coura-geous man. He chose a certain path in life, it proved to be a misguided one, but there, he chose it, he can say that at least. As for myself, I cannot even claim that. You see, I *trusted.* I trusted in his lord-ship's wisdom. All those years I served him, I trusted I was doing something worthwhile. I can't even say I made my own mistakes. Really—one has to ask oneself—what dignity is there in that? [p. 243].

The obsessional person's shame over cowardly betrayal of impor-tant self-inclinations may be vaguely conceived but, at the same time, highly motivating. Advocacy for the indwelling self often appears in the form of stubbornness and angry insistence on rights and boundaries. Tenacious defense of trivial personal rights (to a parking space or a refund after poor service) may juxtapose with a willingness to succumb to others' wishes and to the wishes of the ego ideal standards that promote a mechanical self. By defending the trivial and surrendering the essential, the conscience can find some sort of uneasy balance between the desire to carry the flag for one's own feelings and the opposing need to struggle to satisfy an ego ideal of self-denial.

Many obsessional people are caught in an endless back and forth between pursuit of a perfected, robotic self and assertion of a more feeling-centered self. Often, major conflicts appear around appetites, because appetites (for food, sex, leisure, and so forth) are core self-expressions the parent may have had great diffi-culty accepting and gently taming. So the child identifies with the power of rigid control and feels proud of its operation within her but is also ashamed of it (and resentful) when she senses she has adopted it in trade for something more essentially "herself," and so she rebels. Others may embrace a posture of constant rebellion against authority (see Patricia, Chapter Seven), but the hostility and anxiety evident in the stance betray an underlying inclination to identify with the restrictive authority.

For the obsessive-compulsive person, the assertion of self (to the extent that self is defined by appetites or affiliative "weak" feelings) can stir fears that she is displaying her shamefully out-of-control wants and fears or her bad, guilt-provoking desires, and so she hastens back toward strangulating self-control. The only real solution of course is to reform superego functioning so that a range of emotions and wishes are tolerated and to amend ego ideal functioning so that the ideal of the mechanically controlled self no longer dominates. The indwelling self needs to become lovable to the internal parent, which can happen when the internal parent is reinvented based on identification with the therapist and the values inherent in the therapeutic process. The reforming of the superego will occur in tandem with revised expectations of others' responses to a more impassioned self. Also crucial for change is the broadening of the ego's capacity to tolerate those emotions that have been denied as overly associated with vulnerability.

SHAME OVER DAMAGED INTERPERSONAL RELATIONS

One more area in which the obsessive-compulsive's conscience may judge her as shameful (and often guilty) is that of interpersonal relations. The same person who neatly disposes of the tiger under the table often cauterizes human ties in ways that her surviving empathic capacity finds shameful, both morally shameful because she harms others and shameful as a primary defect of humanness. The defect is experienced when the person views others' warmer human relations and judges something lacking in the self.

Sidney one day repeatedly criticized every extrapolation I made about his feelings and then complained late in the hour that the hour seemed like an "intellectual exercise." Asked what focus might be more meaningful to him, he began to circle around the notion that his wife's distress over her parents' move to another country did not bother him much, but he did have some concern that he was not appreciating his partner's feelings, which were alien to his own experience. He seemed to be catching sight of his own insensitivity as through a glass darkly, and the perception filled him with conflicting emotion over whether to give his coldness status as a reality or not. He often held others in contempt for their emotionalism or inefficiency or financial ineptness, but occasionally he registered the effects his judgments had on others and that registration brought a subterranean rumbling of conscience. He also felt a current of shame when he perceived that his relationship with his therapist had none of the warmth that his wife described in her therapy; however, he tried to combat the shame by complaining that he was being shamed *by* the therapist, whom he saw as suggesting that his therapy experience was deficient.

Mr. Stevens provides a second example of shame over the destructive aspects of the obsessive-compulsive approach to human relations. A lively housekeeper in his employ, Miss Kenton, repeatedly insinuates herself into his well-guarded personal space with hints of warmth, friendliness, and erotic interest, all of which he rebuffs with a coolness verging on ruthlessness. The following passage occurs as Mr. Stevens remorsefully reviews the degeneration of his relationship to Miss Kenton and begins to nurse a growing concern about the destructive impact of his emotional amaurosis. In the passage, which is replete with shame imagery, we see Mr. Stevens desperately attending his dignity as Miss Kenton tries to approach him on a human plane (Ishiguro, 1989):

As it happened, when she entered my pantry that evening, I was not in fact engaged in professional matters. That is to say, it was towards the end of the day during a quiet week and I had been enjoying a rare hour or so off duty. As I say, I am not certain if Miss Kenton entered with her vase of flowers, but I certainly do recall her saying:

"Mr Stevens, your room looks even less accommodating at night than it does in the day. That electric bulb is too dim, surely, for you to be reading by."

"It is perfectly adequate, thank you, Miss Kenton."

"Really, Mr Stevens, this room resembles a prison cell. All one needs is a small bed in the corner and one could well imagine condemned men spending their last hours here."

Perhaps I said something to this, I do not know. In any case, I did not look up from my reading, and a few moments passed during which I waited for Miss Kenton to excuse herself and leave. But then I heard her say:

"Now I wonder what it could be you are reading there, Mr Stevens."

"Simply a book, Miss Kenton."

"I can see that, Mr Stevens. But what sort of book—that is what interests me."

I looked up to see Miss Kenton advancing towards me. I shut the book, and clutching it to my person, rose to my feet.

"Really, Miss Kenton," I said, "I must ask you to respect my privacy."

"But why are you so shy about your book, Mr Stevens? I rather suspect it may be something rather racy."

"It is quite out of the question, Miss Kenton, that anything 'racy', as you put it, should be found on his lordship's shelves."

"I have heard it said that many learned books contain the most racy of passages, but I have never had the nerve to look. Now, Mr Stevens, do please allow me to see what it is you are reading."

"Miss Kenton, I must ask you to leave me alone. It is quite impossible that you should persist in pursuing me like this during the very few moments of spare time I have to myself" [pp. 165–166].

But Miss Kenton was continuing to advance and I must say it was a little difficult to assess what my best course of action would be. I was tempted to thrust the book into the drawer of my desk and lock it, but this seemed absurdly dramatic. I took a few paces back, the book still held to my chest.

"Please show me the volume you are holding, Mr Stevens," Miss Kenton said, continuing her advance, "and I will leave you to the pleasures of your reading. What on earth can it be you are so anxious to hide?" . . .

She reached forward and began gently to release the volume from my grasp. I judged it best to look away while she did so, but with her person positioned so closely, this could only be achieved by twisting my head away at a somewhat unnatural angle. Miss Kenton continued very gently to prise the book away, practically one finger at a time. The process seemed to take a very long time—throughout which I managed to maintain my posture—until finally I heard her say:

"Good gracious, Mr Stevens, it isn't anything so scandalous at all. Simply a sentimental love story" [p. 167].

Mr. Stevens later comes to recognize, however fleetingly, the destructiveness to self and other of his coldly "professional" behavior. Lonely in his later years, he reviews with regret and shame the pivotal points in his relationship with Miss Kenton, all of them moments when he turns from her coldly after she has approached him with affection, woe, or humor.

Mr. Stevens' story concludes drearily, as he registers his alienation from human society and imagines relieving this shameful and grievous situation by pursuing a more human course. In the scene to follow, he stands by the seashore observing strangers interact (Ishiguro, 1989):

> As I watch them now, they are laughing together merrily. It is curious how people can build such warmth among themselves so swiftly. It is possible these particular persons are simply united by the anticipation of the evening ahead. But, then, I rather fancy it has more to do with this skill of bantering. Listening to them now, I can hear them exchanging one bantering remark after another. It is, I would suppose, the way many people like to proceed. In fact, it is possible my bench companion of a while ago expected me to banter with him—in which case, I suppose I was something of a sorry disappointment. Perhaps it is indeed time I began to look at this whole matter of bantering more enthusiastically. After all, when one thinks about it, it is not such a foolish thing to indulge in—particularly if it is the case that in bantering lies the key to human warmth.
>
> It occurs to me, furthermore, that bantering is hardly an unreasonable duty for an employer to expect a professional to perform. I have of course already devoted much time to developing my bantering skills, but it is possible I have never previously approached the task with the commitment I might have done [p. 245].

So here we have Mr. Stevens moved by his life's emptiness, ashamed of his alienation from others and their ways, and wanting to venture onto a terrain ("bantering") previously held as foolish, yet he is able to imagine such agrestic growth within himself only by containing it within the old structures of duty, work, professionalism, and commitment, so that in the end his fantasy of engaging with others through bantering indeed does sound foolish and clumsy, and pitiable.

Thus, Mr. Stevens's inner standards give him at least three reasons for shame: shame if he lapses into humanness, which his ego ideal judges with contempt; shame for abandoning his essential humanness and allowing himself to become a person enslaved and devoid of inner direction and values; and moral shame for treating human feelings as superfluities.

ADDITIONAL NOTES ON THE EGO IDEAL

Lasch's (1984) discussion of the concept of ego ideal (which he does not distinguish from "ideal self," as Schafer does) illuminates the structure's complex roots, which include both narcissistic strain (that motivates compensatory grandiosity) and ordinary creative strivings toward ideals. Lasch reviews those writers who understand the ego ideal primarily as a pathological structure that promotes regressive perfection-seeking through fantasy (e.g., A. Reich). He also discusses writers who emphasize the mature ideals and willingness to value something beyond the self that the ego ideal can signify. Lasch integrates these polar positions in stating the following:

> In view of the lack of agreement about its properties and development, the ego ideal might appear to be a nebulous and useless concept. But if we pursue the problem a little farther, we see that the difficulty in characterizing the ego ideal indicates precisely why the concept is indispensable. It calls attention to the links between the highest and the lowest forms of mental life, between the most exalted aspirations for spiritual transcendence and the earliest illusions of omnipotence and self-sufficiency. It shows how the impulse to restore those illusions expresses itself in regressive fantasies of a magical symbiosis with the world or of absolute self-sufficiency but also in a loving exploration of the world through art, playful scientific curiosity, and the activities of nurture and cultivation. The ego ideal is hard to define because, more than any other psychoanalytic concept, it catches the contradictory quality of unconscious mental life. In the words of Samuel Novey, it refers to "that particular segment of introjected objects whose functional operation has to do with proposed standards of thoughts, feeling, and conduct acquired later than the Oedipal superego, but having its roots in the early pregenital narcissistic operations against [separation] anxiety. . . .
>
> Partial descriptions of the ego ideal, in the psychoanalytic literature, result from a failure to grasp its contradictory qualities and to entertain both sides of the contradiction at the same time. Some writers idealize the ego ideal, seeing only its mature and mitigating features. Others see only its regressive side [pp. 179–181].

Though I do not wish uncritically to endorse all of the developmental concepts Lasch summarizes in the passage above, I do find very useful his separation and *integration* of regressive and progressive interpretations of ego ideal (and ideal self) functioning. The regressive aspects remove the individual's perfectionistic strivings to a private domain in which fantasy is manipulated as if it were reality. The progressive elements bring perfectionistic strivings into commerce with daily reality, including interpersonal reality; the person struggles for high attainments within those spheres. Whether or not one sees the ego ideal's perfectionism as the inevitable, universal legacy of lost intrauterine bliss, as Lasch does, or as related to normative infantile needs around omnipotence, as some self psychologists would, one still can see it as capable of taking mature or regressive forms.

The regressive aspects of ego-ideal formation are well captured by Reich (1960), who describes the narcissistic adult's utilization of a grandiose ego ideal. She discusses "magical denial" (p. 220) as the infant's only defense against a catastrophe that is experienced as already having taken place. Such denial says, "'It is not so. I am not helpless, bleeding, destroyed. On the contrary, I am bigger and better than anyone else. I am the greatest, the most grandiose.' Thus, to a large extent, the psychic interest must center on a compensatory narcissistic fantasy whose grandiose character affirms the denial" (p. 217).

Schafer (1967) briefly discusses the universal human need to create ideal forms, an important topic that has relevance to the ideal self and to other aspects of psychic functioning. He states:

> Inherent in human thought is a tendency to create ideal images, to stabilize and elaborate them however vaguely and unstably, to search the environment for their counterparts, and to perceive and assess the environment (and the self) in terms of its correspondence to these ideal images. In this conception, *every wish creates an ideal* [p. 160].

In the obsessive-compulsive, one set of ideal forms emphasizes her own functioning and its flawless, dispassionate nature. The destruction of aspects of the indwelling self is implied in that ideal, but there is also an act of creation and certainly one of ambition and striving that may support extraordinary achievements.

The unusually high level of investment many obsessive-compulsive individuals make in the ego ideal is an outgrowth of conflict, since the child who surrenders much of her indwelling self seeks to reinvest in some substitute self that can give satisfaction; she abandons ordinary, natural responsiveness to people and events and establishes, instead, an elaborate set of "desirable" behaviors, which bring self-congratulation if they can be produced.

In the chapter to follow, I will take a closer look at Annette's and Sidney's shame experiences. The aim of this second look will be to extend the clinical context of the discussions, so that shame's relationship to other emotions and personality dynamics can be examined. The roots of the type of shame under consideration are multiform. They reach into the earliest child–caregiver inter-actions but also into later identifications (which give shape to ideal selves and to superego strictures) and dynamics of conflict and defense.

CHAPTER 3

Shame in Obsessive-Compulsive Personalities

Expanded Contexts

> There was a good chance that it would at least make Shigekuni acutely aware of the stern and watchful eye of the law. He would see all the amorphous, steaming, filthy detritus of human passions processed right then and there according to the impersonal recipes of the law. Standing by in such a kitchen should teach Shigekuni a great deal about technique.
>
> —Yukio Mishima *(Spring Snow)*

The aim of this chapter is to reintroduce and extend the clinical and literary data from Chapter Two in order to look more closely at central shame concerns of the individuals under consideration. In using Mr. Stevens as a subject for discussion, particular interest will be paid to the interactions between early shame experience and later, hypertrophied superego activity, as well as to driven pursuit of ideal self-images. Annette will be reconsidered primarily with regard to her use of shame as a resistance to insight and personality change. Sidney's denial of shame and his defensive preference for considering himself a victim of shaming will also be discussed.

THE INFLUENCE OF EARLY HELPLESSNESS ON SUPEREGO AND EGO IDEAL

The obsessional adult's heavy emphasis on superego activity, featuring concepts of right and wrong, easily distracts us and the person himself from tracks left by early, interpersonally generated shame experience. Early experiences of helplessness, possibly

69

including shame, contribute to the superego development that then obscures the prior experience, for example, if infantile help-lessness and shame over failed efforts to engage Mother in play lead to later conviction that excessive play is "bad" and must be controlled (Miller, 1989). The obsessive-compulsive individual's emphasis on perfection with regard to self-control similarly can mask early shame experience and other forms of helplessness.

In pursuit of the tracks of early shame, let us turn again to Mr. Stevens and reconsider his exchange with Miss Kenton concerning his dimly lit room and cloaked reading material (Ishiguro, 1989). Clearly, Mr. Stevens lacks a real developmental history, but there is some value in the exercise of generating hypotheses about his early experience. In my first look at the quoted passage, I focused on Mr. Stevens's destructiveness toward human warmth, without much attention to the roots of that orien-tation, other than Mr. Stevens' identification with a father who valued "dignity" and disdained emotion. In considering further Mr. Stevens's anxious rejection of Miss Kenton, we can begin by highlighting the notion that, in some homes, shaming responses to self-expression occur very early, prior to language or to objec-tive self-awareness. Wurmser (1981) attends this realm of human relations when he considers punitive or disinterested caregiver responses to the infant's first efforts at interpersonal influence.

Mr. Stevens's telling of his life history focuses on his father and his father's modeling of dignity, which Stevens eagerly absorbed and appears to have amplified by outdignifying even his father, but his mother, indeed *any* mothering person, is entirely absent from the story. Additionally, we note that the qualities often asso-ciated with motherliness (warmth, ease, flexibility) are lacking in Mr. Stevens's personality. If, for the purpose of argument, we can treat Mr. Stevens as an actual person, a number of hypotheses flow from the observations about his reserved character. The argu-ment already put forth was that Mr. Stevens's internalization of his father's (and culture's) dignified behavior led to suppression of the indwelling self, which in earlier life would have been freely experienced. One reasonable additional or alternative argument would be that Mr. Stevens suffered from indifferent or hostile responses to his own expressiveness from early in life; thus, he was inclined to abandon those increasingly pain- and conflict-laden aspects of self even prior to a well-articulated understanding that his father admired dignity and disdained emotionality.

The maturation of the capacity to view the self as an other brings with it the means to evaluate and direct the self. Pairing these self-managing capabilities with an available paternal model that idealized self-renunciation would have allowed the child Stevens to imagine he had found a way out from the infant's painful experiences of being real and emotional in a nonresponsive surround. Thus, he takes distance from genuineness due to the early discouragement it brought and also because the shame-pride system his father promoted added another level of punishment for humanness and—a new element—proffered the reward of pride for self-renunciation. Now at least there came the possibility of dignity, of goodness, even of "greatness" if one could excel at suppressing the indwelling self. Thus, someone of significance to the to-be-obsessional person offers the child an exit from the shame of being unrecognized and unrewarded. The child can stop being his shameful self. He can adopt the parent's ideals or ideals found elsewhere and become an overcontrolled false self the parent will admire or at least the ego ideal will admire. We will see these same dynamics with Sidney.

A parallel development, in the realm of the superego, leads to moralistic condemnation of those emotions and impulses that have led to experiences of shame. Thus, as indicated earlier, the child comes to believe that those experiences that have brought shame are "bad" and not to be pursued. He takes pleasure and finds power in the act of condemning feelings or behaviors that once resulted in shame.

There is a second slightly, but significantly, different developmental path that also seems plausible for Mr. Stevens. According to this alternative formulation, the young boy may not have suffered so much from *shame* early on but suffered more from other forms of pain that follow from a child's attempt to relate to caretakers who are unengageable or hostile. Thus, his pain might have been the pain of frustration, helplessness, rage, and loneliness. Stevens's adult personality structure, which strongly emphasizes the dignity of self-renunciation (and shame of humanness), would have served as a way to keep the child Stevens clear of the level of relating that was pain-laden, whether that early pain consisted of shame or other emotions.

If we return once more to the quoted scene with Miss Kenton, we might think of Mr. Stevens as tempted, in the present, by an image of motherly warmth and sensuality that is highly dangerous

to him, not just because of superego strictures against sexuality
or fear of the reenactment of early shaming, but because opening
himself to the possibility of warmth may mean vulnerability to
infantile rage, depression, or flooding linked to the frustration
of early wishes. Thus, he stays on the higher ground of "dignity"
by using his ego ideal's advocacy for cold perfection to beckon
him as far as possible from areas of danger.

We might additionally conjecture that later overinvestment in
the ideal self or in the judging, shaming aspects of the superego
would have served to provide Mr. Stevens with an alternative
love object that substituted in part for the absent mother. He
readily could love and admire his own wise conscience (and be
loved by it in return). The "I expect you to do everything on
your own, in adult fashion" theme of his conscience would have
further protected him from missing a mother, while offering the
solace of pride if he could manage to do without.

Stevens's pride over dignity again places us in the territory of
the ego ideal. Mr. Stevens's ego ideal is neither the regressive
pursuit of fantasied omnipotence Lasch portrays (of which we
will see better examples in the chapters on narcissistic disturbance) nor the mature striving for transcendent experience in
love or art also described by Lasch. Stevens finds his perfection
in the minutiae of daily life, while also using such minutiae as
a bulwark against regression. What he loves is order and precision, and he is loved by his superego to the extent he can embody
those qualities. Mr. Stevens's perfectionism is essentially private
and is isolated from meaningful commerce with others.

SHAME AND RESISTANCE TO
PSYCHOTHERAPEUTIC CHANGE

Annette demonstrates the role of overt childhood shaming and
also a number of more circuitous routes to adult shame. Annette,
whose dominant character formation is obsessive-compulsive,
evidenced major anxiety concerning all representations of the self
enlivened by passion, both sexual and aggressive. Movement toward
assertiveness or sexual aliveness regularly brought complaints of
feeling dumb, foolish, or self-conscious. She attributed these
unpleasant feelings to others' demeaning behavior toward her
and also to longstanding "low self-esteem," which she blamed on
experiences of humiliation at the hands of a temperamental, often

explicitly critical father. Verbally reviewing these two arenas for shaming (present and past) seemed satisfying to her in the moment but brought little change in her readiness to function more freely in life. She continued with excessive worrying, obsessive checking and doubting, and chronic fatigue.

A lengthy period of therapy work led me to the impression that Annette's fears of being stupid and foolish did indeed take shape and gain their specific content in relation to Father's outspoken, periodic disapproval. When she spoke to herself about feeling like a fool or heard in others' remarks a relentlessly demeaning voice, she regularly related the present experiences to her father's words. However, the prolonged and rather stubborn maintenance of Annette's shame feelings and their positioning, alongside the obsessive behavior, as clear impediments to sexuality and self-assertion suggested additional early determinants of the adult shame and important dynamics related to current attachment to pathology.

Annette's portrayals of her mother presented her as the more loving and more loved parent. But Mother, though periodically doting, was chronically exhausted, as well as being uncomfortable and ineffectual with active children. When her daughter angered her with rebellious behavior, she withdrew into silence for days. According to Broucek's (1991) objectification theory, Mother's inability to respond appreciatively to Annette's inner experience would have generated shame. This notion remains a hypothesis since I was not able to find unequivocal support for it. What seemed clearer was that Annette felt threatened with loss of intimacy with Mother if she held to her investment in the spirited aspects of self. She also felt guilty about Mother's unhappiness and exhaustion, which she judged to be contingent on Annette's own activity. Thus, Annette's restriction of her expressions of assertiveness and sexuality by reducing herself to an inept, obsessionally constrained, retreating individual served to return her to a guilt-free partnership with Mother. Both the experience of shame and the effects of shame bonded her with Mother.

In contrast with Mother, Father sometimes responded joyfully to Annette's excitement and sometimes reacted shamingly. Fluctuations in response depended on Father's own emotional state, which was influenced by alcohol. Unlike Mother, Father was more likely to engage with an excited or curious Annette, who would stay up late into the night hungrily consuming his stories and telling her own. Annette recalls being excited by Father's responsiveness to her, but frightened by it as well. Father was alcoholic and impulsive, and he did not provide adequate limits and structure. Her pleasure with Father pulled her away from Mother, only to send her spinning off into an exciting but frightening new realm. At times of excitement with Father, she was especially needful of Mother's presence, since Father could be overstimulating, but it was at those times that Mother seemed most absent. The lively self was threatened by terrifying images of death (which meant loss of self-definition and loss of the emotionally alive mother) and by indistinct, but terrifying, feelings about punishment. Thus, it became safer, as Annette's character consolidated, to grow increasingly preoccupied with Father's shaming interactions with her, rather than the exciting ones, and to restrict her own excitement both through highlighting its link to shame and through obsessive-compulsive vigilance and orderliness. Sexual excitement was also associated with sadism toward her mother and brothers and with damage to her weakly mother, so it carried many levels of danger.

Aggressive feelings were similarly restricted by an obsessive-compulsive mind-set and by shame. Annette negated most possibilities for vigorous or decisive action through her obsessional back-and-forth movements or through her masochistic insistence on misery, which will be further explored in Chapters Six and Seven. But if she ever did break free and move a bit more assertively, shame quickly entered to pronounce her or her activity foolish or flawed. Aggressiveness signified kinship with Father, whose temper could be eruptive, while Mother was seen as incapable of utilizing or withstanding direct aggression. Thus, to limit aggression through obsessionality or to react with shame to any aggression experienced served to reinforce close affiliation with Mother. An example of restricting aggression with shame would be the time Annette came late for therapy and talked about "feeling dumb," instead of exploring her self-assertive choice to be late rather than forego an activity of some importance to her.

For Annette, shame often was active in the relationship to the therapist. The therapist's inclination to explore Annette's entrenchment in spiritless obsessing elicited in Annette angry humiliation about being told she was not all right the way she was. The humiliation immediately would shift attention away from the deadening effects of the obsessing and onto Annette's

shame. The eruption of shame at those junctures can be understood not just as "low self-esteem," as Annette would put it, and
not just as reawakened scenes of early shame experienced with
a critical father, but also as a learned use of shame to block any
input aimed at opening the door to emotion and movement. The
humiliation stirred when her attachment to obsessing and misery
were identified probably was intensified by Annette's unarticulated knowledge that she wanted to preserve the deadening
obsessive-compulsiveness the therapist was attempting to explore.
When a person is ready to give up a behavior or attitude, he is
not so humiliated by having it articulated since there is an awareness that a remedy for self-esteem will be found just around the
corner he is turning. But if a person is determined to keep a
behavior because it feels vitally protective, then having the destructive aspects of that behavior exposed feels humiliating and
frightening. Since the person feels he cannot move away from
the problematic behavior in order to restore self-esteem, he will
use the complaint of "being humiliated" to attempt to move the
therapist to restore his self-esteem by retracting the offending
interpretation.

Also important to Annette's humiliated response to such
confrontations was the unarticulated pride she had attached to
her state of inertia, as if immobility represented a grand accomplishment, a unique balancing act that was her own special work
of art, which the therapist devalued through efforts to promote
movement. An example follows of an exchange that might have
occurred in Annette's therapy. The passage demonstrates some
of the dynamics that promoted stasis within Annette's personality organization. Other such dynamics will be explored in the
context of masochism:

> Annette: I'm really tired today [sounds dreary and fatigued].
> I took a nap before I came here. It's lucky I woke up. I
> think I might be getting a headache, too. The animals [at
> the vet clinic where she works] were so wound up today.
> Therapist: Why so tired?
> A: I told you. The animals were wound up. I didn't get enough
> sleep last night either. [She starts to yawn and struggles to
> keep open her eyes.]
> T: You're getting sleepy now?
> A: Yeah. [pauses] Elliot and I had dinner with my parents last
> night. My mother was complaining about my youngest brother.

He doesn't do anything to help around the house. My mother complains but she doesn't really encourage him to get off his butt. She enables him.

T: What about here? Should I be encouraging you to be more active here?

A: What? Oh, I see. I didn't mean that.

T: You get sleepy and turn off the lively parts of yourself. You don't get wound up like the animals you work with.

A: [suddenly looks angry, clams up]

T: You're feeling angry?

A: [nods] I'm about to lose my temper.

T: Are you feeling like I'm pushing you? Criticizing you?

A: Yes.

T: How could I be helpful?

A: Leave me alone. I'd like to take a nap.

T: An expensive nap.

A: [laughs]

T: My intent isn't to criticize you, but to explore why you can't allow yourself more lively experience . . . which relates to the things you talk about wanting, like a better social life and sex life.

A: I don't know why I get so mad. I just get so uncomfortable. [She begins cautiously to explore her anxiety.]

Annette's sense of being humiliated by the therapist, who has pointed to her defenses, undoubtedly draws on early experiences of being demeaned by her father but seems intensified by her intuition that she must hold to the behavior that makes her vulnerable to criticism, the only alternative being to face the aspects of herself about which she is deeply anxious. Furthermore, Annette's identity is anchored to her obsessing, worrying, and fatigue, though she regards these traits ambivalently. She sees how they restrict her, yet they represent her power over circumstance, and they signify as well her individuality, her closeness to Mother, and the strict conscience in which she historically has taken pride. Later discussion of masochism will consider how such behavior serves to extract nurturing attention from others.

Annette brings to mind a comment by Broucek (1991):

In other words, the sense of self, if not based on effective interaction and communication with other persons, may instead be based on effective inhibitory activities in relation to oneself. Thus, with certain patients one cannot modify their defenses without also seriously disturbing their sense of self and producing profound depersonalization experiences [p. 29].

During much of her adolescence, stimulated by sexual fantasy, Annette felt unreal. She had become more effective in stopping the self than in using the self to engage with the world. Associated with stopping the impassioned self was the fantasy of controlling vital relationships by doing so. For example, she would make Mother love her by being a zombie. The importance self-restriction can assume in personality formation is addressed by Zerbe (1993) when she examines the anorexic whose sense of self is constructed around refusing appetites, rather than using appetites to interact with the world.

For Annette, shame and obsessive-compulsive restriction of behavior work in tandem as two levels of self-limitation, which are used primarily with regard to the vital self: the obsessive-compulsive organization aims to keep the bull from getting out of the stall; shame sends it back in if it eludes containment.

DENYING AN EMOTION: SHAME SUPPLANTED BY COMPLAINTS OF BEING SHAMED

For comparison and contrast with Annette, we can reconsider Sidney, the discussion of whom will double as a transition into next chapter's topic of narcissism, since he has many narcissistic, as well as obsessive-compulsive, dynamics. Sidney is more compulsive than he is obsessive: like Annette, he is careful with time and money, is morally scrupulous, and is perfectionistic and intolerant. While Annette's need to do things with mechanical perfection vies with her need to identify with an ineffectual mother, Sidney's perfectionism is unattenuated. He cannot stand to waste time or make errors, and he has contempt for others' inefficiency and sentimentality, though such contempt burdens his conscience. He constantly plans upcoming activities and makes lists of all that must be done. When his progress through a list is impeded, he feels preoccupied and dysphoric.

Sidney felt forced into therapy by a particular compulsive behavior that was emblematic of dyscontrol; the symptom infuriated and humiliated him by demonstrating the failure of his lifelong determination toward self-control. His symptomatic behavior corresponded to Salzman's conceptualization of obsessive-compulsive symptomatology:

> The term *obsessive-compulsive neurosis* refers to a wide variety of phenomena that may be manifested at any time in a person's life. It refers to thoughts, feelings, ideas, and impulses that an individual cannot dispel in spite of an inner desire to do so. The compelling nature of the activity—even though it may be illogical, undesirable, and unnecessary—is the central issue. Generally such thoughts or feelings are alien to the individual's usual attitudes and are experienced as being somewhat strange, even outrageous, sometimes disgusting, and, at times, frightening. Their presence is embarrassing and quite distressing. It is an intriguing development—particularly in the face of current notions of free will and freedom of choice—because despite all the wishes, desires, and active opposition of the person, he is forced by some internal pressure to concern himself with a variety of experiences that may be distasteful or frightening [pp. 13–14].

Sidney is also well described by Salzman's description, "It is his unwillingness to settle for anything less than the best that makes him feel superior to others and is frequently responsible for arrogant and contemptuous attitudes toward those who will settle for 'second best'" (p. 54).

With respect to shame, Sidney is opposite to Annette in that he is quick to enumerate his areas of pride and to deny that he experiences shame. Sidney finds no safety in advertising his shame and humiliation as Annette does; for him, these emotions are thoroughly unacceptable. Humiliation serves a self-protective role only when it engenders the accusation that the other person in the interaction is behaving so as to humiliate Sidney: in that case, one does not feel ashamed, but feels *shamed*, and therefore entitled to anger and retaliation, which push the other person to a safe remove and eliminate any wishes for closeness Sidney otherwise might feel.

Sidney sees many aspects of life and most aspects of the psychotherapeutic situation as engineered to elicit shame. He would stop short of saying he actually *feels* shame in those situations but would keep his emphasis on the other's intention to evoke shame or the other's behaving so as to shame him. Thus, with Sidney, in contrast with Annette, we see a more active fight against shame, which is seen as a particularly noxious, detested state out of keeping with his prideful sense of himself. While Annette may feel indignant and entitled to self-pitying complaint if someone belittles her, Sidney will feel fury. When Sidney, on occasion, does feel shame, he strives fiercely to eliminate the precipitating behavior.

From the outset, Sidney took therapy to be a badge of shame and failure. To engage in the process was to acknowledge a flawed part of the self. A complimentary word about a job well-done within the therapy hour was an insult, since the work of therapy was defined as so beneath him, so predicated on helplessness, that he should be able to toss it off effortlessly and move on to something more worthy of him.

This associating of therapy (and therapist) with the needy, ungoverned, and therefore humiliated self seemed an essential setting of the stage for the therapy relationship. This particular stage setting represented a tenacious resistance to commitment to the therapy and to valuing of it. Yet the choice to be so helpless that he absolutely required another person's aid (a choice he, after all, had made, however ambagiously) seemed also to be an assertion, on the part of the indwelling self, that he was not an island and did not fully wish to be one; he wanted to explore the realms of dependency that had been obstructed for him as a child. One might say, looking from this point of view, that even the attaching of profound shame to the act of seeking therapy had not deterred him from his goal of human connection. Though he defined therapy as humiliation, he attended, or endured, his sessions regularly, though caught in an obsessive debate about the value of the experience. One motivation to remain in therapy seemed to be the wish to defeat and humiliate the therapist, in order to restore dignity to a defeated self. But also active was the wish to make a human connection, which required dethroning the belief that vulnerability signifies humiliation.

I will not discuss the unfolding of Sidney's treatment in detail but will mention a few patterns relevant to shame experience. The first time I met with Sidney and experienced his formidable resistance to needing or wanting anything from me and noted as well the disgrace that surrounded his seeking of therapy, I found myself trying to imagine a childhood situation that might correspond to such feelings. What came to mind was a child who asks his mother, "Mom, will you go to the park with me?" and the mother's response is, "What's the matter with you? You can't go by yourself?" In other words, the wish for human companionship inherent in the request is not recognized and valued as being simply that, but is reinterpreted as a deficiency with regard to autonomy. Anything the child needs, or wants, that has to do with human exchange, play, or intimacy is seen as a shameful insufficiency.

As the treatment unfolded, it became clear that Sidney needed to cast the entire relationship in shame terms, in part to reenact his childhood experience of being a failure because of being human, but also to keep distance from the therapist and to dramatize, through a distorted reenactment, the difficulty of achieving mutuality with his parents. Though he felt successful in most other areas of his life, in therapy, Sidney felt like a failure; he vacillated between feeling ashamed of his failure and faulting me for setting up a situation designed to defeat him.

Therapy stood apart from the rest of his endeavors in being difficult to do and impossible to comprehend; therapy was mystifying: it could not be grasped. He often felt "in a blur" in treatment and only on occasion did he "wake up, and see the room." He despised the fact that in therapy he felt constrained; he sat and fixated the floor molding and felt like a fool. The whole venture was a humiliation.

The impossibility of therapy seemed to parallel something impossible in his communication of needs and wishes to his parents. When I asked about that parallel, he found himself describing his relationship with Mother in the same words he had used to describe the maddening treatment. He said of his communications with Mother, "It should be so simple," meaning, "What I'm saying isn't hard to understand but I never get through to her." As he began to describe his inability to get Mother to understand him, he started to cough and had to leave the room and spend the remaining few minutes of the hour in the bathroom. When he returned, he remained standing as if to end the hour and prevent any return to the discussion of Mother and any return to the brief moment of working harmoniously around significant material. His remedy for emotional discomfort was usually to redouble efforts at controlling his feelings, thoughts, and expressions.

Sidney continued to construe everything in treatment as a task or test he must fail. Once, he became quietly furious with me for ending a session by posing a broadly conceived question. I later learned that he had experienced the whole session as me asking him questions that he "failed" at answering. When I ended the session with a particularly "difficult" question, he felt he had no chance whatsoever to "succeed" with this question, given the shortness of time and the challenging nature of the question. He felt I expected him to resume next week with this same topic; he saw that expectation as unfair because, by then, his mind would have moved way beyond this topic. He would fail next week, too, right from the beginning of the hour.

My own experience of the hour had been that Sidney was atypically withdrawn and detached, and I had asked a few questions as an effort to engage him, to draw the two of us closer. My reaction to his concern about forgetting the therapy material between sessions also brought in the theme of closeness: I wondered if he wanted more frequent sessions, something I had recommended earlier but he had refused. To venture such a query seemed a personally risky act, given the likelihood Sidney would respond with a smirking dismissal of such a comment. Therapy at this stage seemed like a game of "hot potato" in which humiliation was tossed back and forth between us. Sidney seemed to be saying, "Someone will be humiliated and defeated here, and it isn't going to be me."

Sidney's insistence on keeping therapy an impenetrable process raised questions about what it would mean to him for therapy to be understandable, manageable, and comfortable. Each time this question was posed, he laughed and said triumphantly, "Then I'd leave." His notion was that the only task of therapy was to overcome its impossible nature; then he would terminate. He could not allow himself the fantasy of a comfortable relationship that could continue on. Keeping therapy intractable was the only way to keep it going.

Sidney perhaps was reenacting an early experience of only getting contact when he was in a state of shameful neediness: one must be broken down to be engaged. But he also was insisting, through his behavior, that our relationship not depart from the model of difficult engagement established with early caregivers. He would complain about the impossibility of our relationship but require that difficulty to persist. He would forewarn me of ways in which other caregivers had failed him, yet it felt inevitable that I, too, though cautioned, would fail in precisely the same ways. When on one occasion he experienced an easy give-and-take between us (just what he had hungered for), he immediately destroyed its value by arguing that if therapy was this easy after all, then today's accomplishment meant nothing. So after weeks of protesting the lack of rapport, he devalued the day's painless exchange as valueless because it was easy. Many hours had this structure of a doing and undoing sequence in which he established some communication and then blew it to bits by denying or doubting its meaningfulness. Often, I was left paralyzed in every effort, an experience that presumably once belonged to Sidney.

One day, I conveyed to Sidney my impression that he felt ashamed, as a child, for having any human desires. I used the playing-in-the-park analogy and wondered if he now feels I might say to him, "Why do you want me to go to the park with you? What's the matter with you? Are you *incapable* of going by yourself?" Though normally he would have balked at any reference to his upbringing, Sidney deepened the interpretation in what seemed to me to be his first act of taking in, digesting, and using something I offered him. He said he thought his shame was not the issue, that he used shame in order to protect himself from disappointment. In other words, if he says to himself, "It's shameful to ask Mother to go to the park," he stops himself from asking for the company and need not face asking and being hurt if Mother says, "I'm busy," or if she misconstrues his request and offers to take him to the beach when he wants to go to the park. Thus, Sidney was pointing to shame that is not a function of a child reacting to objectification nor is it the activity of a critical superego identified with a rejecting parent; it is an ego mechanism for keeping the self off unsafe ground. Though I expect shame *was* a primary issue, not only a defense, his work around the interpretation seemed meaningful, not only in content but in form.

As much as Sidney complained that "my" process was mystifying, I experienced him as confounding as he reformulated events between us in order to wash away traces of contact or sharing. The early part of the treatment often felt as if he were saying to me, "I want to go through that door (that takes me closer to you)." He goes through the door; he joins me on the other side. He frowns and says, "That wasn't a door I went through."

I say, "Yes, it was a door."

"Okay," he says, "If it was a door, then I must not have gone through it."

"You went through it," I say.

"Well," he says, "then it must be that you're over on the other side of the door."

"No," I say, "I'm on this side; we're on the same side."

"Then I was mistaken," he says, "I didn't want to go through the door; I hate doors; I'll go back." He desires a connection; he pursues it; then he undoes what he did, often through complex manipulations of reality that feel like moves in a chess match where I must somehow outplay him to get him to accept we have been playing together.

I try to step back from that kind of exchange, to say, "Look at what you're doing. Is it really what you want to be doing? Do you really want to insist we must play against each other, even though you've been complaining that we don't play together?" For Sidney, to accept "playing together" means, "Now I am with you, you can hurt me; I have surrendered control." He says, "In therapy, I struggle even to know there's another person in the room."

Historically, while Annette maintained a loving connection with Mother by disavowing certain vigorous aspects of the self, for Sidney, the wish to love and be loved itself became highly shameful, and the associated sense of vulnerability bred hatred. To need affection or to need to give affection were felt to be deeply shameful needs. Self-control, independence, and pridefulness became the defenses both against shame itself and against disappointment and frustration if one expressed needs that went unrecognized and unmet. To have a need was both a shameful defect and a dangerous point of vulnerability to frustration and disappointment.

Listening to Sidney, one had little sense that his needs were taunted or ridiculed while growing up. But they seemed to have been not heard or misheard over and over, leading to fury and to confusion about whether he was somehow defective in communicating or defective by virtue of needing or was the caregiver massively defective in listening and responding. Any of these explanations portrayed an intolerable reality.

If Annette's strongest statement was, "I will not be a person of passion because that separates me from Mother and leaves me in an uncontrolled state, neither of which I can stand; I would rather be insecure and stupid and ashamed," Sidney's might be, "I will not be a person who needs human warmth because then

I will be ashamed and infuriated and disappointed when my need is disregarded, and I will not be a person who shows human warmth to others because then I will be shamed for my lack of self-control."

Sidney and Annette are alike in attributing many of the shame experiences in treatment to the therapist, who is seen as creating the patient's shame. Shame is not experienced as internally generated due to one's own sensitivities but is seen as the other's misstep in relation to oneself. Thus, the patient's solution to shame in the therapy is for the therapist to be very circumspect about his words. This pressure for caution becomes one way that the patient controls the therapy interactions so that no unsafe ground is tested. For example, Sidney is shamed by any comment that suggests he has some investment in keeping the therapy relationship antagonistic or ineffectual. Angrily complaining about such shaming lets him push the therapist away from that threatening area of exploration and push him beyond connection with Sidney altogether.

Sidney fears that any partner in interaction will dump all that is bad, degraded, or inadequate onto him and take all that is pristine and perfect for himself. He openly takes pride in opposing that outcome, in saying, "I'll fault you before you'll get anything bad to stick to me." But he feels troubled by his inability to work with others and wonders whether the persistent friction between himself and others points to a personal defect, the presence of which defeats the original determination to be free of shame.

My willingness to "share the blame" by acknowledging my own contributions to difficulties in the therapy seemed gradually to relax Sidney so that he could tolerate looking at some of his own shortcomings without feeling defeated. Also important in the therapy were simple acts of taking notice of his needs, including concrete needs around time or money. Seeing that his ordinary needs would be respected appeared to obviate his fear that he would be a nameless, faceless nothing forced to fight for recognition or deny desire for it.

Shame speaks with many voices in obsessive-compulsive contexts. It is the therapy's ally, the true voice of the indwelling self saying, "What damage have I done to myself by disowning my feelings? What contemptible thing have I done to others who wanted to relate to me?" And it is the therapy's adversary, the voice of the harshly critical superego that paralyzes the self with shame and guilt whenever free movement is attempted. Shame in the obsessive-compulsive speaks as well to the need to hide the offendingly active and defined self behind an ineffectual, belittled self. And shame is the voice of the rejected child-self saying, "I cannot bring Mother close, which makes me feel small; thus, I prefer to deny my needs and to find solace through self-control."

CHAPTER 4

Shame in the Background

Narcissistic Disturbances

Mind in its purest play is like some bat
That beats about in caverns all alone,
Contriving by a kind of senseless wit
Not to conclude against a wall of stone.

It has no need to falter or explore;
Darkly it knows what obstacles are there,
And so may weave and flitter, dip and soar
In perfect courses through the blackest air.

And has this simile a like perfection?
The mind is like a bat. Precisely. Save
That in the very happiest intellection
A graceful error may correct the cave.
                    —Richard Wilbur ("Mind")

SELF-PSYCHOLOGICAL THEORY AND SHAME

Narcissistic disturbance is the context for this chapter's examination of shame and shame theory. Morrison's (1989) book, *Shame: The Underside of Narcissism*, explores this shame context, so I will draw heavily on that text, in which Morrison reviews Kohut's thinking on self-development, notes Kohut's inattention to shame, and undertakes modifications of Kohutian theory in order to carve out a larger place for shame.

Many definitions of narcissistic disorder have been advanced in the literature. Broucek (1991) provides a simple, but useful, phenomenological definition by stating, "To the extent that one is excessively preoccupied with or dominated by concerns about one's image, one's status, or oneself as an object for others, to that extent one is narcissistic" (p. 6). Social critic Lasch (1992) objects to "the equation of narcissism with 'selfishness of the extreme form,' in the words of Daniel Yankelovich" (p. 57). He goes on to say, "The terms have little in common. Narcissism signifies a loss of selfhood, not self-assertion. It refers to a self threatened with disintegration and by a sense of inner emptiness" (p. 57). Lasch's definition emphasizes the inner sense of deficiency. Broucek's definition stresses the narcissistic individual's preoccupation with self-image, which presumably reflects discomfort with the inner self. In pointing to the self-bolstering activities of the narcissistically disturbed individual and to the inner sense of vulnerability, Broucek's and Lasch's concepts intersect those of Kohut (1977). Kohut (1977) sees narcissistic personality disorders as "(1) defects, acquired in childhood, in the psychological structure of the self and (2) secondary structure-formations, also built up in early childhood" (p. 3). The latter include defensive and compensatory structures.

As one comes to know the inner space of narcissistically troubled people, one witnesses a struggle with deep concerns about being deficient and not matching the perfectionistic images of self that are held as indispensable, and one sees people who respond to their concern with denial of deficiency and with exaggerated demonstrations of power or importance, sometimes alternating with a painful awareness of flaws. Contrasted with those to be considered in the later chapters on masochism, the people I will discuss in this chapter do not present with constant depressive misery or defeat. They tend more toward expansiveness and assertions of power and importance, which alternate with expressively conveyed suffering.

Stylistically, their expansiveness separates them from the determined obsessive-compulsives of the previous chapter, as does a greater emphasis on controlling the environment than on restricting the self. Reich's (1960) description is helpful. She refers to the denial of defect and the "compensatory narcissistic fantasy whose grandiose character affirms the denial. It is as if the person is saying, 'It is not so. I am not helpless, bleeding, destroyed. On the contrary, I am bigger and better than anyone else. I am the greatest, the most grandiose'" (p. 217).

Shame represents a lurking danger for narcissistic people. Many fear the moment in which shame over some overwhelming, unintegrable deficiency will flood them or perforate their inflated pride. There is a feeling that the self contains some defect that is beyond facing, that must, at all costs, be masked. Thus, shame is feared as a traumatic affect, which gives it a different status and feel from the major types of shame discussed in relation to obsessive-compulsive characters. For them, shame more quietly lights a path, establishes boundaries, tells one where it is safe to walk, where one must avoid.

Thinking of shame in the context of narcissism, I think of Fred, addicted to alcohol and drugs, who literally would fight to the death before admitting the most trivial of errors, who, in therapy, would constantly bid for words of praise. Fred conformed to Mayman's (1974) description of "the shame personality." Every ride in his car was a competition with drivers who might outperform him. Every mislaying of his keys was a potential humiliation if his wife spotted them while he was helplessly looking. A query about an overdue bill sparked fury because he felt such shame over his difficulty making money. I think also of Jeremy, to be discussed at length in the next chapter, to whom his therapist mentioned at the end of one session, "You are ashamed of that quality in yourself." Jeremy came to the next session angry. He felt his doctor had assaulted him, had "zinged" him at the end of the hour with this intolerable idea of being ashamed. To feel ashamed meant to be shameful; it meant he had something about which he needed to feel ashamed. He found that idea intolerable, in part, because he expected himself to be perfect, in part, because the idea resonated with a feeling of deficiency he carefully skirted. His fear of shame was, in part, his fear of some awful idea about the self that would sink into him and stay with him and could not be banished with rage or denial. By using this word, *shame,* his doctor had undermined him, had whisked the rug out from under his feet. In this context, the fearsome idea seemed to be, "You are no good," not, to borrow Wurmser's terminology, "You are unlovable." The focus was on the self, not as embraced or rejected by the other, but standing alone and subject to self-observation. It is probable that the experience of defect derived from a sense of being unlovable, but it is important to note that the known terror was of being imperfect in and of himself.

Before proceeding into a discussion of Morrison's (1987, 1989) self-psychological thinking about shame and narcissism, let me introduce the notion of omnipotence. Though one could argue for distinctions between "omnipotence" and "grandiosity" (the former specifically emphasizing the self's *powers,* the latter the overall resplendence of the self), I am choosing at present to merge the concept of omnipotence with that of grandiosity as roughly equivalent terms referring to the self's stature and power. I do so in order to bring into relationship a number of writers who use these words. In this chapter, since the emphasis will be on self-psychological theory, the term *grandiosity,* with its stronger connotation of specific self-images, will dominate.

Broucek (1991) offers us yet another term, *idealized self,* stating, "I prefer the term *idealized self* to *grandiose self* because the latter term is somewhat deprecatory" (p. 59). Broucek sees the idealized self as a "fantasy system" that consists of "families of imaginatively elaborated 'scenes,'" including for example, "those in which one is gloriously triumphant, heroically successful, extraordinarily competent or sexually attractive, admired by others, and so forth" (p. 59). It is not hard to see that Broucek's descriptions fit some of the case material from the previous chapters, specifically, Mr. Stevens's fantasies of himself as the "great" butler, admirable in his dignity. Neither Sidney nor Annette permitted themselves the free rein on fantasy that would allow for such elaborate, conscious fantasy systems, but Sidney certainly adhered to a notion of the near-perfect self that came close to being an "idealized self" or a grandiose or omnipotent one.

The concepts of grandiosity, omnipotence, and idealized self relate to the earlier discussed constructs, ego ideal and ideal self, in that the person utilizing grandiosity, omnipotence, or idealized self imagery strives to deny any distinction between the ideal self and the actual self. She needs her ego ideal to judge her to be, in fact, as magnificent as her imagination can render her.

In the obsessional characters already considered and the narcissistic characters soon to be considered, the sense of self features many images of perfection (again, roughly, grandiosity, omnipotence, or idealized self). The character of the perfectionism may differ between these two clinical contexts, with the obsessional person emphasizing perfection in adherence to routine or in the exercise of restraint and responsibility and propounding her right not to be interfered with in the execution of her tasks. In those with primarily narcissistic disturbances, the idealized self often has a more exhibitionistic, flambuoyant, overtly powerful feel to it, as conveyed by Broucek's definition. The obsessive-compulsive is apt to seek perfection in self-restraint, while the narcissistic person's perfection features the self on display or the self in heroic action. She wants to wave a magic wand and see traffic open up before her like the Red Sea parting or to tell a joke that cripples a roomful of people with laughter. The omnipotent demands of the narcissistic individual often are more obvious than those of the obsessive-compulsive. In the obsessive-compulsive, the burdened, restrained quality of the personality may obscure such demands, as may superego objection to the aggressive quality of the perfectionistic press such expectations on others. In both clinical contexts, the idea of creating and sustaining perfection stands as a counterpoint to various experiences of helplessness.

A simplified version of Kohut's (1971, 1972) self-developmental theory (as it pertains to shame) and a similarly streamlined rendering of Morrison's (1987, 1989) shame theory may be of value at this juncture. Kohut grounds his schema of development in the controversial idea that the infant begins life making substantial use of two psychic states, one of which is grandiosity. The early grandiose sense of the self is shared with the mother, or other caretaker, through exhibitionism. The infant's exhibitionism must be responded to warmly (mirrored) by the caregiver in order for the infant gradually to modify the grandiose sense of self so that the mature self is vigorous, competent, and ambitious, but no longer dominated by an archaic sense of power and greatness.

According to Kohut, the second infantile state relevant to self-development is the child's experience of the "idealized parent imago" or the "idealized omnipotent selfobject." In this state, the infant relates to the *other*, not the self, as perfect and powerful. To the extent that the idealized other offers an empathic response to the child's admiring interest, the baby shares in the object's perfection, and her self-esteem is enhanced. Kohut believed that the two types of experience alternate in the infant, rather than one regularly antedating the other. He also believed that empathic responses from others are crucial to the positive outcome of both types of infant experience. Empathic responses lead to modification of early grandiosity and to attenuation of early idealization. Gradually, images of perfection shift to "guiding ideals" and aspirations.

Important to shame theory is Kohut's additional notion that repeated empathic failures lead to the splitting off of the early grandiose images of self and other, so that these images are retained in their original, unrealistic form and cannot be well integrated into the personality. Whenever the original aims of the child are split off, rather than being modified and integrated, the "nuclear ambitions" of the self are not realized and the self that operates in the world is depleted of vigor.

Though he is keenly interested in what happens to the *self-esteem* of the person whose personality is depleted by such splitting off of core ambitions, Kohut has relatively little to say about shame per se. What he does say is that shame is the response to the flooding of the ego with grandiose-exhibitionistic libido. One important prior condition for such shame is the splitting off of the grandiose self. The person who has split off her early grandiosity, rather than modifying it so that it can be retained as ordinary ambition, is highly shame-vulnerable because split-off exhibitionistic libido suddenly may flood the ego. Kohut (1971) describes a person experiencing "shame, because revelation at times is still accompanied by crude, unneutralized exhibitionistic libido" (p. 149). In other words, when a narcissistic person attempts to share the self with another, she does so in a way that activates and exposes her split-off, infantile grandiosity, and such exposure leads to shame. Another passage in which Kohut (1972) explicates the relationship between archaic exhibitionism and shame reads:

> On the other hand, the archaic grandiose-exhibitionistic (body-)self will from time to time assert its archaic claims, either by by-passing the repression barrier via the vertically split-off sector of the psyche or by breaking through the brittle defenses of the central sector. It will suddenly flood the reality ego with unneutralized exhibitionistic cathexes and overwhelm the neutralizing powers of the ego, which becomes paralyzed and experiences intense shame and rage [p. 373].

Shame for Kohut is not an emotion in which the ashamed person makes a *judgment* that her own behavior is deficient, because the behavior is infantile and out-of-control or it is maladaptive; shame is, in its essence, a judgment-free, largely physical experience of flushing, shrinking, and gaze aversion, which occurs automatically in response to exposure of grandiose-exhibitionistic claims and without superego judgment that the self-expression is problematic. Shame is intimately tied to narcissistic disturbance of self-structure.

Morrison (1989) is critical of Kohut's schema because of its omission of an important role for the ego ideal or ideal self; such a structure would serve as a basis for the self to *judge* its traits and behavior. Morrison indicates that Kohut originally believed that the ego ideal has a role in "controlling the exhibitionistic drive components and thus in preventing shame" (p. 72), but

Kohut later abandoned this notion, perhaps, according to Morrison, because Kohut saw the ego ideal as a concept too closely allied to drive theory and object relations theory. Kohut leaves us with flooding exhibitionism as the only cause for shame. Morrison disagrees with this unitary-cause theory of shame.

Morrison (1989) argues that shame occurs when the self judges itself deficient in relation to the ideal self, a term he prefers to ego ideal, but does not clearly distinguish from it, though contextual use sometimes suggests a definition for "ideal self" that, like Broucek's (1991) definition of "idealized self," emphasizes fantasy images of the self, not just abstract values against which one compares one's behavior. A bridge that might be used to establish some connection between Kohutian theory and Morrison's suppositions is the notion that flooding exhibitionism (Kohut's concern) is experienced as a failure to approach the "ideal shape of the self," which is Morrison's phrase, and thus flooding exhibitionism is shameful. Morrison perhaps would endorse the stated bridging idea but would argue, quite correctly I believe, that the ideal self concerns itself with a *range* of self-characteristics, not just the expression or containment of infantile exhibitionism and grandiosity.

Morrison (1987, 1989) takes pains to position his own shame thinking within the context of Kohut's general developmental theory. He talks about the grandiose self acceding developmentally to the idealization of the parent (who is experienced as a need-fulfilling "selfobject"); he departs from Kohut in seeing these two developmental experiences as more sequential than coincidental, but he agrees with Kohut's notion that both postures are critical ones. And of course, Morrison again diverges from Kohut when he conjectures that the later development of the ideal self is crucial to shame experience. The ideal self is understood to be a set of internal representations of how the self should be. In explanation, Morrison (1989) states:

> I believe that the ego ideal—and particularly the ideal self—provides a framework for understanding shame from an internal perspective. The values, idealizations, and internalized parental expectations of perfection, which form the content of the ego ideal, have been structuralized and no longer require the presence of the external object as guide. . . . It is failure to live up to this ideal self—experienced as a sense of inferiority, defeat, flaw, or weakness—that results in the feeling of shame [p. 36].

Though there is some lack of clarity on this point, I believe Morrison feels that the representations that make up the ideal self derive, at least in part, from the early grandiose self and the idealized parent imago. That is, the notions of perfection in the self and the other move into and find a final home in the ideal self. They do not, however, seem to represent the full composition of the ideal self, since Morrison also makes reference, as in the above passage, to "values" and to "internalized parental expectations of perfection" (p. 36) that contribute to the ideal self. What *is* clear is that the *notion of perfection* lives in the ideal self. Morrison states:

> This constellation of optimal, experience-near qualities and ideals forms the *ideal self*—the representation of the goal of perfection in the subjective experience of the self. The ideal self is thus an endpoint in the development of the cohesive and stable self—from grandiosity to idealization of the selfobject to final internalization of the "self as it aspires to be": cohesive, independent, vigorous, and embodying values and ideals [pp. 79–80].

Without considering all the theoretical fine points of Kohut's and Morrison's thinking, we now can review some key elements, as they pertain to shame. Kohut (1972) believes that shame is the outcome when "the flow of exhibitionistic libido becomes disturbed" (p. 395). What we call shame consists of an element of discharge and an element of blockage: "It is this disorganized mixture of massive discharge (tension decrease) and blockage (tension increase) in the area of exhibitionistic libido which is experienced as shame" (p. 395). Kohut acknowledges a relationship between shame and disturbed self-regard, and at times his contextual use of the word *shame* seems to imply a concept more like Morrison's, in which shame is elicited when one compares the actual self against inner standards. For example, in discussing attempts to cover up verbal slips, he says, "our defensive activity is primarily motivated by our shame concerning a defect in the realm of the omnipotent and omniscient self" (1972, p. 384). Despite such statements, Kohut's articulated concept of shame fails to focus on self-judgment.

In taking interest in shame as a "blockage" of exhibitionistic tension (which also has a discharge element), Kohut fits with the "braking" theorists, including Freud, Knapp, and Tomkins, each of whose interest in shame relates primarily (though not exclusively) to its control of other tendencies in the person, rather than to the shape shame gives to consciousness or to shame's role in initiating other psychological responses. These writers vary with respect to which specific tendencies they see countered or controlled. Kohut takes a narrow view of shame's functioning by considering only exhibitionism and grandiosity and not any other self-related energies that shame might interrupt. In contrast, Tomkins (1963, 1987) talks of interest and enjoyment as muffled by shame; Wurmser (1981) talks of active looking and showing; Knapp (1967) discusses the sexual instinct. Lewis (1992) states, "If, as I believe, the self-conscious emotions of shame and guilt serve as interrupt signals to inform us that the actions we have taken have failed, the interrupt clearly serves the biological function of enabling the organism to reconsider and alter its strategy" (p. 71). Lewis's notion of what shame interrupts clearly differs from Kohut's in that it is not grounded in Kohut's notions about self-structure. A comprehensive shame theory needs to consider the "interrupt" functions of shame and to consider as well the other forces set in motion by the *experience* of shame, including the wish to avoid future shame and the interest in using shame's braking capabilities toward a variety of self-protective aims.

Morrison's (1989) contribution to shame theory is his argument that the ideal self is a normal and important self-structure that mediates the generation of shame. Shame occurs when a person has failed in relation to the ideals that constitute that structure. Morrison's thinking is similar to that of a number of others (see H. Lewis [1971], M. Lewis [1992], Piers and Singer [1953]) who see shame as an emotion generated when comparison is made between the self and some standard, but Morrison brings the idea into relationship with a self-psychological theory of development and of pathological narcissism.

Morrison's concept of the ideal self (or ego ideal) is, in some respects, difficult to grasp. At times, he suggests that the ego ideal is strongly reflective of the perfectionism Kohut sees in the early developmental phases (of grandiosity and idealizing of the parental selfobject). In other words, the ideal self is just what the words suggest: it is *ideal* and it is unattainable; it is "the goal of perfection in the subjective experience of the self." There is a problem with this notion, which I believe Morrison encounters. If the ideal self is the unattainable self and if failure to match the ideal self is shame generating, then we would all feel ashamed all of the time. Morrison seems to conclude that the ideal self in the *narcissistic individual* is indeed perfectionistic, highly influenced by infantile grandiosity and, thus, constantly shame generative, whereas the ideal self in the person not narcissistically organized is less removed from the actual self. Broucek (1991), too, endorses this division, as does Schafer (1967) who states, "Given favorable parental conditions. . . . ideals will not be pitched at so great a distance from the human capabilities of the individual child (or the human species) that all realistic action will seem futile to him and despair or magical thinking seem the only way out" (pp. 144–145).

Another notion Morrison (1989) introduces is that of "approaching" the "ideal shape of the self," rather than matching it. The thought is that "approaching" the ideal self is good enough for most people; some gap between ideal and actual can be recognized without shame. It is in pondering the nature of the ideal self in the average, not especially narcissistic person that Morrison's thinking seems least developed, though he clearly believes the ideal self operates actively in people who are not narcissistically disordered.

My own thinking about these concepts has led me to question how the ideal self (retaining here Schafer's distinction between ego ideal and ideal self) operates in the average person, especially with regard to shame generation. Certainly, *ideals and values* are important to mature people, and the ego ideal can be said to operate to compare actual behavior with ideals and values, but the ideal self suggests something more embodied, as is conveyed in Broucek's descriptions of the "idealized" self; it suggests actual images of the self succeeding grandly in various poses. Such images are used by most people as part of pleasure-generating fantasies about the person one would love to be, and they are used for narcissistic soothing, but I don't know that they are present as a set of self-expectations one must attain or approach in order to forestall shame.

One could argue, as many have, that there is less disparity between the real and the ideal for the average person than for the narcissistic person (i.e., the average person's ideal self is not so unrealistic or grand) or one could argue that the ordinary person simply does not utilize ideal self images as a model for behavior. Alternatively, one might argue that highly idealized images

of self are present as a beacon or reference point for nonnarcis-
sistic people and are as perfect in nature as for the narcissistic
person but that the average person differs from the narcissistically disturbed one in having no pressing need to reach the beacon;
therefore, stopping short of it is not shame generative. Most people
likely have multiple sets of ideals, some clearly fantastic and not
utilized to measure actual behavior, others pitched within range
of actual capabilities and useful in judging real performance.

As indicated earlier, I am intrigued by the notion of ego ideal
Lasch (1984) propounds, following Novey. Here I must set aside
for the moment Schafer's distinctions, since Lasch's concept implies
roles for both ego ideal and ideal self, as well as ideal object and
general "ideals." Lasch's concept of ego ideal emphasizes the link
between perfectionistic strivings (which may take healthy or
unhealthy forms) and the universal quest for deep connection
with other persons or forces (e.g., nature), a notion allied with
Broucek's "primary communion" and self-psychology's notion of
the ongoing need for self-selfobject relatedness. The ego ideal as
thus defined is not just about the self and its assets, but about
the self's relatedness to the surround: it concerns ideal or desirable forms of self–other connection. Schafer (1967) seems to be
exploring similar terrain when he talks about the human need
for "ideal forms." One can see as well, in the inspired passage
to follow, some anticipation by Schafer (1967) of Kohut's emphasis
on the need for an idealized parent imago:

> On the other hand, as a benevolently curious or empathic thera-
> pist, the analyst may, for some patients, fill an ideal form that has
> lain empty for many years. And, in expressing appreciation of the
> analyst, such a patient may say or imply, "This is how I wanted
> to believe a parent could be," or, "This is the idea of a good parent
> I once created." Winnicott speaks in one place of a patient's "creating"
> his analyst (1948). In this limited respect, it is not a repetitious
> transference phenomenon we are contemplating: it is a form of
> remembering and of renewed invention and reality testing; it is a
> fresh and hopeful attempt by the patient to find a fit for leftover
> and tenaciously held ideal forms, or perhaps even to create mean-
> ingful ideal forms for the first time [pp. 167–168].

Following Schafer, one might conjecture that for some individuals—disappointed in object relations and in the surrounding world
in general (which includes nature, art, religion, society, and so

forth)—the ideal *self* may become the primary satisfaction for one's thirst for the admirable. This line of argument is rather different from one that conjectures that approaching the ideal self is necessary to forestall shame and secure self-esteem.

Concerning the generation of shame, I would hypothesize that, in the individual mature enough for self-reflection, shame occurs when a person feels *deficient.* To be less than ideal is not the same as being deficient. Being less than ideal generates shame only in someone for whom anything short of perfection equates with inadequacy. Fred would be an example. If he buys a toy for his little girl and finds that the toy is junk, he feels that *he* is junk because he shouldn't have made a mistake in choosing the toy. Though Wurmser's (1981) position on this question differs in some particulars from my own, he, too, believes that failures vis-à-vis the ego ideal are not invariably shame generative. He states:

> What is necessary in addition is that the inner wishful image of the self be 'betrayed' and that certain self-critical, self-punishing, and reparative processes be set in motion. Only then does shame arise. If these criteria are not fulfilled, the failing of ego standards leads to loss of self-esteem, but not to shame [p. 73].

Revisiting once more the relationship between Kohut's shame ideas and Morrison's, we note that Kohut recognized that shame can operate as a mechanism for stopping certain flowing energies. Though Kohut did not emphasize the functioning of such an energy-blocking mechanism very early in development (since he was primarily concerned with shame as an aspect of adult narcissistic disturbance) we can posit that a mechanism of this type indeed could operate early on, since it could antedate objective self-awareness.

Though Kohut joins other writers in talking about shame in terms that allow for early, pre-OSA shame experience, I hasten to add that his ideas about such shame differ significantly from some of the others who consider shame in early infancy. Consider as an example Broucek (1982, 1991), who thinks of early shame as a response directly induced in the child by seeing certain facial expressions on the face of the caretaker (or seeing no facial expression when one is sought). Even though Broucek and Kohut both emphasize the unresponsiveness of the caregiver, they differ with regard to *how* caregiver misattunement instigates shame. While Broucek sees shame as an immediate response to the parent's emotion, as does Nathanson (1992) (though Nathanson considers shame stimuli other than parental misattunement as well), Kohut (1971, 1972) sees shame as a highly *indirect* result of mirroring failure in that mirroring failure leads to thwarted, therefore split-off, grandiosity, which leads to periodic flooding grandiosity, which produces shame. We should keep in mind that all these theorists may own a bit of land in this development in that, depending on a variety of shifting factors, an infant not well responded to may feel shame, fragmentation anxiety, or other feelings not yet considered such as rage or the intensification of urges to engage the other.

In contrast to Kohut, Morrison (1989) seems to have little interest in the shame variants that might operate prior to fairly elaborate self-concepts and outside the sphere of concept formation; his contribution is to introduce the important notion that negative judgments about the self mediate shame. One can question some of the particulars of Morrison's view that the *ideal self* is the specific set of concepts that generates shame, and one can argue that shame sometimes occurs in the absence of defined self-concepts, but the broad notion that negative self-assessment does frequently produce shame seems incontestable.

There is, nonetheless, reason to remain alert to examples of shame that might follow Kohut's theory of shame genesis. We might see, for example, a man who is ashamed when he has to remove his shirt. His shame is supported by self-critical notions about his poor muscle development; thus, it seems to fall in line with Morrison's thinking about failure vis-à-vis the ideal self. But further inquiry reveals a fantasy that his chest should and could be as developed as Arnold Schwarzenegger's. Even though this fantasy suggests a split-off grandiose self structure, we still might assume the correctness of Morrison's hypothesis that the gap between real and ideal generates the shame. The point at which one would shift some toward Kohut's supposition would be the moment of perceiving that the "scrawny chest" image the man carries does not, in fact, represent the "real" (which diverges from the ideal) but, instead, represents a defensive effort to keep the grandiose fantasy split off. One then could argue that it is the emergence of the overstimulating, grandiose fantasy that generates the shame, not the gap between the real and the ideal.

Occasionally, one sees moments of acute embarrassment that seem to conform to Kohut's notion of shame generated by the sudden revelation of a grandiose sense of the self.

In jettisoning the notion of shame as an early appearing brake or blockage of some kind (whether on interaction or excitement), Morrison (1989) gives up a concept that I believe is a useful bridge to later life, active uses of shame as a characterological method for using superego affects (shame and guilt) to inhibit parts of the personality experienced as dangerous to the ego (see especially Chapters Six and Seven). He also gives up the essential idea, extensively developed by Wurmser (1981), of shame as an emotion enlisted by the punitive superego in order to curtail the self's free activity. Morrison focuses on failures to achieve the ideal self and not on "bad" actions that elicit punishment, whereas Wurmser emphasizes the use of shame affect to stop behaviors around which internal conflict centers. When, as Wurmser suggests, the superego makes a judgment against the self that takes the form, "That behavior is shameful; stop it," we have concurrently a self-appraisal and a directive to the self. The self-appraisal may flow from stable, considered values or from perfectionistic ideal self-images (Morrison's emphasis), but it can flow as well from self-annihilating needs that have developed in pathological interpersonal settings.

A concept that Kohut positioned centrally and Morrison retains is that of the grandiose self. Much controversy within psychoanalytic theory has centered on whether infantile grandiosity represents a normal developmental phase or a product of strain or trauma. Morrison's writing reflects the controversy. He states (1989, p. 54) that he prefers Kernberg's (1975) view (which is the view that the grandiose self is a pathological development), yet certain of his discussions of the normal transformation of early grandiosity into the later "ideal self" structure would seem to require that he see early grandiosity as a normal phase.

An alternative stance on this difficult question is that it probably makes sense to posit some feeling of entitlement in the infant, which is not linked to a grandiose self-concept but is simply a naive expectation that one's wishes all will be met and an associated readiness for rage if they are frustrated; such rage occurs in a child who has very limited capacity to recognize others' needs and wishes or to comprehend the reasons her own wishes cannot all be granted. The early propensity for rage and helplessness in connection with unmet needs (for food, for play, for engagement) would, in the course of normal development, give way to an acceptance of delayed gratification without such delay having any special significance with regard to self-concept or self-esteem. But if early frustration and rage are excessive and the environment cannot be trusted to provide reasonable gratification with reasonable speed, then gradually, as cognitive development allows, the early, cognitively unelaborated expectations of gratification may be conceptually elaborated with what can now be called "grandiose" ideas about who I am and what I deserve. So now enter feelings such as: "I am perfect, no one dares criticize me; no delay is acceptable; effort is beneath me"—all of which constitute the usual narcissistic mind-set. Some such development, in fact, may occur for a great many young children; later development would then determine whether the child's grandiosity becomes entrenched and, perhaps, split off, or gradually surrendered.

The Kohutian assumption of normal infantile omnipotence is nicely conveyed in a brief fictional passage by Madison Smartt Bell (1985):

> From each window, the baby could see the lights of the city fanning out in all directions to the horizon's limit. Simon, his mind so far unformed by the strictures of conscious thought, assumed that the chains of light were baubles already his own [p. 100].

Baby Simon assumes that he owns all the lights in the city, that they are his toys, which enhance him. While one can imagine such a view of the infant's apprehension of his world, as Bell does in portraying an infant destined to become a terrorist, I am not persuaded of its accuracy as a model of ordinary infant consciousness.

I find the notion of an infantile grandiose-self hard to assimilate, in part, because it is difficult to conceive of grandiosity as a largely preconceptual experience, which it likely would need to be if occurring a priori as a fundamental infantile mind-set. A second, alternate hypothesis with regard to infantile grandiosity (which answers the above objection) is that it is a transient, normal development in the older infant, in response to ordinary pressures of development; when developmental strain is excessive, the ordinarily impermanent posture may become fixed.

The notion of infantile grandiosity as a temporary, normal development is in keeping with Modell's (1968) thesis. Modell argued that the infant needs to develop a positive sense of "identity," through empathic parenting, before she can relinquish the magical (omnipotent) world that she has established early on for the purpose of creating illusory control in a situation of otherwise intolerable dependency. A positive identity, containing a sense of a "beloved self," renders the baby less object-dependent, therefore, more tolerant of the separation and object-loss that define ordinary reality. Once achieving that reality tolerance, the child can surrender the magical world. Modell states:

> [T]he very conditions of excessive dependency lead to anxiety and the creation of a private inner world. For the dread of loss and abandonment (Rochlin, 1965) provides the motive force for the creation of another world, a world that is more in keeping with the child's wish—the magical world, the world of interconnectedness between symbol and the object symbolized. In this world, separation and death are denied, for possession of a symbol of the object guarantees the existence of the object itself [pp. 85–86].

I find much value in Kohut's thoughts about infantile exhibitionism (roughly, Wurmser's delophilia) and about the need for caregiver responsiveness to such self-expression. However, I think Kohut's theory would be strengthened by keeping the notion of exhibitionism, or self-expression, separate from any notion of a "grandiose self," since the former need not be embedded in the latter. In my view, exhibitionism is one subset of a larger set of important expressive and interactive behaviors that require caregiver responsiveness; it would not stand apart as the essential behavior requiring mirroring. My argument is in keeping with Socarides and Stolorow (1984/1985), who thoughtfully consider the importance of caregiver responsiveness to *all* infantile emotions as a precondition to the integrated experience of those feeling states. Thus, my objection is not to Kohut's emphasis on parental empathy or on exhibitionistic feeling and behavior, but to his notion of a crucial, early self-organization designated as "the grandiose self" and to the associated notion that empathic failure leads primarily to splitting off of that grandiose self rather than to more broadly conceived disavowal of whatever affects the parent has not helped the child to assimilate. Speaking to this issue, Socarides and Stolorow state:

> An absence of steady, attuned responsiveness to the child's affect states leads to minute but significant derailments of optimal affect

integration and to a propensity to dissociate or disavow affective reactions because they threaten the precarious structuralizations that have been achieved. The child, in other words, becomes vulnerable to self-fragmentation because his affect states have not been met with the requisite responsiveness from the caregiving surround and thus cannot become integrated into the organization of his self-experience [p. 106].

GRANDIOSITY AND SHAME

What then would be the relationship between grandiosity and shame? I will use case material to explore that association but can preface the case presentation by positing that shame in the narcissistically disturbed person, as in any person, occurs as a direct response, unmediated by self-concepts, to a shaming other, and it occurs in response to a judgment that one is deficient, which the self makes against the self. The narcissistically troubled individual differs from others, as Morrison and others have noted, in that her notion of what is acceptable in herself is pitched at such a high level that the shame of falling short becomes a constant danger. Her grandiosity functions to protect her from helplessness of various sorts, as Reich stated, and one form of helplessness that may have threatened her earlier in development is shame, especially within the child-caregiver relationship.

Certain other contexts for shame also are likely in the person with narcissistic disturbance, for example, shame over the child-like narcissistic rage to which she is prone. Here I refer not to an automatic, judgment-free shame that erupts in order to curtail the rage, but to a conscious judgment that the behavior is insupportable. From an evolutionary or adaptive perspective, such shame might be seen as having the value of arresting dysfunctional rage, but the fact that the emotion operates through *conscious appraisal* adds to its levels of significance.

Before moving on to case material, which dominates the chapter to follow, I would like to acquaint the reader with a set of concepts, "the dialectic of narcissism," that is central to Morrison's views on narcissism. Morrison uses this group of interrelated concepts in order to clarify shame's position within the field of narcissism and to place shame in a different relationship to Kohut's major concepts (the grandiose self and the idealized parent imago) than

Kohut does. It is instructive to observe how Morrison utilizes Kohut's overall developmental framework to create his own much broadened theory of shame's operation.

Morrison's (1989) "dialectic" is defined by the notion that experience moves between two poles, the first of which is the "archaic sense of self as flawed, inadequate, and inferior following realization of separateness from, and dependence on, objects" (p. 66). At the other pole is "narcissistic grandiosity and desire for perfection" (p. 66). Morrison does not state, as others might, that grandiosity is a *response* to vulnerability. He simply states that there exists an ongoing tension between the two postures: grandiosity being one, and the sense of being separate, object-dependent, and flawed as the other.

Morrison goes on to identify two additional postures, each of which can be thought of as a subset of the grandiosity pole and a solution to the vulnerability pole of the dialectic. One posture is that of autonomy, self-sufficiency, and isolation (in other words, the self is alone and complete); the other is that of merger with a perfect other. These two grandiose postures are noted as well by Lasch (1984), who says, "The minimal or narcissistic self is, above all, a self uncertain of its own outlines, longing either to remake the world in its own image or to merge into its environment in blissful union" (p. 19). In describing the two grandiose solutions, which interact in a second dialectic, Morrison states, "Similarly, a metaphorical dialectic exists between the wish for absolute autonomy and uniqueness and the wish for perfect merger and reunion with the projected fantasy of the ideal" (p. 66). Making a concluding statement about the two dialectics, he says, "Thus, shame and narcissism inform each other, as the self is experienced, first, alone, separate, and small, and, again, grandiosely, striving to be perfect and reunited with its ideal. Uniqueness and specialness may be imagined in terms of total autonomy and independence, or worthiness for merger with the fantasied ideal" (p. 66). Both postures within the second dialectic make use of the concept of "the ideal," which sometimes is seen as existing within the self and sometimes within the other, with whom the self then seeks to merge. Morrison is somewhat vague as to whether the dialectic he proposes should be understood to be a pathological or universal structure.

Morrison (1989) describes the desired merger with the ideal other, a merger of which the self hopes to be worthy, by saying, "the essence of narcissistic concern is a yearning for absolute uniqueness and sole importance to someone else, a 'significant other'" (p. 48). This quotation demonstrates that the quest for uniqueness need not be a pursuit of isolation, but may at times be a desire for uniqueness in the eyes of an idealized other.

Morrison argues shame's relevance to the narcissistic dialectics in that shame would attend the experience of being small and flawed, and it would attend experiences of falling short of the perfect, grandiose self or being "unworthy of merger" with the idealized other. Finally, shame may appear as a response to impulses to merge, which may be experienced as weaknesses.

Since Morrison's formal shame theory centers on the notion that shame follows from failures vis-à-vis the ideal self, I believe one would have to posit that *ideal self failures* occur in all of the above shame-producing circumstances and mediate the generation of shame. Presumably, the ideal self organizes around images of the person being either grand in isolation or grand enough to merge with the idealized other. When she feels she does not match such images, she feels shame.

Within Morrison's (1989) schema, shame's entry into any clinical picture should depend, in part, on the extent to which we are talking about *perfection* as an ambition of the ideal self. A goal of perfection is a prescription for shame, since one inevitably falls short of perfectionistic designs. What follows is Morrison's statement about the relationship between the ideal self, shame, and the dependency aspects of the narcissistic dialectics:

> Thus the self's failure to approximate its "ideal shape" as contrasted with the representation of the "actual self" (Sandler et al., 1963) leads to the sense of self-defect and shortcoming that is central to the experience of shame. This sense of defect represents either feelings of unworthiness for merger with the ideal or feelings of dependence and lack of autonomy, resulting in the *need/longing* for merger itself [p. 67].

As I stated earlier, I do not agree with the idea that shame follows from every failure to meet an ideal self image, nor do I think that an ideal self structure is a precondition for shame; but I do find merit in the cluster of hypotheses positing that *in narcissistically disordered individuals* ideals are perfectionistic, they are highly invested as goals toward which to strive, and they are shame generative when the individual cannot achieve them. Put differently, for those individuals who are hugely invested in idealized images of the self, evidence that the person cannot become the imagined self will bring shame unless the evidence is denied. These individuals generally are classified among the narcissistic personality disorders.

The grandiosity pole of Morrison's dialectic seems to include both the experience of captivating an admiring other with one's own magnificence and that of merging with a respected and adored other. At a purely descriptive level, the pair of experiences intersect reasonably well Wurmser's (1981) drive-centered notions of the infant engaged in showing the self to the object and in connecting with the object through looking. And of course, at a descriptive level, the corresponding concepts in Kohut's developmental theory are the grandiose self versus the self engaged in idealizing and joining with the parent imago.

I think there would be broad agreement among theorists that Morrison's images of the flawless self and the adored, unflawed object, taken in their extreme, perfectionistic forms, provide usable reference points in thinking about narcissistic disturbance, though other, similar frameworks might be equally serviceable. Morrison's theory becomes more controversial if one ventures beyond the descriptive level to consider the proposed genesis of the perfection-oriented structures. Despite his intermittent endorsement of Kernberg's (1975) notion of defensive grandiosity, Morrison, according to my reading, integrates the notion of the thwarted, primal grandiose self and idealizing self into his understanding of patient transferences and appropriate therapeutic response. Morrison perhaps is attempting to integrate Kohut's view with Kernberg's views by using the notion of a "dialectic" that makes reference to *two* early views of the self, one reflecting grandiosity, the other vulnerability. Or perhaps he is implying (along the lines of Lasch and Novey) that there exists normally, as an existential inevitability, an early grandiose self that represents the universal response to the pain of separateness.

Even though Morrison's theory positions the perfectionistic ideal self as a mediating structure that generates shame, his clinical thinking sometimes suggests that shame is a *direct response* to inadequate mirroring from objects, which can occur without mediation by an ideal self structure. For example, when his clinical material portrays shame in a boy who is spurned by an idealized father, Morrison is clear in stating that a child's rejection by a parent will bring shame, with no apparent interposition of an ideal self against which the child compares himself. In discussing the case of Mr. Dowland, Morrison (1989) states:

> It seems that he got into major trouble in traversing the second pole of the bipolar self-idealization with regard to his father. This narcissistically vulnerable man [the father] was impatient and rejecting of his son's personality and his strong attachment to him, generating in his son deep shame and humiliation [pp. 98–99].

If the boy's shame, in response to Father's mistreatment, is dependent on the child's recognition that he does not approximate his ideal self, that mediating element has been omitted from Morrison's description of the events.

It would seem reasonable to argue that the ideal self, as the concept is utilized by Morrison, could not exist prior to objective self-awareness, except perhaps in inchoate form as impressions accumulate regarding what is good (roughly, pleasure promoting) in self and others and what is not. But the ideal self would not coalesce as a shame-generating structure until objective self-awareness was established, since shame generation depends on comparing the actual self with ideals, which requires looking at the self as an object. In Broucek's (1991) words, "the *idea* of the self and the *ideal* of the self are both brought about by objective self-awareness" (p. 56).

Morrison's theory, wedded as it is to the ideal self as the sole shame-generating circumstance, neglects shame generated interpersonally with little conceptual mediation. In contrast, Broucek's notion of heightened shame in pathological narcissism weaves in the distinction between early, pre-OSA experience and later, OSA-dependent experience. He argues that the infant met too often by an unresponsive caretaker *experiences shame.* That is, the infant does not just split off her wishes for mirroring (Kohut), which might lead down the road to a malformed, shame-generating ego ideal (Morrison). No. The infant *experiences shame.* That early set of shame experiences then predisposes the toddler to find in her new objective self-awareness a threat (i.e., the self she now sees and judges is a self already diminished by shame) and to form and cling to an extremely idealized self-version as a compensation for the intensified shame associated with self-awareness. Broucek (1991) states:

> [T]he child who arrives at objective self-awareness with a weak-
> ened sense of self and significant shame experiences will have a
> stronger need to aggrandize himself in the form of what Sandler
> and Joffe have called the "idealized self." In Kohut's self
> psychology . . . this "idealized self" is labeled the "grandiose self"
> and its defensive functions are not acknowledged. Grandiosity is
> taken to be the natural original state of the self along with the
> need for an idealized selfobject [p. 58].

Returning now to Morrison, we can see that, even if we were
to suppose that Morrison's ideal self antedates OSA, like Kohut's
grandiose self (which means that it is an experience of one's own
greatness that must originally be largely preconceptual in nature),
Morrison's notion of *shame* generated by the ideal self would
have to await OSA, since shame generation depends, in Morrison's
view, on a comparison between the actual self and the ideal self.
Such comparison would not be possible prior to objective self-
awareness.

As indicated earlier, Broucek's view that the infant experiences shame well before objective self-awareness is a controversial
one. Many writers see shame as a response mediated by a later-
developing, self-evaluative structure. Lewis (1992) criticizes the
idea of "automatic elicitors" of shame, that is, the notion that
certain outside stimuli automatically generate shame without the
need for the self to judge itself with regard to standards, rules,
or goals. I agree with Lewis that the shame-eliciting stimulus
has to have meaning for the subject and be experienced as averse
to self-esteem, but I think the exception to his no "automatic
elicitors" (p. 31) idea would be the facial, vocal, and postural
expressions of the caregiver, which have meaning innately due
to our human inheritance, without requiring any prior experience of standards, rules, and goals. Nonverbal affective expression
is a language we are born to understand. It is indigenously meaningful to human beings. Here, I am expressing Broucek's notion
and Nathanson's, as well as my own. It is a notion that allows
for some form of shame prior to objective self-awareness and the
associated concepts of self.

Case material in the chapter to follow will allow a deeper look
at questions pertaining to the concepts of grandiosity and early
versus later shame forms, as well as concepts not yet introduced
relating to narcissistic transferences. I will also begin to pose

some questions about treatment of narcissistic disturbances. These questions interface with questions about shame theory and self-developmental theory.

CHAPTER 5

Narcissistic Disturbances

Case Examples and Discussion

> He thought he kept the universe alone;
> For all the voice in answer he could wake
> Was but the mocking echo of his own
> From some tree-hidden cliff across the lake.
> Some morning from the boulder-broken beach
> He would cry out on life, that what it wants
> Is not its own love back in copy speech,
> But counter-love, original response . . . .
> —Robert Frost ("The Most of It")

GRANDIOSITY AS A SHAME SOLUTION

Jeremy entered treatment complaining of significant depression and of concern he might return to alcohol, an old addiction, to manage his depression. Thirty-two years of age and unattached, he talked initially about a series of technology investments that had in the end gone badly. He had made a small fortune in a high-tech business that cashed in on a brief period of great success for another company. For a short time, he lived the good life and felt on top of the world, but he squandered the money and soon returned to a familiar state of longing for success. A subsequent investment promised even greater riches, but he researched the opportunity poorly and failed to uncover a fatal flaw. In the end, he lost money, including money borrowed from his family. A prized fantasy of finally extracting his critical father's admiration was dashed. Instead, he felt humiliated, and depression followed.

Jeremy's interpersonal style was jovial and expansive; he described himself as the life of the party, and though he sometimes resented the demands of that role, he felt odd and conspicuous if he stepped out of it. He liked to do things on a grand scale.

111

Tiresome daily tasks annoyed him and he resisted completing them. Dreams of elaborately imagined, fantastic successes brought him delight and solace.

In everyday life, Jeremy felt he could overcome basic laws such as those regulating time. He could do two things at once or get places in half the time needed. He refused to acknowledge reality's strictures. When reality presented itself as an impediment, he reassured himself, saying, "I'll do it *my* way," which meant, "I can circumvent that obstacle; it might stop others but it won't stop *me*." He contested reality and felt enraged when reality asserted its power with him.

Jeremy admired whomever sported conspicuous signs of success, whereas ordinary accomplishments elicited his contempt. He divided the world into winners and losers and constantly rank-ordered other people and critiqued his own and others' performances. Little existed for him that was free of judgment. Even a meal must be closely evaluated for excellence.

Jeremy was the older son of an infertile couple who adopted both their boys. His father was a flashy, articulate, rather judgmental and dogmatic parent, one who always knew "the right way" to do things. His mother was a sketchier figure, subordinate to Father while the boys were growing up, perhaps somewhat depressed, though responsible in attending to basic needs of the children. Jeremy recalled her reluctance to spend time with the kids after school. A schoolmate's lively household contrasted with his own family's subdued afternoon tenor. Jeremy returned home from school to find his mother immersed in her arts and crafts. He recalled her telling the two boys to take their wild play out of the house. In therapy, he seldom talked about his mother, though he spoke frequently of his father. The imbalance was striking. All of what was problematic in the self was referred back to the relationship with Father, as were certain ideals and assets.

Jeremy remembered no distress about the idea of being adopted, except for one panicky moment in adolescence when certain implications of adoption suddenly struck him. In thinking about his adoption, he recalled being told by his father that he was "chosen" by his parents, "because he was special." As a young child, he became attached to that idea and maintained his belief in it, even though he witnessed the realities of the adoption process when his younger brother joined the family.

Early months of treatment were filled with communications about Jeremy's system for evaluating self and others, which heavily stressed material wealth and other conspicuous emblems of success. He hardly conceived of what "inner experience" meant and found it almost unimaginable that a person whose accomplishments in the world were not outstanding might achieve any sense of worth. In his mind, an ordinary person was a cipher. The therapist's mildest questions about the possibility of finding value in activities that did not set one apart as unique precipitated in Jeremy a dysphoria bordering on panic. He felt he was being asked to hand over his most cherished dreams about himself, about his specialness. He couldn't imagine relinquishing the idea that the one who finished first, the one distinguished as special, was the one of value. Though he recognized the distress his value system brought him, the only solution he envisioned was to become wealthy and famous.

My primary basis for seeing Jeremy as narcissistically disturbed were his constant focus on his self-image, his notion of being special (set apart from others and superior to them), and the associated insistence that ordinary rules of reality did not pertain to him. At times, there was a hostile entitledness about him. Routinely, there was a persistent denial of being an ordinary mortal. If held to customary standards (e.g., with respect to appointment scheduling), his response would range between moderate anger and flooding fury. Though occasionally he seemed slightly embarrassed by grandiose ideas about himself, they seldom brought him real shame, except when reality forced recognition of a great schism between the imagined self and the actual self.

As a point of reference from another text, it may help to introduce as a rough typology Broucek's (1991) division of narcissistic disturbance (endorsed by Morrison) into the "unconflicted egotistical" individual, the "dissociative" type, and the person who vacillates between the two presentations, showing an "unstable equilibrium." Though not a precise match, Jeremy looks most like Broucek's egotistical narcissist, who "is unabashedly self-aggrandizing and seemingly shameless" (p. 59). Broucek goes on to state:

This type, which I have designated the unconflicted egotistical type, displays a seemingly total lack of tension between the idealized self and the realistic self, and thus there is an apparent absence of shame. It might be more accurate to say that these individuals lack a well-formed, realistic self-representation [pp. 59–60].

Broucek's description, which corresponds somewhat to Jeremy's presentation, suggests grandiosity without associated shame, something Kohut's theory of shame would not predict. Though Jeremy experiences shame, shame does not follow predictably from his grandiosity, which is not so fully split off as in some of Kohut's case presentations.

Broucek conjectures that the "egotistical narcissist" may form the basis for Kernberg's (1975) often pejorative theorizing about narcissism, whereas the "dissociative narcissist" may approximate the individuals Kohut had in mind and regarded with empathy. Like any typology, Broucek's captures some things and not others. At a descriptive level, Jeremy fits Broucek's "egotistical narcissist" fairly well, though his early history does not look much like the histories Broucek links with such presentations. Also, Jeremy could marshall considerable awareness of the distinction between his realistic and idealized selves, despite intermittent confusion about what is actual in the self and what is fanciful. In comparing Jeremy to Broucek's three types, it is important to note that Jeremy's grandiosity pertains more to his wishful fantasies about himself than to his view of his current reality. Thus, while he aspires to be perfect and imagines himself far greater than others in his potential, he is most unhappy with his actual attainments and sees a few select others, including his therapist, as outpacing him in real terms.

The terms of Morrison's dialectic of narcissism speak to Jeremy's concerns, especially the "grandiose" aim of captivating an admiring other with one's own magnificence, thus securing self-esteem. Jeremy's foremost wish is to be extraordinary and admirable, in others' eyes and, thus, in his own. Personal power and glory preoccupy him; anything short of perfection is valueless and thus shame generating. In fantasy, he sees himself as a shining light, of unparalleled brilliance, admired by all but needing no one.

Jeremy also finds some gratification in idealizing select others and seeking their acceptance. Historically, the major idealized figure was his father. During treatment, I initially took that role and elicited feelings of "adoration" and admiration. His early experience of me was of someone omniscient who doled out valuable wisdom at will. If I offered him no astounding insights, Jeremy preserved the idealization by seeing me as withholding those insights, rather than lacking them. Only later did he see himself and me as closer to equal; at that point, he began to find value in his own ideas as well as mine.

Some questions can be raised about the nature of Jeremy's grandiosity and his object idealization (and denigration) and also about the connection of his shame to the notions of grandiosity, object idealization, and ideal self. Treatment implications of the theoretical discussion will also be considered.

Clinically, it seemed most useful to conceive of Jeremy's grandiosity primarily as a healing effort, in relation to shame and other forms of helplessness. As he traversed childhood, Jeremy developed an elaborate fantasy of being unique, perfect, chosen, and invincible. His sense of living outside the rules of reality followed from this fantasy. Shame did not seem to follow naturally from his indulgence in grandiosity, as Kohut's work would predict, except when others highlighted the unrealistic nature of his thinking or, occasionally, when he stepped outside his grandiose fantasies and viewed them as unreal and maladaptive, nor was his grandiosity experienced as something that flooded him or escaped from control. Even when others pointed out his grandiosity, he did not regularly feel ashamed. He was more likely to feel frightened or to argue against the idea of surrendering what had sustained him and become a source of great fantasy gratification.

The idea of being special also had significance as a link to others. By being special, he would preserve the valued other's interest in him. In therapy, he proudly asserted that he could keep me fascinated with "his case" through the interesting way in which he presented himself; verbalizing his idealized views of me also served in fantasy to control me, since he imagined I would be gratified by his enthusiasm for me and so I would take special interest in him. Paired with the omnipotent fantasy of controlling the other person's interest was the burden of *needing* to generate interest within another. He did not feel he could safely assume such interest and free himself of the task of entertaining and pleasing the other. Greeted in the waiting room before each hour, he would offer a joking comment to begin the process of entertaining me. He had to "entertain" (amuse, engage) in order to be "entertained" (received, welcomed).

It is important to note that, in Jeremy's fantasy world, the self that pleases the other is an apparently self-sufficient, performing self, not an intimate, interactive self. One does not love and receive love from the other; one impresses and is impressed by him. Occasionally, Jeremy appeared to be cultivating an isolated self-sufficiency, but further exploration usually showed him living within a fantasy in which his uniqueness was admired by a valued other or a whole stadium or amphitheater of others.

EARLY STRAIN AND ATTACHMENT TO THE FANTASY WORLD

Jeremy's fantasy of specialness likely represented a solution to a number of childhood problems. Among those would be the fact of his adoption, which was a piece of reality onerous for a child to integrate without resorting to some kind of compensatory fiction. Jeremy's father gave him a leg up into the restitutive fantasy of specialness by providing the adoption story of the "chosen" and "special" child. One can imagine that, as a boy, Jeremy saw the specialness concept as an egress from the diminished, displaced feeling that would come with knowing he was not wanted and was given away and, perhaps equally stressful for this particular child, knowing that he did not "belong" with his adoptive family in some objective way that probably corresponded frighteningly to an inner feeling of not fully belonging, a feeling that had long been present due to parenting limitations. The image of "having the floor disappear beneath your feet" was an especially evocative one in Jeremy's therapy and seemed to refer to the latter aspect of the adoption revelation, that is, the loss of connection with the adoptive family upon coming to understand his birth circumstances. Another perspective on Jeremy's embracing of specialness is that he, as a child, felt *required* to pursue specialness (if not, he might be given back: he was chosen because he was special), and thus it was psychologically economical for him to find as much defensive value in that stance as possible.

Jeremy's fantasied specialness generated for him an alternate world, which in therapy he came to call his "play world," a better place reminiscent of Modell's (1968) "magical world" of infancy, to which Jeremy could fly away when the ordinary world that contained the horrid adoption idea became uncomfortable. The play world was not a domain to be integrated with the ordinary but to be separated and protected from it. It was a place where he dwelled alone, though often he peopled the play world with admiring audiences. The play world was filled with material treasures above all else, but sometimes also with images of creative activity that allowed expression of some of his deeper feelings of love and longing.

The therapy relationship for a long time belonged more to the play world than the "real world" and was asked to obey its rules. Jeremy imagined he could achieve perfect, thrillingly revealing treatment hours from which he would carry off a precious package of insight. If I had little to say or my comments were not sufficiently focused to allow Jeremy to take home a laserlike insight, Jeremy radiated frustration, and he prodded me with question after question to give him what he wanted. If he received a special insight, I was "so smart," "so good" at my job.

The play world stood in contrast with the ordinary world of imperfection and interdependence and was, to some degree, "split off" from commerce with daily reality. One world was everything, the other nothing. One was a Christmas ornament, shiny and perfect. The other was sullied and earthbound: it was beneath him. At times, his imagery echoed that of the Christ story. He was the special child, put on earth for a noble purpose. The "two-worlds" imagery was also suggestive of the two families—biological and adoptive—that must have held sway in his imagination, in however unintegrated a form.

Jeremy's attachment to the world of specialness and perfection had many implications for his day-to-day experience. It promoted narcissistic rage when life persisted in its plainness and failed to conform to the specialness expectations. The spirit of the play world was: "Seek and ye shall find, knock and the door shall be opened." Not getting everything he wanted brought shame because he assumed that perfect satisfaction was an option and that those sufficiently special ones do get all their needs and wishes met with a wave of their magic wand.

Jeremy's real life was a profound, enduring source of shame and anger because it failed to distinguish him from others as the smarter, more talented, superior person who existed so gloriously in the play world. One could say that to fail to greet commonplace functioning with shame would have been a threat to his play world, since his shame signified adhering to standards of perfection. The same was true for Sidney, discussed in Chapters

Three and Four, for whom a word of praise was often an insult, a suggestion he should be satisfied with ordinary achievements when he was "capable of very much more."

Because the play world derived from the need to deny what was intolerable in the ordinary world, Jeremy had to maintain the unacceptability of the day-to-day world as a precondition for holding fast to the play world. Good things in the ordinary world represented a threat to the play world. Good things in the ordinary world (including good things in the ordinary self) needed to be denied, devalued, or blighted through anxiety. He could not sustain for long an effort to make positive things happen in the real world, since those positive things would call into question the need for the treasured play world. Simple pleasures (a golf outing, an opportunity to see a show) had to be spoiled. Narcissistic dangers in the ordinary world had to be amplified, which led to exaggerated shame responses and to dissatisfactions that soon persuaded him of the need to return to the superior world of his own making.

Thus, one sees how a two-worlds structure can become self-sustaining. The ordinary world increasingly is depleted of good feeling and stocked with bad feeling, which reinforces the original conviction that an alternate, special, private, entirely controllable realm is needed. Functioning in the real world becomes actually impaired, which imbues one's everyday self with considerable shame. When Lewis (1992) describes the "global" orientation of narcissistic individuals (p. 72) and notes their associated tendency to judge and condemn the *whole* self, which he sees as a primary cognitive bias, he may also be picking up the defensive desire to discard the whole of the self as it exists in the day-to-day world, in order that one may exit that unpredictable world and go to the safe remove of the perfect world created in fantasy. Thus, for some, it is not so much a primary cognitive bias toward inclusiveness that is operating as it is a motivated tendency to discard the whole of the ordinary self.

A similar dynamic is evident in traumatized individuals who cannot afford any feeling of safety in the ordinary world, for fear such comfort might tempt them out of the protective remove established as a refuge from extraordinary dangers. It is necessary to be panic-stricken in the grocery store and the city park, since the world that holds the grocery store and the park also holds the abuser; if you embrace one, you may find the other.

FATHERING PROBLEMS AND
THE FANTASY WORLD STRATEGY

I have speculated thus far about the disturbing adoption idea as a contributor to Jeremy's grandiosity. Other factors may have been equally important, especially the personalities of his parents and their parenting styles. As indicated earlier, Jeremy's father was task-oriented and judgmental. Though he told his son that he had been chosen for adoption because of his specialness, the father's daily communication was, "You are not good enough." The father's choice to present adoption in terms of specialness may have derived, in part, from his own perfectionism, which conveyed to the child a message that he could not reach Father's standards. This communication would have elicited shame and anger and a need to escape the certainty of failure.

Jeremy's father's attitude toward his son is well described by Broucek's notion of objectification. The father seemed disinclined to relate to what was inside his son, to the self composed of thoughts and feelings. Father and son seldom enjoyed simply being together, sharing ideas or appreciating commonplace pleasures. Father was present as an evaluator, a dispenser or withholder of rewards. Jeremy felt good if Father said, "You've done well," or if he offered a material reward for chores competently performed, but Jeremy had no memory of having fun playing a game with his father or taking a walk or singing a song. As I indicated earlier, I agree with Broucek that objectification is a generator of shame, though it would appear to be one of a *group* of such shame generators.

Jeremy's response to objectification was to try to become the glittering surface he thought his father desired. Jeremy had about him less of a sense of a hidden or carefully veiled self than the obsessional Mr. Stevens and more of a sense of a false self replacing an indwelling self. The shining surface, modelled in part after Father's own charm, substituted for the depth.

Jeremy's self-formation looked like the development Lasch (1984) describes when he considers American society as a whole. Lasch talks of consumerism as "encourag[ing] a new kind of self-consciousness that has little in common with introspection or vanity. Both as a worker and as a consumer, the individual learns not merely to measure himself against others but to see himself through others' eyes" (p. 29). He goes on to say:

He learns that the self-image he projects counts for more than accumulated skills and experience. Since he will be judged, both by his colleagues and his superiors at work and by the strangers he encounters on the street, according to his possessions, his clothes, and his "personality"—not, as in the nineteenth century, by his "character"—he adopts a theatrical view of his own "performance" on and off the job . . . the self becomes almost indistinguishable from its surface. . . . When people complain of feeling inauthentic or rebel against "role-playing," they testify to the prevailing pressure to see themselves with the eyes of strangers and to shape the self as another commodity offered up for consumption on the open market [p. 30].

Jeremy began treatment concerned with his inability to be the perfect production or performer. Only later did he begin to complain about conflict between pressures to perform and wishes to leave the stage and simply be. In treatment, there arose the novel notion that a session might be valued as an experience of being together, sharing, and enjoying work and play rather than as a means to attain a great gift of insight to be carried out at the end of the session and held aloft and admired, like a polished jewel, throughout the week. But such notions were anxiously resisted, since they threatened fantasies of greatness that represented the most dearly held of Jeremy's pleasures.

In the play world, Jeremy could attain the perfection he imagined would attract and delight his father, and he could do so without effort or setbacks because, in the world of his invention, he was a luminous being whose magnetic force could not be resisted. Given the nature of Jeremy's ambitions, shame was inevitable and, as indicated, was in some ways courted by him as a persuasion to remain in the play world, where perfection could be achieved by little more than a gesture in the desired direction.

Shame was even more prominent than it might otherwise have been because Jeremy had a compulsion to fail and, thus, to fall far short of his high standards. The compulsion seemed overdetermined. In part, it served his attachment to his magical world of specialness. Jeremy's need to fail also seemed to serve his need to maintain a masochistic tie to his father, by which the two of them connected through interactions in which Father reprimands and shames his son for his impractical, highflying, dreamer's nature and the son feels rebuked and ashamed. If Jeremy assumed the identity of the bad child in need of correction, he could connect with Father; he could give Father the position of tutelary superiority he desired.

It is worth noting that there existed some confusion and complexity about the *object* of Father's criticism and shaming. Two apparently identical but, in fact, dissimilar things were conflated in Jeremy's mind and appeared as a single focus of Father's denigration. Jeremy's reluctance to function in the real world was one of the two objects of criticism, and in a sense, that refusal needed to be criticized by a concerned parent. But the other object of Father's scorn—apparently identical to the first but, in fact, distinct—was Jeremy's indwelling self, which was creative and emotional and different from Father's, as Jeremy experienced him. It was traumatic for Jeremy to have Father reject his indwelling self. By confusing that natural self with his defensive impracticality and difficulty functioning realistically, he obscured the trauma by hiding his Father's unjustified rejection behind an understandable spurning. Jeremy would behave badly—for example, by squandering family funds—and his father's rejection would follow and seem right, as did the profound shame that Jeremy felt. This type of dynamic will be explored more fully in the chapters on masochism.

Turning back now to the relationship between Jeremy's constant self-criticism and his specialness fantasy, we can conjecture that those two self-aspects were intertwined in yet another way. Jeremy watched over his performance of daily tasks as if he were doing microscopic brain surgery. He pretended he was doing something special and highly consequential at every moment. If he was two minutes late for an ordinary meeting, he acted as if he had been tardy to a global summit. This pretense of being engaged in momentous matters added tremendous stress to his life, and shame, too, because small failings were amplified and became intolerable; often, it gave him an excuse to escape the stress by slipping off to his play world. The pretense also gave him relief from the strain of seeing that his daily life was much like the lives of other mortals; it let the play world penetrate the ordinary.

Jeremy's self-critical consciousness, which held out possibilities of ticker-tape triumph or cataclysmic failure, also functioned to keep him in a world where judgment and assessment were paramount, and immediate experience of the self, of others, of

nature, music, food, or sex lost significance. He was deeply alienated from the natural experiences of the body and heart and
intermittently he was painfully aware of this estrangement. Broucek
(1991) describes Jeremy well when he compares pathological narcissism with normal narcissism, as follows:

> In "pathological narcissism" one has been more thoroughly
> captured by self-images and the exaggerated concern for how one
> appears to others and to oneself. One has lost the unself-conscious
> sense of self with its possibility for recovering primary commu-
> nion with the world and its ability to dissolve, at the affective
> level, the sense of distance and alienation from others [p. 57].

HYPERTROPHIED OBJECTIVE SELF-AWARENESS
AS SELF-PROTECTION RELATED TO EARLY STRESS

Jeremy's constant self-monitoring and self-judging can be understood as hypertrophied objective self-awareness. Jeremy continually
judges himself and others with a critical, outsider's eye, as if he
is a thing, not a center of experiences. He seldom suspends such
activity and simply feels alive in the world. Every moment of
sensation, analysis, or emotion is heavily overlaid with judgments
about performance and appearances.

Broucek (1991) argues that the very young child who experiences excessive shame may find the maturational leap into objective
self-awareness particularly stressful, since the child already carries
negative feelings about himself, to which now likely will be added
negative ideas and concepts about the self. But in the discussion
of obsessional individuals, we considered that OSA might in some
instances be experienced as higher, safer ground where one can
know some control over early dangers. Once a child can take
himself as an object to be viewed and evaluated, he also can begin
to imagine *designing* the self so that it is praiseworthy and safe
from various threats.

Jeremy's telling of his family story suggests he may have experienced his mother as fairly remote. We can at least conjecture
that such unresponsiveness might have brought early shame or
stressful feelings of frustration, anger, and aloneness. Objective
self-awareness may have offered a leg up out of a variety of early

pain states, although, as Broucek stresses (personal communication), the higher ground is attained at great cost if one abandons the indwelling self.

A particularly noteworthy feature of Jeremy's objective self-awareness was that it had the sound of his father's voice. His father seemed to have been the more emotionally present of the two parents; thus, to carry around his father's voice, even with its censorious tone, may have felt like a relief from the experience of a disengaged mother. The internalization of Father's caviling voice was bent to some advantage through an associated fantasy of triumph that said, roughly paraphrased, "If you finally do everything perfectly, the sea will part, you will be on the other side in the golden land you deserve."

The developmental schema pertaining to Jeremy's objective self-awareness is quite conjectural; I present it to focus attention on the variety of different pictures that might emerge clinically depending on the prior experience a child brings to OSA and on how he makes use of the developmental shift into that phase of life. It seems likely that the child badly stressed in infancy would find in objective self-awareness new threats, and to the extent that ego development promotes security, he might also discover possibilities for safety.

One can argue that, in Jeremy's narcissistic disturbance, we see an individual who has shifted the whole of his psychological focus from relatedness with others to perfecting the self as if it were a work of art. If he could not have a loving, mutual relationship with another, perhaps he could be admired from a distance, like a magificent sculpture. He began one hour with the frightening realization that he did not really want wealth and possessions; he wanted the feeling of admiration he believed such attainments guaranteed him. He longed for such regard, although he found such a yearning shameful and barely could acknowledge it. After his associations took him in the direction of both parents' emotionally cool natures, he ended the hour with a sudden nervous recognition of the discomfort he felt receiving love and warmth. He could long for admiration and aim to achieve it, but the idea of seeking love and relatedness discomforted him. Both he and I were struck by the importance of this realization and were impressed, too, by the prolonged period of treatment disruption (linked to an eruption of time and money conflicts) that immediately followed it and threatened to nullify it.

A different hypothesis with regard to Jeremy—one also stressing early relatedness—is that the infant-mother relationship was fairly comfortable, but the later imposition of the adoption information precipitated a traumatic experience of having the ground disappear beneath his feet. After that trauma, relaxed comfort seemed dangerous, and the images of Mother as detached and Father as critical were exaggerated defensively, so that the boy would never again rest easy with the idea of safely belonging. His approach became, "Spoil your pleasures before fate does it for you. Enjoy only those pleasures of your own making, over which you have perfect control." The surest reconstruction probably combines the two lines of inference and portrays a child somewhat strained early-on by a mildly depressed, periodically disengaged mother and an unempathic father; that child is further troubled later in development by the stunning adoption idea.

SHAME AND THE IDEAL SELF
IN NARCISSISTIC DISTURBANCE

With reference to Morrison's construct of the ideal self as the primary generator of shame, there is little question that Jeremy carries through life an ideal self that is grossly unreachable, and there is scant doubt that, given his personality structure, falling short of that ideal self is a major producer of his adult shame experiences. But that observation need not lead us to conclude that failed pursuit of the ideal self is the universal precondition for shame. Borrowing from Winnicott's (1965) much-utilized notion of the "good-enough mother," I would argue that, in the post-OSA individual who makes judgments about the self, the crucial shame-generating structure is not the ideal self but is better called the good-enough self, which consists of good-enough behaviors and inner states. To varying degrees, people do carry images of ideal behavior and ideal forms of the self, but ideals generally are not meant to be behaviorally matched; they are beacons, or sources of fantasy pleasure. In addition to such ideals, people have notions about behavior that is adequate or good-enough. And paired with these notions are ideas about that which surely is not good enough, is flawed, is shameful. Shame is felt when one is not good enough, when one is deficient.

There is, of course, an important subset of individuals—Jeremy being an example of that group—for whom the definition of "good enough" is that which is perfect, special, or unique. For these people, highly invested fantasies revolve around images of the ideal self. In treatment with Jeremy, when shame over imperfection regularly interrupted his ability to explore an important area, it became important to say, "Okay, so you are ashamed of that, you see it as less than ideal, but is it possible to accept that imperfection in yourself and yet go forward and explore it?" The query asked him whether he needed to equate imperfection with shameful worthlessness.

It is also true that there are moments in any person's life, or passages in development, when one may reach for some remote goal, become deeply invested in it, and then feel ashamed when the lofty goal is not met. I suspect that, in most of these cases, the shame comes less from falling short of an ideal than from the foolishness one feels in having valued a goal so deeply, perhaps advertised publically one's intention to achieve it, yet one is unable to meet the goal and must return to more ordinary ambitions. The experience is close to the shame of "false confidence" I discussed in a case study in my 1985 book (p. 108). An example might be an artist in a whirl of excitement about the possibility of some high attainment, perhaps an academy award following a nomination for fine acting. It is not the awardless state that is pitiful, but the wearing on one's sleeve of one's excitement and great expectations, which leaves one vulnerable. This shame is a variant of the shame of unrequited love. You have let the world see and let yourself see your delight in the fantasied gratification, but now the goal is to be denied, suggesting you were not so worthy as you dared to imagine. You must return to ordinariness, which is not normally a shameful place to reside but may become so after flights of fantasy. Thus, the shame is stimulated by unveiled narcissistic wishes, which often bring active shaming in childhood, sometimes in the form of teasing. This dynamic for shame production begins to sound like Kohut's theory of shame, except that I am not assuming, as he does, a permanently split-off grandiose self as a necessary precondition.

Shame then is the sense of deficiency. Deficiency, in some cases, may be defined in relation to a perfectionistic ideal (including, but not limited to, goals of perfect self-sufficiency or of worthiness for merger with an idealized other [see Morrison]), but it can be evaluated by more commonplace standards of behavior. It is also important to note that the measure of inadequacy need not be an abstract standard (such as Lewis's standards, rules, and goals). The mark of deficiency may be the disgusted or contemptuous or indifferent look on another's face or the tone of his voice, which causes the person suddenly to view himself as valueless. These concept-free measures would be especially powerful in early life, before our judgment of self is heavily mediated by *ideas* about the self and ideas with which to gauge our behavior.

IS SHAME THE CENTRAL AFFECT OF NARCISSISM?

Morrison (1989) argues that shame is the central affect of narcissism. Since the inflated self and the self-protective attachment to the inflated-self posture are so prominent in many individuals we label narcissistically disturbed, and since breaching such self-inflation regularly brings shame, there is apparent good sense to Morrison's assertion. Lewis (1992) appears to hold a similiar view. He states:

> The extreme pathology of prolonged shame produces narcissistic disorders and the disintegration of the self system. . . . Narcissistic disorders generate a wide range of symptoms including grandiosity, rage, inferiority, overidealization, entitlement, and a lack of empathy. *For me, the inability to cope with shame and humiliation underlies these pathological disturbances* [emphasis mine]. Narcissists seek to avoid shame, and, when avoidance fails, engage in emotional behavior that masks their underlying feeling [p. 11].

I am not fully persuaded that shame stands apart as the primary problematic emotion in every case of narcissistic disturbance, even when shame is defined to include feeling bad about oneself, low self-esteem, and the like. The assertion that shame is the central affect of narcissism may rest on attention to a subset of narcissistic cases or on a failure to consider the full range of protective roles that enhanced self-attention may play. The narcissistic individual's insistence on his own power and uniqueness defends against a number of danger situations and the associated emotions. These emotions include clearcut shame feelings but likely also include helplessness to control objects who are neglectful or abusive (leading to frustration, rage, fear, and loneliness), helplessness to prevent weakness in objects (which can lead to guilt in the child, and anxiety) and helplessness to control traumatic circumstances such as one's own physical illness or injury or separation from loved ones. Shame is a highly important affect in narcissistic contexts, in part due to the original, personality-forming stresses on the child and, in part, to the structure of his defenses, but it is not, in my opinion, the central affect of narcissism any more than rage is, or desolation, or frustration. In order to see shame as uniquely important in narcissistic disturbance, we would need to offer an unreasonably broad definition of shame that included not just the usual shame variants such as humiliation and embarrassment, but all states that relate to the sense of personal comfort and security.

What *may* be true with the more egotistical type of narcissistic disturbance, though I remain uncertain on this point, is that an important part of the person's psychic life is organized around avoiding a particular piece of reality that has been interpreted as a crucial self-defect. In Jeremy's case, adoption might stand in that position, though the therapy did not incontrovertably support such a conclusion. In the case of Fred, repeatedly abandoned by his father both physically and emotionally, that position was occupied by the idea of not being good enough as a son to sustain his father's interest. Fred's therapy was one in which the identification of shame and pride concerns, the recognition of shame's relationship to impulsive behavior and to other emotions (especially rage), and the increasing tolerance for shame all were crucial aspects of the work. Fred brought to therapy a profound fear of shame and a lifetime of grandiose, sociopathic behaviors (including addictions, fighting, and felonies) aimed at bolstering a sense of invincibility and phallic pride. Fred's psychopathology was largely organized around the terror that facing reality could devastate his self-regard. The ability to face painful realities, including the reality of childhood rejection and that of a number of his own adult behaviors, was essential to his psychological growth. Empathic mirroring of his strengths had value, however, only after he faced his limitations and withstood the associated shame could he begin to find some real self-acceptance. At that point, his appreciation of his assets was genuine and not just a mimicry of others' encouragements.

A contrasting example of narcissism, with grief, guilt, and disillusionment all appearing as important elements in its substrate, came from a young man, Davis, who sought therapy for depression and self-defeating behavior. He was deeply invested in ideas of superiority to others. He saw very few people as worthy of his attention. In a playful and good-natured, yet ultimately serious, way, he talked of his own specialness, his sense he was meant to be a king, saint, or philosopher. He disdained friendships and involvements with ordinary activities, such as college courses. Whatever he began to invest in, he dropped halfway, whether the effort was directed toward a class, a book, a movie, or a relationship. He regularly came to therapy halfway through the allotted time and contemplated reducing sessions to half the original frequency. Early analysis of conflicts over commitment led not so much to a sense of shame underpinning the exalted self, but more to a dread of attachment, given early experiences of deep attachment that resulted in painful loss, disillusionment, and insoluble feelings of guilt (when both parents got depressed and mother divorced father). Shame had significance in a number of ways in this clinical picture. Davis felt shame over identification with parents who were weak. He felt shame over his own simple humanness, his failure to be a king or a saint. The real social and sexual immaturity that resulted from withdrawing from life brought shame, but he often obviated that shame by reframing his immaturity as superiority. Despite these important areas of functioning in which shame figured, a shame-dominated sense of self did not emerge as the essential experience that determined his difficulties.

Many have talked about grandiosity as a denial of defect (Reich, 1960) and a defense against shame, and indeed, as with Fred, it often is that. Another path to grandiosity (and the shame to which it leaves one vulnerable) has its provenance in extreme object unavailability. Grandiosity is, in part, an attempt to substitute the self as a lovable and sufficient object of attachment for the longed-for, but absent, other. I believe this was part of Jeremy's dynamic, because his adoptive parents were characterologically somewhat remote and his biological parents were situationally entirely unavailable. The same development might occur if the other is too fragile to engage with the indwelling self, as seems to have been the case with Davis and his father. Kohut (1984) and his followers emphasize the need for the other as a foundation for the development and sustenance of the sense of self. That need figured prominently for Davis as did his desire for an other who is truly not-self, especially the other as an object of love, a longing reflected in the few lines from Frost that precede this chapter.

Also relevant here is Lasch's (1984) argument that narcissism is a diminishing of self that can result from the insubstantiality of the external world with which one interacts. The self is defined in relation to the substantial other, and if such self–other interaction is attenuated, the solidity of the self suffers. Lasch's analysis is an analysis of our "culture of consumption," which, in his opinion, leads to narcissism (in the society as a whole) because it "dissolves the world of substantial things . . . and replaces it with a shadowy world of images, and thus obliterates the boundaries between the self and its surroundings" (p. 52).

TREATMENT CONSIDERATIONS

Morrison (1989) sees the therapist's mirroring of infantile grandiosity as the basis for the patient's increased ability to internalize selfobject functions. The following passage conveys key aspects of Morrison's thinking about the psychotherapy of shame-prone people:

> In shifting attention to the ideal self and the ideal parental imago, I have proposed the role of "transmuting internalization" of functions from the idealized selfobject into the self. . . . This process may occur, as I have noted elsewhere (Morrison, 1986a, 1987), through integration of empathically mirrored infantile grandiosity and perfection into the ideal self and its projective identification into the idealized selfobject [p. 80].

Though I agree that a successful therapy often involves significant internalization of therapist functions (especially, the non-judgmental consideration of one's mind and heart), I am uncomfortable with the notion that an essential therapeutic function is the mirroring of infantile grandiosity and perfection. Perhaps I am splitting hairs but it seems more accurate to say that the empathic therapist responds to the patient's genuine emotions and abilities. It is sometimes the case that a patient's newfound ability to share his inner life brings him to reveal grandiose fantasy; for example, an inhibited man who has privately nursed certain grandiose views about his wit and intelligence or his sexual stamina begins to reveal those visions to the therapist. But I don't think it is the mirroring of that grandiose content per se that promotes growth. The grandiose self-appraisal may be a function of inexperience in judging one's abilities (which have been walled off from contact with ordinary life), or it may represent the conflation of genuinely creative trends with sadistic fantasies of triumph, in which case the latter aspect can be interpreted (otherwise, it likely will lead to guilt and a move back toward inhibition), or it may be a defense against vulnerability or against reciprocal relatedness. What is important for the patient's growth is not the mirroring of grandiosity, but the encouragement and acceptance of joy and activity in the self and joy in the possibility of the self acting meaningfully in the world. The therapist need not delight in the particulars of a patient's unrealistic idea that he can become a CEO of a major company in six months' time, nor must he deny what defensive significance such a fantasy might have, but he can respond to his patient's budding pleasure in the active, enthusiastic self.

As an example of grandiosity in a treatment setting, I think of Andrew, a man in his forties, neglected throughout childhood and intermittently exposed to parental violence. Andrew lived a robotlike life and kept his talents, desires, and self-appreciation sequestered. Life carried on around him, and he knew little engagement in or memory for events that transpired close at hand. He seldom faced life without interposing complicating intellectual activity that converted interactions into carefully plotted scripts. As Andrew experimented with showing his strengths, at times, they emerged in therapy as grandiose, unrealistic ideas about his greatness. These notions were conveyed with an eruption of delighted laughter and a deep smile enlivening a usually fatigued, immobile face. I responded appreciatively to the lively and self-loving aspects of his images of personal and business triumph and commented on the ways in which his inventiveness and pleasure in the self had been punished, but I did not feel I needed to mirror the most grandiose elements in his self-presentation, some of which seemed related to the previously isolated status of his self-love, some to terror over worthlessness, and some to his wish to use his creative energies to triumph over others or otherwise to defeat intimacy and mutual respect.

The sadistic elements in Andrew's grandiosity needed to be interpreted and differentiated from ordinary pleasure, since they shaded into fantasies of rape and coercion, about which he felt guilty and ashamed and which damaged his relationships. My countertransference was a guide in my response to Andrew's grandiose fantasy. At times, I felt *forced* to admire him and, at those moments, inclined to harbor private reservations about his capabilities; my resistance seemed to pair with his impulse to extract admiration forcibly. Analysis of Andrew's relationship to these intimidation fantasies was crucial to contacting fears that the only way to engage others was to get them to prod or push him or to reverse roles and become the coercive one. An important image was that of a diver or racehorse who stands ready and able to perform his athletic feat. If he stands still, he feels others' hands and voices pushing him from behind, but if he moves forward, he is entirely alone. No one moves along with him or waits beside the pool or at the finish line to embrace and congratulate him. Absorbing and initiating coercion had become special forms of pleasure for Andrew, but ones that brought guilt and damaged relatedness.

A therapeutic stance of indiscriminately mirroring Andrew's grandiose fantasy would have neglected the sadistic and self-protective roles of his images of overtaking or overrunning others. It was possible to respond to his enjoyment and appreciate its value as a state of the self without joining in an assertion of his superiority over others or sharing his sadistic pleasure in disabling others.

Andrew repeatedly described his own work as "amazing." He offered mocking dismissals of others' competing efforts. Questioning his experience of his work as "amazing" revealed a fantasy that, by laying out remarkable wares like fine silks at a bazaar, he would *guarantee* an attentive and appreciative response, or if such a response still were withheld, against all evidence of his genius, the other's idiocy would entitle Andrew to a rageful attack. Behind the fantasy of displaying such irresistible wares was a fear that, if he showed his actual work, which indeed was impressive but had no magical power to coerce appreciation, he might be gravely disappointed in the response or even retraumatized by someone neglectful who, like his parents, left him believing his best efforts were nothing. Thus, the delighted claims of amazing work did not seem best understood as the resumption of natural childish grandiosity; they were a self-protective effort to control interpersonal events and an angry refusal to accept what life brings.

With regard to Morrison's thinking and its relationship to Kohut's, another point of confusion for me concerns my assumption that grandiosity at times mitigates shame and other painful emotions. Morrison (1989) seems quite clearly to agree, referring on occasion to "defensive grandiosity" (p. 176), but his extended comments portray grandiosity less as a defensive posture and more as an immature posture, essentially a developmental arrest. Thus, the patient whose early selfobject needs were thwarted continues to experience and express those needs, and they appear prominently within the therapy relationship. Morrison advocates responding empathically to these developmentally early needs and recommends focusing interpretive comments on defining the familial context in which such needs were thwarted. This approach seems sound as a partial response to particular varieties of grandiosity and as an initial response that can be followed by interpretive work if the mirroring fails to result in improved self-regard. Gedo (1975) reminds us that Kohut's own work around persistent grandiosity sees therapeutic progress as dependent on interpretive comments that occur when grandiosity, or idealization, are inevitably disrupted within the therapy. He states that "the indefinite acceptance of the patient's idealizations is therefore the exact antithesis of Kohut's technical recommendations for analytic work with narcissistic personalities" (p. 490).

One of the potential points of confusion in this type of discussion concerns the *phenomenology* of grandiosity. In his discussion of "defensive grandiosity" in manic-depressive patients, Morrison (1989) is referring to demands for need gratification from the selfobject (often paired with a readiness to externalize bad-self aspects onto that same object). This particular variety of "grandiosity," which he also calls "dependent demandingness" (p. 177) does indeed look like the rageful expression of thwarted infantile needs, as Morrison argues, which can at first be accepted uncritically by a therapist, even explicitly welcomed if it comes from someone previously unable to feel entitled to much of anything. But in time, if the expression of entitlement persists, one must begin to address the maladaptive, defensive role it has assumed. For example, a patient may continue ruthlessly to demand flawless empathy from a therapist, rather than risk trusting that the therapist will see the patient's needs and provide for them adequately of his own free will.

An example comes again from Andrew, who took at times an arrogant stance within which he felt entitled to force his therapist to gratify whatever he defined as his needs. Interpretive work around his fear that no kindness or empathy would be given willingly by others let him relax the coercive efforts that brought him guilt and shame. An important moment in the treatment, pleasurable for therapist and patient alike, was a moment when he recognized some bit of kindness or generosity flowing from me to him and realized that he had not compelled or extracted it in a way that was designed to cause me pain, but had allowed whatever gift it was to come naturally, out of my inclination to give. In the past, any kindness or understanding I had given him had been tainted by his assumption that I gave to him only because he afforded me no choice. He had both reveled in and regretted this "rapist" image of himself.

There are some forms of "grandiosity" that should be identified as defensive as soon as the patient can tolerate that interpretation. For example, a patient who regularly carries on about his amazing mental agility while barely keeping afloat in school does not benefit from having the therapist stop at mirroring his grandiose self. He would profit more from a tactfully communicated interpretation of his need to deny poor performance, which then could lead to consideration of inborn or neurotic limitations on his effectiveness. The "grandiosity" in this example differs in feel and significance from the grandiosity of the patient who demands that his therapist meet his each and every need, understand him unerringly, and so forth. The latter focuses on the patient's angry need for the therapist to be flawless and to treat the patient as the sun around whom he revolves. The former focuses on the patient as an object of others' admiration. Both types differ from the joyful expansiveness of a person newly exploring areas of vitality; that person may recognize with good humor that his exuberant self-love may not reflect exceptional talents or accomplishments, but still he delights in what for him is an important new experience in living.

THE IDEALIZING SELFOBJECT TRANSFERENCE

Kohut (1971, 1977) introduced the notion of the cohesive, idealized parent imago and an associated transference structure, the idealizing selfobject transference. Morrison (1989) frequently refers to this variety of transference in discussing shame-prone individuals. Kohut talks of the idealizing selfobject relationship as an experience beginning in infancy and extending into later development; idealization of the parent imago co-occurs with the experience of the grandiose self. I have earlier questioned whether grandiosity or idealization are meaningful to the very young baby. They both emphasize evaluation of an individual as highly worthy, which does not seem like an infantile cognitive experience. However, clinical and developmental data do support the notion of parental idealization in the somewhat older, post-OSA child, and it is important to consider how such idealizations affect self-esteem, shame vulnerability, and transference structures.

There is ample evidence that young children see their parents as powerful, immensely capable, and admirable figures, unless the parent's behavior is so deficient that such views cannot be maintained. This idealization probably is explained in part by cognitive immaturity, in part by wishful thinking, and in part by accurate assessment of the relative capability of parent and child. Schafer (1967) emphasizes the latter point. He states:

> It is not, however, simply that perfection is "ascribed" to parents, as Freud put it. To attribute this development to idealization does not quite cover the situation fully. In the limited terms that a child can think and test reality with, the adequate parent *is* omniscient and omnipotent. He can talk, move, understand, provide, and solve problems like a god. He is an ideal object [p. 165].

Loving admiration for the parent is, indeed, valuable to the developing child both in fulfilling inherent needs for attachment and in building self-esteem through association with admired figures whose love and respect one experiences. If the parent's behavior is such that admiration cannot be sustained or if the respected parent makes it clear that he does not love and admire the child, the child is injured and becomes prone to shame, and he may be left seeking something approaching an ideal form, which can be admired. Ironically, adults reared under such circumstances may deny some of their own resources (thus promoting shame) in order to boost the impression of a parent's resources, so as to promote a sense of security with that parent and pride in him.

There are questions to be asked about the "idealizing selfobject *transference*." Often, when idealization of the therapist is an issue in the patient's mind and, thus, is made an issue in the therapy, we are not talking about a simple reinstatement of a child's love and admiration for a parent. Elaborate notions about the therapist's perfection and superiority (to other therapists, to the patient) often work counter to the patient's self-esteem while fulfilling covert self-protective functions that must be examined. The therapist must be careful to note whether the patient's affection for or admiration of him promotes a healthy valuing of the work the two do together and of both parties' contributions to the work and the relationship or whether the patient's high esteem for the therapist represents a point of contrast with his view of the self or of others.

Idealization of the therapist frequently represents a divvying up of good and bad qualities between therapist and patient. If the bad qualities are assigned to the self, the relationship with the idealized therapist generates shame, envy, and hatred, not self-esteem. If the bad qualities are assigned to the therapist, the relationship generates sadistic triumph, which may be gratifying but signifies the ongoing need to misuse others in order to elevate or purify the self. Such behavior may produce a slurry of emotions that combine gratification with guilt and shame and with grief over the absence of genuine relatedness with a valued other.

As an example of assigning all goodness to the therapist, I think of Roxanne, a woman emotionally abused in childhood by a paranoid, likely schizophrenic, mother. Roxanne saw me as kind, educated, and generous. She showed deep affection toward me and she feared losing me. At times, she used me as an internalized parent image to whom she could turn for support in her efforts to treat herself with more consideration. Roxanne's affection and admiration had a genuine and healthful aspect to them and represented a recognition of my efforts on her behalf and also a realization of differences between me and her cruel mother. But also present in her picture of me was a pairing of my supposedly perfect, valuable self with her no-account self. She thought of offering to clean my office as payment for sessions. My time was more important than hers, my ideas more valuable, my motives purer. Any kindness or flexibility from me was regarded as extraordinary and not her due. The bad-self, good-other split, which obviously echoed an early childhood apportioning of value between her and her mother, served her self-structure in many ways. This type of dynamic will be further discussed in the chapter on masochism.

Another type of idealization is seen in individuals who show a profound dread of the therapist's human imperfections. Here, I think of Betty (see Chapters Six and Seven) who needed from her therapist an image of parental perfection. Only absolute goodness would protect her from the power of her abusive mother and from the terrible experience of finding the world empty of anyone to respect and love. She sought something clearly and completely distinguishable from the bad, because she so profoundly feared the bad and its capacity to overwhelm goodness. Her need for a purely good other also grew from a need for reassurance that her aggression would not spoil her loved one and from her need to remain in a protective dyad in which she was the worthless child to whom the good parent would remain loyally bound.

Since Betty's need for an ideal other derived, in part, from traumatic disillusionment, it brings to mind Kohut's thinking about the young child's need for a parent who is worthy of idealization. However, Betty's idealization speaks to the need for a good object as a true "other" as much as to the need for a selfobject who forms the basis for one's self-regard, thus Kohut's thoughts about the idealizing transference do not address all of what was at stake for Betty when she clung to the image that her therapist was flawless.

An idealizing transference was also important to Fred, the young man whose self-concept was deformed by a deep sense of having been unacceptable to and rejected by an abandoning father and less embraceable by Mother than the two sisters with whom she could share feminine interests. Fred idealized his father, in part to keep rage at bay, in part because it was intolerable to lose the idea of a good father who would support Fred's own masculine self-esteem (as Kohut describes). His idealization of Father coexisted with degraded images of Father, even experiences of Father as so dangerously disgusting that the slightest contact would contaminate Fred with Father's shameful inferiority, thus Fred could not handle a book that had been Father's without interposing a protective cloth barrier. Both the extreme idealization and the excessive denigration demonstrated the great tension Fred experienced around the question of Father's worth and also the great fear concerning how Father's worth, or lack of it, would influence Fred's own value and sense of security. His fear that his father, clearly viewed, would be weak was consonant with Goldberg's (1989) critique of Freud's analysis of Hamlet:

> What may have been frightening for Hamlet in his father's death was not his own "murderous" wishes, but the fact of his father's weakness. If his tall and might[y] [sic] warrior father, presented as a ghost—as a man of steel—can be easily felled by his weak brother, then we are all unprotected, vulnerable mortals! [p. 602].

Fred's spotty idealization of his father was reproduced with me. He treated me as an authority figure, sometimes calling me "Ma'am," and he presented himself as a messy, disorganized, foolish, emotional child who predictably forgot his payments, stained my chair with chocolate or coffee, and came unkempt to sessions. To the extent that he, like Roxanne, could think of me, the idealized other, as accepting him, there was a transient good feeling of worth, but little lasting gain in self-esteem or reduction in self-abasing behavior was achieved through this experience. Those changes occurred only when he learned to confront his own limitations and the reality of his father's shortcomings. One could, of course, argue that his experience of an empathic idealized other allowed for the growth in reality contact, which, indeed, may be the case; however, it is important to highlight that the shift in reality-relatedness was a precondition of lasting growth in self-esteem and one that was hard-won and did not flow directly or easily from experiencing a mirroring or idealizable other.

Just before Christmas one year, Jeremy began to use the word *adoration* in describing certain of his feelings for me. As indicated earlier, one function of Jeremy's idealization was to control me. He felt that, if he flattered me and left me feeling gratified and appreciative of his contact with such a "nice guy," he could assure himself that I would like and value him, which was of great importance to him. If he let his feelings about me range more broadly and honestly, he felt no security about my continued emotional availability to him.

Gedo (1975) reviewed concepts of therapist idealization and subdivided the phenomena into three subtypes:

1) idealization of the analyst as a whole oedipal object, defensive against hostility

2) pseudo-idealization, which is a more archaic, defensive use of idealization of the whole object, to protect against traumatic disillusionment (which brings narcissistic rage)

3) true, Kohutian "idealizing transference," which "tends to be silent and relatively impersonal, reflecting its archaic origins at a time when the parent is still part of the child's inner world as a self-object [p. 504].

Gedo's paper raises many questions, not all of which can be considered here. The case examples I have given would appear to distribute among his three types, though some combine elements of two or three subtypes. Betty's idealization best fits Gedo's second type, though the traumatic disillusionment she fears would bring not only narcissistic rage, but grief, abandonment anxiety, and aloneness. Roxanne's idealization, like Gedo's first variety, seems defensive against hostility, though the object toward whom hostility is directed may be the pre-oedipal mother, as well as the oedipal mother. Fred's dynamics and Jeremy's look like those of Kohut's patients. One would expect their idealizations to be true Kohutian idealizations, but their idealizations are not so silent or impersonal as Gedo predicts. They are, however, less anxiously concerned about disillusionment than is Betty or others like her, perhaps because their concern is less with the object's flaws than with the object's failure to admire the self. Each had a parent who disappointed him not so much through pathetic or reprehensible behavior as through the failure to love the child and admire him. Each enthroned the therapist as an admired person and then looked for reciprocal admiration.

Though I did not see this development with Fred or Jeremy, one does see in many treatments the kind of quiet assuming of a good other and good process that Gedo describes as the "true, Kohutian 'idealizing transference.'" He further explains the genuine idealizing transference as follows:

> [It] did not involve placing the analyst on an undeserved pedestal: in fact, it had more to do with idealizing the analytic process than the person who performed it. . . . In genetic terms, this imagery was related to that early phase of her childhood when the mother had been an ideal nurturing figure in the oral sphere [p. 499].

Though I have seen what I believe to be the kind of transference Gedo has in mind, the context generally has not been that of conspicuous narcissistic disturbance. With narcissistically disturbed individuals, I have noted either denigrating transferences (which glorify the patient by comparison with the the devalued therapist) or the noisier idealizations described with Fred and Jeremy or a combination of both. Also common are attempts to be "above" having any feelings for the therapist. The quieter, apparently unconflicted idealizations to which Gedo refers I associate with those healthier individuals who appear to have had good, childhood selfobject experiences, who retain in adulthood a capacity for idealization, a topic Kohut (1984) discussed. When psychopathology does not interfere with its emergence, such idealization appears to constitute part of the universal response to a relatively anonymous therapist who fits the mold of "the stranger" as discussed by the sociologist Simmel (1950).

It may be the case that, in the way that nature provides us all with immature cells that can be differentiated and utilized to heal an injured body, so nature affords us the possibility of psychological growth by allowing us, even as adults, to assume a childlike posture of trust in relation to a human environment perceived to be benevolent and wise, a posture that may be a precondition of major psychological change beyond childhood. This experience of trust in the healing goodness and power of the physician appears to be close to the "silent and relatively impersonal" idealizing transference to which Gedo refers.

I believe that such a stance of the patient is matched by a complementary set of therapist behaviors, which occur when the therapist recognizes the childlike faith the patient has placed in him and responds, as to a young child, with his own best self, meaning that he is more giving and more scrupulous than in many other aspects of his life; he, in fact, comes closer to the patient's selfobject expectations of him than he might if his relationship with the patient took place in another context. Obviously, there are exceptions to this scenario, but I believe that it holds true in many instances.

In closing the discussion of idealization, it is important to recognize, as Kohut clearly did, the positive roles idealization can play in a mature personality. I was reminded of that topic when listening to a radio interview with a Tibetan monk who served as the Dalai Lama's translator. Asked about his early interest in becoming a monk, he described first a childhood memory of the Dalai Lama coming to his school. He was chosen, along with one girl, to put a wreath around the Dalai Lama's neck. That early experience of specialness achieved through intimate connection with an exalted adult figure made an enduring impression on the child. Future contacts with monks consistently impressed him with the monks' "serenity," which was "serene but strong, and gentle." From the stories this man told of his early contacts with the Dalai Lama and other monks, one gained the sense of a child finding a path to a self that would not be buffeted by powerful passions, but would command them (he would be serene and strong). Also, he would be gentle, not cruel, so he would have mastery over any sadism within the self. Thus, his own monkhood preserved the sense of contact with a wonderful other, making for a good self, while it offered resistance to specific disturbing passions and provided sublimated, constructive use of them. Through his own monkhood, which developed from contact with idealized others, his need for personal efficacy and morality were well served and probably his need to express passion as well, in that monkhood might gratify a fantasy of loving closeness with a father figure.

NARCISSISTIC RAGE AND SHAME DYNAMICS

A full consideration of narcissistic rage and its relationship to shame poses many more questions about fundamental concepts of personality development than I can discuss in this context, but I would like at least to point to some of the relevant issues and make a few observations. In considering narcissistic rage and its association with shame, it is important to bear in mind that "shame" or "the shame family of emotions" are terms intended to designate particular moments of feeling, not pervasive internal situations such as "low self-esteem" might suggest.

Kohut carefully considered narcissistic rage in his 1972 paper. Using the biological notion that "fight and flight" are alternative responses to attack, he suggested that narcissistic rage is the narcissistically vulnerable individual's "fight" response, whereas "shamefaced withdrawal" is his typical "flight" response (p. 379). Thus, shame and narcissistic rage are placed in relation to each other by Kohut, though his consideration of narcissistic rage in this context is far more extensive than his consideration of shame.

Kohut goes on to differentiate narcissistic rage from other forms of aggression by identifying two distinct aspects of its phenomenology, which are "the need for revenge, for righting a wrong, for undoing a hurt by whatever means, and a deeply anchored, unrelenting compulsion in the pursuit of these aims" (p. 380). He goes on to say, "In its typical forms there is utter disregard for reasonable limitations and a boundless wish to redress an injury and to obtain revenge" (p. 382). In assessing the psychodynamics that produce vulnerability to narcissistic rage, Kohut states, "Yet underlying all these emotional states is the uncompromising insistence on the perfection of the idealized self-object and on the limitlessness of the power and knowledge of a grandiose self" (p. 385). Later, he states that the grandiose-exhibitionistic self, when narcissistically injured, "like the evil stepmother in Snow White . . . cannot ever find rest anymore because it can never wipe out the evidence which has contradicted its conviction that it is unique and perfect" (p. 385). Thus, Kohut's clear contention is that the special experiential qualities of narcissistic rage—its vengefulness and implacability—follow from the need to reestablish a conviction, once disturbed, that the self is unmarred by flaws or limitations.

Writers wishing to give shame a more prominent place in psychological life increasingly have tended to view narcissistic rage primarily through its relationship to shame. The notion is advanced that shame is the "underlying," problematic emotion that narcissistic rage obscures. Morrison's (1989) analysis of a treatment episode demonstrates the clinical application of the theory that narcissistic rage is a response to and a fight against shame. Morrison's exposition aims to highlight the differences between his shame-based intervention and what he believes Kohut's theory of narcissistic rage might prescribe:

> [S]he acknowledged her fury that the taxi driver had been ignoring her needs and treating her as insignificant. From Kohut's (1972) perspective, her rage was a response to lack of control over the taxi driver; she wanted to "obliterate" him because of his noncompliance.
>
> Treatment might have consisted of clarifying this feeling, accepting her frustration, and waiting for the ultimate analytic transformation of her narcissistic strivings and rage into appropriate assertiveness and aggression. However, her rageful response became clearer when I asked her about her use of the term "insignificant." Associations followed about her own "puniness," her "weak femininity," her observation that the taxi driver had been a "big, burly, stupid man." She, by contrast, had felt passive and helpless—a theme that had been discussed many times before—and she had felt "embarrassed and humiliated" (shame equivalents) by her own weakness and insignificance to him. Elaboration of her own shame feelings followed.
>
> This vignette illustrates the place of (sometimes sudden) shame in eliciting many rage responses and the potential utility of analyzing the underlying shame in gaining a fuller understanding of the rage.

As with many of the other shame-related responses considered in this chapter, analysis of rage in treatment often stops at the manifest level, without further sensitivity to the underlying shame [p. 103].

We can see from the above paragraph how Morrison's thinking diverges from Kohut's. Kohut presumably would argue that the point of the woman's narcissistic rage is to reestablish control over the selfobject environment, thus shoring up the self, but no assumption is made that lack of control necessarily brings the affect, shame. Shame would occur only if the frustrating situation unleashed a display of unmodified, archaic exhibitionism. In contrast, for Morrison, shame over personal insignificance is the prime mover in the situation. It is the experience of shame that triggers the woman's rage, which can be labeled "narcissistic rage" because of its specific character, which satisfies Kohut's and others' criteria.

Here and elsewhere, Morrison's analyses elucidate a shortcoming of Kohut's thinking about narcissism, which is its failure to appreciate fully the role of shame as a *motivating force* within the personality. As Morrison and others amply demonstrate, shame is a stressful, even traumatic, emotion that speaks to a person's estimation of his value and propels behavior, including other emotions. However, what Morrison may be undervaluing in the clinical analysis above, which Kohut generally appreciates, is the importance of what I will call "psychological structures" (i.e., recurrent patterns of response with specific aims) in generating emotion and in driving behavior. Thus, Morrison's analysis would pose the question, "Why has narcissistic rage been generated in this woman?" and it would answer the question by saying, "Because shame generated the rage." But a psychological structures approach would bid us ask, "Why was shame generated?" and would answer, "Because this woman's personality is structured to require absolute power over the selfobject environment." Clinically, both levels of analysis are needed. It is necessary to tie the woman's rage to her shame but also to understand the internal structures that promote her shame. Morrison's own theory approaches the latter task through the concept of the "ideal self," but he does not introduce that construct into the clinical analysis above.

As I have indicated before, questions can be raised about the particulars of Kohut's ideas about self-structure, but it is nonetheless important to recognize the general importance of such structures for establishing susceptibility or resistance to specific emotions. Some clinicians or theorists agree with Kohut that pathological grandiosity derives from the developmental failure to modify an original infantile grandiosity, due to caregiver deficiencies in empathy. Others argue that pathological grandiosity is a psychological stance *created de novo* due to caregiver failures of empathy. Clinically, these two positions are not such a world away. Both speak to a profound attachment to a grandiose self-experience, an attachment that leaves an individual vulnerable to narcissistic rage and, in some cases, shame, when his control over the environment proves to be less than absolute.

What I have found most useful in practice is to weave together the concepts of grandiosity, shame, and narcissistic rage by using a statement of the individual's experience that would sound something like this: "If I am not fully powerful, then I am nothing, which means I am deficient, and ashamed, and enraged." Sometimes people bypass the shame aspect of the formulation and simply feel: "If I am not fully powerful, I am enraged." In these cases, of which both Fred and Jeremy are good examples, the clinician can watch for and introduce the shame element, which is linked to an identity element. It has been my impression that the significance of the shame component is variable. For some individuals, including Fred, internal images of a shameful self are sources of profound feeling and must be addressed regularly and repeatedly. The concept of the disgraced self becomes a central point of reference and is inextricable from the notion of environmental control, since it is the inner experience of wounded pride that environmental control aims to obviate. In other cases, shame is in fact less important. The person is not as concerned about pride and deliverance from shame as he is about power per se.

Thus, I agree with Morrison that shame often is important in eliciting narcissistic rage, and a focus on rage frequently serves to protect a person against suffering shame's characteristic misery. But narcissistic rage is not reliably reducible to a shame byproduct, against which it then defends. Narcissistic rage results from perceived helplessness in a range of circumstances seen as affecting one's well-being; that well-being includes but is not identical to one's self-esteem, and the helplessness at issue may have greater or fewer elements of shame, depending on the circumstances that produce it and on the individual's make-up. Early helplessness frequently results in perfectionism, which establishes a psychological structure that predisposes toward later shame, with or without the interposition of narcissistic rage.

It may be useful at this juncture to reconsider Morrison's female patient in the light of the notion that lasting structures contribute to the generation of moments of feeling. Morrison's patient utilizes a psychological structure that leaves her perceiving as infuriating slights all experiences of lacking perfect authority. It would be important to explore, as Morrison does, her shame-linked images of self and other (e.g., puny self versus big, burly other), but equally salutary to examine what motivates her to distort ordinary situations, such as being kept waiting by a slow-moving cab, so that they become tests of her power and, inevitably, demonstrations of her insignificance. She must find some safety or solace in thus defining the world.

Narcissistic rage would appear to occur very early in development, certainly before objective self-awareness and before the later forms of shame, which depend on viewing the self as an object. In the experience of narcissistic rage, the emphasis is on some error of commission or omission that the outer world has perpetrated against the self. The rage says, "This should not be done to me, how dare they do this to me? I demand better; I am entitled to the gratification of my needs." The sense of the frustrated, helpless, churning self is at the center of the experience, and that image of self is paired with an image of the offending other.

As an example of narcissistic rage that is intertwined with images of an ashamed self but driven more by object-hunger or the longing for a mutually loving and admiring relationship than by moments of shame, we can consider Mary Shelley's (1831) *Frankenstein,* in which Dr. Frankenstein creates a living being, then completely rejects his creation as abhorrent. The "monster" becomes *truly* monstrous—that is, he becomes destructive of goodness—only when powered by narcissistic rage over his creator's rejection of him, which leaves him not just lacking in regard for self but utterly alone, without companionship in an alien world. Frankenstein's creature says:

> I am thy creature, and I will be even mild and docile to my natural lord and king, if thou wilt also perform thy part, the which thou owest me. Oh, Frankenstein, be not equitable to every other and

trample upon me alone, to whom thy justice, and even thy clemency and affection, is most due. Remember, that I am thy creature; I ought to be thy Adam; but I am rather the fallen angel, whom thou drivest from joy for no misdeed. Every where I see bliss, from which I alone am irrevocably excluded. I was benevolent and good; misery made me a fiend [pp. 73–74].

Rejected by his creator, the monster might come to view himself with shame, and his narcissistic rage might attempt to counter his shame, but such rage is more than a struggle against shame. It is his statement of fury toward the one he sees as causing his misery, including his shame; it is also his effort to reestablish intimacy and mutual admiration between himself and his creator. Thus narcissistic rage speaks to the relatedness pole of experience, not just to the self-feeling aspects. It conceives of shame, degradation, deprivation, or other forms of pain as unfairly inflicted on the self by the other and within the other's power to remediate. The monster says to Frankenstein, "Make me happy, and I shall again be virtuous" (p. 74).

Similar arguments can be offered about certain experiences I will call "narcissistic hunger," which are not best conceived as efforts to obviate shame but as positive efforts to generate self-love and a sense of connection with a loved other. I am referring to instances in which one longs for a relationship with a loved and admired person through which that person recognizes one's value and wishes for one's companionship. As an example, I think of a young woman whose father had left the family when the patient was an infant and her older siblings were five and six. The family myth was that Mother and the older children were hurt by the father's departure, but not little Evelyn, because Evelyn had no relationship with Father. But Evelyn was burdened with a longing for a relationship, both an actual father–daughter relationship with its quotidian routines and the *idea* of a father–daughter relationship, which would confer on her the sense and status of being wanted. She may have been ashamed of herself as someone who mattered so little that Father did not stay with the family in order to be with her, but more pressing than any specific shame feeling was a hunger for acknowledgment. She did not talk of feeling shame at her school's Father's Night, but spoke repeatedly of ritually counting the family photos that portrayed her sisters with her father and then counting those of her and her father so she could make a case in her head to present to her father, a case that argued, "See what you owe me; see how unfairly I've been treated." She also told of going to community fairs with her father and sibs, during visitation meetings, and regularly and intentionally getting lost so that her father was forced to come find her after an announcement of her whereabouts had been made over the public address system. The recurring scene of Father calling out for her return over the loudspeaker, and pleased later with their reunion, seemed to counter her ongoing pain of unwantedness. When her efforts to create what she needed with Father failed, she felt narcissistic rage, which was not just an obscuring of shame, but an angry and frustrated response to her inability to secure the relationship for which she hungered. In this case, the treatment effort needed to focus less on shame and more on the pain of longing, which had made it impossible for her to accept a close, adult relationship with a man.

Fred, Jeremy, and Annette all experienced rage feelings similar to Morrison's patient when their control over ordinary situations was imperfect. It proved valuable in each case to look at the broadly operative, underlying assumptions about the self and its powers, not just the associations that linked a particular traffic jam or failed alarm clock with a particular memory of insignificance or a current treatment stimulus. The need to examine broadly operative assumptions is especially important in those people who *habitually* respond to frustration with narcissistic rage.

Fred's narcissistic rage both masked and displayed his guilt and moral shame over his own ethical shortcomings, which included deceptiveness. He might become enraged at a store clerk who insisted he have a receipt in order to return a purchase. In his rage, he berated the clerk for her poor record-keeping, which left her with no proof of the sale. He also condemned her failure to trust him. Privately, Fred harbored guilt and shame over the fact that he was covering up his own poor record-keeping (which shamed him) and forcing the clerk to bear all the responsibility. His rage at her represented a trumped-up complaint over an offense to the self, a complaint meant to obscure his own offenses against another.

An interesting example of narcissistic rage and one that raises theoretical questions comes from the character of Coalhouse Walker in E. L. Doctorow's (1974) novel *Ragtime*. Coalhouse Walker is a proud, fastidious African-American who becomes consumed by unrelenting murderous rage when his perfectly maintained Model

T Ford, an important self-symbol, is obstructed on the road, vandalized, and finally befouled with dirt and human feces. The phenomenology of Coalhouse's rage seems to fit Kohut's notion of narcissistic rage in most of its particulars. I remind the reader of Kohut's (1972) reference to "the need for revenge, for righting a wrong, for undoing a hurt by whatever means, and a deeply anchored, unrelenting compulsion in the pursuit of these aims" (p. 380). Though Coalhouse's response fits Kohut's description of narcissistic rage and matches my own sense that the assertion of self constitutes the core of such rage, describing Coalhouse's response as narcissistic rage resurrects the question of whether a grandiose self-structure, presumably pathological in nature, must underlie this variety of rage. It seems reasonable to argue that offenses against the self that are great and real and truly abusive in their nature produce in most anyone a furious and prolonged determination for revenge. If such a quest requires an internal image of a perfect, pristine, grandiose self that has been offended, then some representation of that pure self must exist in all of us. Alternatively, it is possible that egregious offenses against the self regularly unleash a self-assertive rage, phenomenologically akin to more pathological narcissistic rage, but do not depend on a split-off grandiose structure. It is likely that the course of resolution, over time, of such rage would relate to the original status of the person's narcissism.

With regard to the relationship between shame and narcissistic rage, we can note further that Coalhouse Walker was a self-consciously proud man and a very careful man; most likely, he was a man vulnerable to shame, though we aren't shown that. But to construe his narcissistic rage as exclusively a response to and flight from shame misses the validity of the rage as an appropriately indignant outcry, a statement that he has been sadistically wounded and deserves and demands better from his fellow men. His feelings are not only about what has become of the image of self and the sense of self (which is shame's concern); they are about his need for a relationship of mutual respect with his fellows. Coalhouse Walker is introduced as follows:

> One afternoon, a Sunday, a new Model T Ford slowly came up the hill and went past the house. . . . The driver was looking right and left as if trying to find a particular address; he turned the car around at the corner and came back. Pulling up before the boy,

he idled his throttle and beckoned with a gloved hand. He was a Negro. His car shone. The brightwork gleamed. There was a glass windshield and a custom pantosote top [p. 161]. When Mother came to the door the colored man was respectful, but there was something disturbingly resolute and self-important in the way he asked her if he could please speak with Sarah [p. 162].

Sometime later . . .

[Coalhouse's] car stood off the road in the field. He made his way to the car. It was spattered with mud. There was a six-inch tear in the custom pantasote top. And deposited in the back seat was a mound of fresh human excrement [p. 183].

I want my car cleaned and the damage paid for, he said. The Chief began to laugh and a couple of his men came out to join the fun [p. 184].

The big policeman came to a decision. He took Coalhouse aside. Listen, he said, we'll push your tin lizzie back on the road and you be on your way. There's no real damage. Scrape off the shit and forget the whole thing. I was on my way when they stopped me, Coalhouse said. They put filth in my car and tore a hole in the top. I want the car cleaned and the damage paid for. The officer had now begun to appreciate Coalhouse's style of speech, his dress, and the phenomenon of his owning a car in the first place. He grew angry. If you don't take your automobile and get along out of here, he said loudly, I'm going to charge you with driving off the road, drunkenness, and making an unsightly nuisance. I do not drink, Coalhouse said. I did not drive my car off the road nor slash the roof nor defecate in it. I want the damage paid for and I want an apology. The policeman looked at the Chief, who was grinning at his discomfiture, so that the issue for him was now his own authority. He said to Coalhouse I'm placing you under arrest [pp. 184-185].

As one last example of narcissistic rage that is about shame but also about interpersonal needs, I think again of Jeremy, furious and outraged over being charged for an appointment he cancelled at the last minute, stating as his reason a pressing situation at home. As analysis of his feelings gradually became possible, it grew clear that his rage flowed less from shame than from fear of emotional abandonment. He equated the charge with the distressing idea that his therapist did not care about him or about the work he felt they shared, but only about the fee. His rage was a protest against the doctor's perceived indifference, which buffeted his sense of secure attachment as well as his self-esteem.

Grandiosity was also part of the picture, in that he equated the therapist's caring about him with the therapist's being fully controlled by Jeremy's wishes and by nothing else. He set up a test of his ability to control his therapist (he knew the cancellation policy but chose to believe it would not be enforced) and was determined to see the therapist's independence as a betrayal of the relationship. For him to allow his doctor independent functioning, while also maintaining his investment in the work, led to a kind of vulnerability to his therapist that frightened him. If he maintained his commitment to a person who was not under his control, who would not function as part of his fantasied "play world," he could indeed be disappointed and hurt. The "test" was a set-up for his therapist to fail him but also a bid for her to help him move ahead to a new level of relatedness, in which he could allow others to be themselves and still remain engaged with them.

In this chapter, we have seen how psychological structures related to perfectionism can generate shame in situations that would seem benign absent those structures. Writers disagree as to the nature of the perfectionistic structures and their mechanism of operation. Kohut sees split-off grandiosity as the precondition for flooding exhibitionism, the discharge and restraint of which constitutes shame. Morrison sees the ideal self as a template against which the actual self is compared, with deviations from the model resulting in shame. Though these theories, and others that could be cited, differ significantly, they share the notion that a lasting structure establishes the conditions for shame experience. In the two chapters to follow, we shall see how the need to maintain certain psychological structures motivates masochistically organized individuals to feel and communicate shame.

CHAPTER 6

Shame in the Foreground

Early Roots of Moral Masochism

So in my father's house, which was her home, I tried to cloak my self in an atmosphere of apology. I did not in fact feel sorry for anything at all, and I had not done anything, either deliberately or by accident, that warranted my begging for forgiveness, but my gait was my weapon—a way of deflecting her attention from me, of persuading her to think of me as someone who was pitiable, an ignorant child.

—Jamaica Kincaid ("Xuela")

INTERPERSONALLY ESTABLISHED
MOTIVES FOR EMBRACING SHAME

I begin this chapter with Jamaica Kincaid's words because they point to shame as a posture or stance that carries certain interpersonal benefits. Reading the passage, we might wonder whether the speaker protests too much, whether she, in fact, feels sorry for some things or ashamed of some things. But even were that the case, it remains important that she can use a *stance* of shame to influence her environment and also to affect how she sees herself in that setting.

It is in this chapter particularly that I wish to explore ways in which the recent trend toward isolating shame as a crucial pathogenic emotion, while constructive in many respects, has led not only to underrecognition of other problematic emotions, but also to unfortunate dismissal of previously established insights about the role mechanisms of self-protection play in determining adult affect experience. The prevalent notion that shame is the bedrock of much psychopathology, the gold to be mined psychotherapeutically, has contributed to increasing neglect of the ways in which shame experience and expression intertwines with character pathology and defense. In this chapter, one area of emphasis

151

will be the self-protection some find in the painful experience of shame. Such pain may be generated and communicated in order to exert a variety of influences over internal and interpersonal worlds that are seen as replete with danger. Behaviors aimed at maintaining such self-protection constitute one of the psychological structures to which I referred in the previous chapter.

Lewis (1992) quotes and endorses Nathanson's (1987) statement, "What the therapist sees is not shame, the symptom, but shame, the shaper of symptoms" (p. 119). I would argue that the therapist sees both. Early experiences of painful shame join with other developmental stresses in contributing to later, self-protective use of shame. Thus, shame of one variety can serve as a safeguard against shame of another kind. I will look both at shame as a shaper of symptoms and at shame as a symptom, with particular attention to the latter. I will use a notion of shame experience as roughly divisible into "primary" and "constructed" shame, by which I mean to differentiate shame that is a nearly universal response to a particular situation (e.g., being demeaned in public) from shame selected from among the various emotion options, amplified and broadcast as having some protective value.

In talking about the "governing scenes" from childhood that underlie adult shame experience, Kaufman (1989) builds on the notion that every current shame experience reflects a memory of an old experience (like a flashback or a reliving). My point of view is that a present-day experience (especially if occurring without a compelling external stimulus) is better conceived of as a construction or choice. If it is a choice to relive the past, one must look at why that choice is made. What value does such a reliving have for the person in her contemporary setting?

Moral masochism, which some equate with depressive disorders (Markson, 1993), has in common with obsessive-compulsive disorder, narcissistic disturbance, and psychopathology in general (indeed, with all character development) the firm establishment of behavior designed to achieve control over potentially painful emotions through manipulation of inner and outer realities. What sets masochism apart is the creation of a suffering and deformed self as the specific mechanism for controlling that which has been and might again be traumatic.

Thus, by "masochism" I mean to designate those forces in the personality that lead to the perpetuation of suffering based on a belief, generally unarticulated, that suffering leads either to direct gratification, to respite from pain or helplessness, or to effective assault on that which is hurtful and hated. Shame is one type of pain employed in masochism, though by no means the only type; depression, anxiety, and angry experiences of deprivation are other varieties. Shame refers to those experiences of pain that occur through seeing the self as deficient or at least discomforted and exposed. It is in the context of masochism that we best see the adult actively utilizing powerful shame experience as a way to manage helplessness.

The active use of shame as a tool for managing one's world speaks both to early and later shame developments. The earliest roots of this variety of investment in shame or attachment to it in some cases would include an infant's or young child's experience of needing to be bad or worthless in order to exist for the primary caregiver, to gratify the caregiver, or to be like the caregiver and thus connected to that person. Early ways of being bad or diminished may include experiences of being dirty, stupid, selfish, inept, ill, or babyish.

A brief, preliminary example of masochistic embracing of shamefulness, as well as guilt, comes from Betty, who often chose to accept and internalize badness, attributed to her by her mother, in order to play a necessary part in her mother's world and to avoid perceiving her mother's destructiveness and insensitivity. Betty recalls, at age five, discovering the family cat inexplicably dead. When Mother returned home from work, she told the children the cat had starved to death; she blamed the children for failing to feed the animal. The children then went out and buried their pet, during which time Betty recalls struggling with her mother's claim. She vacillated between accepting Mother's words, which meant feeling that she, Betty, was terrible—she had killed a loved cat—and, alternatively, embracing a second set of thoughts that said that a mother, not a child, is responsible for feeding a pet. We can see how she was torn, even at so young an age, between her wish to use her reason to free herself from the attributed shamefulness and culpability and her fear of the awful aloneness such alienation from Mother's point of view would bring. She also feared her mother's consuming rage if Betty were to hold to her perception of Mother's responsibility. Over and over again, Betty's treatment laid bare her terror in seeing her mother's great limitations, the acknowledgment of which left her too alone and unprotected in her childhood world and, as an adult, unbearably grieved over past maltreatment. She preferred her demeaning self-perceptions and self-abusive behavior, which left her feeling restful and in her place.

MASOCHISM AND NARCISSISM

Masochism and narcissism have many features in common. Many would call Broucek's (1991) "dissociated narcissists" masochistic. Broucek describes this group of people as characterized by "[l]ow self-esteem, vulnerability to frequent shame experiences, and rejection sensitivity, as well as diminished energy and vitality" (p. 60). He also refers to "a subtle air of superiority and entitlement that exists side by side with a more consciously articulated self-devaluation" (p. 60).

Both the narcissistic person and the masochistic one distort reality in order to maintain the illusion of full control over interpersonal life and corresponding object representations. The narcissistic person finds her power chiefly in overt images of might. She feels special, magical, or exempt from ordinary logic, or she feels physically invincible or lucky or above involvement with ordinary others and their trivial concerns. The masochistic person achieves power more covertly and often with less awareness of her investment. She finds power in the intensity and specialness of her suffering (often her shame), in her ability to render herself invulnerable to *ordinary* pain and pleasure, and in the imagined or real effects her suffering has on others, who can be bound to the self in sado-masochistic pairings or in pairings rooted in shared misery or in a suffering person's need to be tended. Both the narcissistically disturbed person and the masochistic person may believe she wields great destructive power, as well as authority to avert destruction. Fred (previous chapter) feels, "I can blow you away with my temper if you dare humiliate me by speaking of my limitations." Betty feels, "I can kill cats or anyone else—my mother says so and I accept it and depend on it."

The masochistic individual and the narcissistic one may share an anxious self-centeredness. The self-centeredness of the masochistic person emerges in a number of ways. One form of self-centeredness is the taking of the suffering self as one's primary object, to be nursed, worried over, and brought to the solicitous attention of others. Others' suffering pales in comparison with one's own. Others' wishes and needs, hopes and dreams, seem incidental by comparison with one's pain. The whole of the ordinary world recedes in import and may have only a shadowy existence, as is the case with a person in deep mourning. The nursing of the self may aim at sustaining the self, at influencing others, and at channeling loving attention that cannot be safely invested elsewhere.

The masochistic person and the egotistical type of narcissistic individual have different relationships to shame. The narcissistic person usually denies shame until treatment makes inroads into her character. When she does acknowledge it, she is likely to react to shame with narcissistic rage as if the shame had been inflicted on her by some careless or inattentive other who might be forced to withdraw it. Even when the inflictor of shame is actually her own conscience, she may rail at others seen as shaming her. She complains less of feeling ashamed than of being shamed.

In contrast, the masochistically organized person is quick to claim shame as one of her core experiences and to assert that the experience is so deep-rooted and excruciating that no one can relieve her of it. She may carry her shame feelings as a conspicuous burden and make certain they are evident to all. Though the pain she feels is real and often profound, the investment in the pain is equally real.

DEVELOPMENTAL PARADIGMS RELEVANT TO SHAME

Thus far, I have been looking at the notion, pivotal to an understanding of masochism, that shame can be utilized actively in an effort to achieve mastery of early strain and trauma. In examining masochism, it is also necessary to consider those shame experiences that themselves may constitute a part of the problematic early strain, that is, "shame, the shaper of symptoms." In order to do so, I will reintroduce some of the available developmental schemata for shame.

Broucek's (1991) paradigm for shame development points to the child's abandonment of the indwelling self, seen as occurring when the caregiver fails to respond to the child's natural forms of engagement and offers only a "still-face gaze." Broucek's belief is that such experience produces shame (an alteration in the "sense of self") in the infant and results over time in the child's forsaking of her indwelling self. This type of early occurring shame would represent a universal human response to a stimulus impinging on the self. It stands in contrast to those shame experiences that the more developed personality adopts in order to achieve power in relation to a specific, threatening circumstance.

In looking at the child's abandonment of her indwelling self, Broucek mainly considers the child's wish to protect herself from a discouraging environment and the shame feelings it engenders. He does not fully consider the role of internal conflicts over utilizing one's capabilities, which may develop in such settings; Wurmser supplies this element to the discussion about early shame.

Broucek's depiction of shame-related early experience is somewhat schematic, both in its emphasis on a single type of parental response and in its focus on shame emotion and dissociation from the indwelling self as the only infant responses considered. Wurmser (1981) enriches the picture by drawing attention to the effects early caregiver unresponsiveness have in evoking anger and in generating discord around those drives or partial drives that the infant uses to connect with the caregiver. The infant's experiences of her drives can be thought of as aspects of her indwelling self, which become mired in conflict. In examining the ways in which the drives to look and show become overburdened and overinvested because they are obstructed as pathways to contact, Wurmser elucidates the fantasied powers to create and destroy that come to attend these activities, thus burdening the personality with magical views about its powers, including its destructive powers. Such developments may be relevant to obsessive-compulsive conditions, as well as to masochism.

Wurmser (1981) divides shame experience into shame anxiety and shame affect. He restricts shame affect to the later developmental stage in which the superego is developed and is utilizing shame (and guilt) as an internally generated means of controlling conflictual behavior. Later stopping of the self through use of shame is seen as modelled after earlier stopping of the self by others: an example would be a mother's scowling interruption of an infant's curious looking or delighted bouncing on her bed. Later, the superego aspect of a person may scowl when she feels curious or inclined to show off.

Wurmser differentiates shame anxiety from shame affect by the use of notions of internalization and superego. As defined by Wurmser, shame anxiety involves the dread of being shamed by an external other. Wurmser's contextual use of the terms suggests it also involves the response to actual shaming. Shame anxiety becomes shame affect when the punisher is internalized so that censure can be generated by the self against the self.

The following passage (Wurmser, 1981) describes shame anxiety, which antedates the shaming superego and is crucial to understanding its eventual character and the threat it poses to inner comfort:

> We come therefore to the phenomenological definition of shame anxiety as *that type of anxiety evoked by sudden exposure and signaling the danger of contemptuous rejection.*
>
> Shame anxiety has characteristically a "freezing" or, paradoxically, a burning ("searing"), numbing quality and is accompanied by a profound estrangement from world and self, present and past. All eyes seem to stare at the shamed one and pierce him like knives. Everyone seems full of taunts and mockery; everyone undoubtedly knows about his profound disgrace [p. 53].

I initially found the above passage confusing in that it seemed to suggest that shame anxiety is a signal emotion that occurs in order to protect against actual shaming, but rereading (in the context of other passages) led me to doubt whether that is Wurmser's intended meaning. I believe he wants shame anxiety to signify the response to actual, early rejections. The passage to follow examines the development of the affect shame, as contrasted with shame anxiety:

> We must assume that the complex affect of shame—in contrast to shame anxiety, its core—always involves the superego; it is therefore possible only after the formation of the superego as a system, probably only after the resolution of the Oedipus complex. In contrast to shame proper, its archaic precursors—notably shame anxiety and the archaic defense by hiding, which later become part of the shame structure—far antedate the oedipal stage [p. 73].

In the following passage, shame affect is not differentiated from shame anxiety, but I believe Wurmser means to designate the earliest form of shame, which would be the experience of the infant from whom the caregiver turns away, refusing to be engaged by the baby's looking or showing:

What are the basic and archaic fears in shame? Provisionally it can be said they are loss of the object and, with it, loss of the self. The other person turns away in contempt. Contempt removes the right of presence and even of existence. He who is not loved stops loving himself; he feels he is "a nothing," "empty," "frozen"— "like a stone." The basic fear to be feared is this total object loss and self-loss [p. 83].

Wurmser later considers why shame is such a prominent emotion for seriously disturbed adults. The conclusion he draws focuses on the role of shame (presumably, shame affect) as a superego force that restricts attempts to exercise power in one's interpersonal world. He states:

Why are shame and the struggle for power so important for many people, particularly for seriously disordered persons? The answer is not necessarily that they have been exposed to excessive shaming— or that shame plays a particular role in the whole family situation—in other words, that they merely responded to borrowed shame, although this may indeed be the case. Rather, as with excessive guilt, shame is rooted in the intensity of the underlying conflict, the conflict of power through perception and expression versus rejection—rejection implicit or explicit [p. 63].

In Wurmser's presentation, shame has a double meaning and set of roles: it signifies the reduced, destroyed state of the child-self exposed to profound rejection; it also signifies the aggressive superego force the self wields against itself, in order to curtail expression much as the early caregiver did. In getting at this doubleness, Wurmser is integrating a number of major trends in the shame literature, including the trend toward seeing shame as an immediate, conceptually unmediated response to another's disapproving or unresponsive face and the various notions of shame (such as Morrison's ideal-self theory) as a self-scrutinizing and self-stopping activity.

A simple integration of the two levels of shame is achieved by saying that earliest shame is the unmediated response to narcissistic injury (including both inattention and mistreatment), and later shame is the inflicting on the self of the narcissistic strain once imposed by the caregiver. Even in the presence of an actively shaming other, later shame involves self-punishment, not just castigation by another. Presumably, the ability to conceive of the self as an object (objective self-awareness) would usher in the second form of shame.

In later discussion of one of his central concepts, *unlovability*, Wurmser (1981) returns to the theme of loss of self and loss of relatedness. He argues that the central fear in shame is being unlovable:

> This allows us now a theoretical breakthrough to the center of this book. If put generally, is this shame then, at its deepest layer, the ever-deepening conviction of one's *unlovability*—in a man because of the surrender to pervasive castration anxiety? in a woman because of the sense of genital defectiveness? and more deeply, in both, because of an inherent sense that the entire self is "dirty," "untouchable," "rotten"—that at one's core one can never be loved? The most radical shame is to offer oneself and be rejected as unlovable. This abyss of unlovability contains such a depth of wordless and imageless despair that any more delimited shame comes as a welcome friend; its visibility and concreteness protect against the gray ghost of that absolute shame. *Basic shame is the pain of essential unlovability.* It is beyond speech. Ibsen called it the crime of "soul murder"—this bringing about of unlovability [pp. 92–93].

As indicated earlier, I have some reservation about Wurmser's use of the word *unlovability* as a descriptor of the infant's experience, not only because it is such an unlovable bit of language but also because it is a summary term that indexes an infant's experience of self by means of a concept of self more appropriate to an older person. I might prefer to divide the concept into small units of experience and say, for example, that the infant feels small and shriveled up and unhappy and finds that nothing she does brings a pleasing response from the other person, that doing the things she naturally does brings little shared joy, but such an itemization fails to convey the far-reaching pain and terror Wurmser seeks to communicate. Indeed, there is nothing so wrong with the term *unlovability* as a summary concept; it just needs investigating with regard to its sources in moments of experience.

Though their language differs distinctly—Broucek's relatively spare, Wurmser's cutting close to the bone—both are reaching for an explanation of earliest, pre-OSA, pre-superego forms of shame as painful ruptures of the pleasure in self and of the sense of relatedness to the other, collapses that bring about profound alienation from the lively, indwelling self, as well as from the human milieu. Schore (1994), too, explores shame of this sort, but he restricts early shame generation to the infant's efforts to find mirroring for his hyperaroused exhibitionism, whereas Broucek and Wurmser consider a broader range of self-expressive states and developmental stages.

Nathanson's (1987) comments on "the bad self" and my own on feelings of "badness" (1985) intersect Wurmser's discussion of unlovability. Nathanson's explanation for the bad self experience is that it attempts to preserve the good mother by relocating to the self the badness the child finds in the rejecting mother. Thus Nathanson, here following Melanie Klein, conceives of the child's earliest self-formation as already defensively influenced; his thinking contrasts with that of Wurmser and Broucek who attach more significance to the child's direct apprehension of real, disturbing affective communications from the mother. In the world portrayed by Wurmser, the child feels destroyed and unlovable as she absorbs the mother's hurtful communication (though such an experience of unlovability presumably might be amplified by the child's defensive exaggeration of her own destructive powers), whereas, for Nathanson, the child's psyche actively preserves the good mother by devaluing the self. Nathanson's concept belongs to the group of "splitting" concepts. If one imputes some validity to both points of view, one finds in the later-developed, judgmental, shaming superego both the internalization of the shaming mother, now wielded against the self by the self, and the perpetuation of the defensively motivated "bad self."

Spero (1984), too, conjectures that defensive splitting is active very early in establishing a shameful sense of self, but rather than consider the bad-self, good-mother split that Nathanson posits he considers the splitting of the self-image into bad and good and the corresponding good–bad split within the object representation:

If the onlooker's real or imagined reaction is humiliating, and is experienced as an intrusion into the ego's private interiority, it is dealt with during early development by changes in the relationship between self and object representations. The combined effect of suddenly being confronted and glared at in a "no escape" context (Greenson, 1967, p. 132), and of being rejected or devalued, is dealt with by (1) splitting the "shameful" and "good" self representation and by (2) splitting the "bad" object representation of the shaming onlooker from its good aspects [p. 266].

Nathanson (1987) claims additionally that the early attachment of a notion of "bad me" to the image of the self can be explained by assuming, following Broucek's reasoning, that shame affect is elicited by the mother's disturbed physiognomy, by her appearing "like a stranger"; however, that affect is uncoupled from the cognition, "bad mother," so that the cognition can be reassigned to the self. The reassignment of cognition occurs because "The relationship with mother is so critical for survival that it is unlikely that the infant could accept a definition of the suddenly unfriendly, unloving, unacceptable mother as 'bad'" (p. 37).

EARLY ROOTS OF MASOCHISM

If we return now to masochism and speculate about the earliest roots of this orientation, we can think about directly shame-related early experience and also about indirectly shame-related early experience. The directly shame-related experience might be the sort described by Broucek (1991), in familiar shame language, in which the sense of self is diminished and the baby is seen slumping, with head down and gaze averted (p. 31), or that described by Nathanson in which the badness found in the unmotherly caregiver is defensively relocated onto the self. Earliest shame might also take the form of feeling frozen, empty, and despairing, like "a nothing," as Wurmser describes. It is worth noting in connection with Wurmser's descriptors that some would attach summary terms other than shame to the states he describes, an observation that highlights the illusory neatness of the "basic affects" categories.

If we shift our focus slightly and think about early responses not so directly shame related, we encounter views such as those of Novick and Novick (1987, 1991) and Markson (1993), who talk of the infant (of, for example, a depressed mother) who has *few experiences of efficacy* in eliciting positive responses. The point emphasized by these writers, which constitutes the bridge from early emotion to masochism, is that the infant who is helpless to engage its caretakers using its ordinary capabilities, especially with regard to pleasurable exchanges, is left with the task of seeking some other way to engage people predictably, some way other than the usual smiles and joyful vocalizations and demonstrations of mastery or playfulness. The child must find a way to make herself interesting to others in order to feel some control in her object world and some inner sense of an efficacious self. It is in this literature that we find the pathway from early stress (whether it is shame stress or other types) to later masochism and, if we extend the thinking, to later masochistic use of shame as one of the emotions of suffering.

Novick and Novick (1991) conjecture and Markson (1993) concurs that the infant under the described circumstances may find that closeness can be achieved (or imagined) through joining with the parent's dysphoric emotion; thus, early on, in order to connect with Mother, one may begin to share in her painful emotion. The connection may be based on an inner feeling of mother–child sameness, or it may depend on sensing that the mother, seeking someone to share her misery, responds with warmth only to a distressed infant, not to a lively one. The infant reaches out to the mother where she is, where she lives, in her state of pain, since the mother does not reach out to the infant in her varying states of feeling. An example is a child whose mother only attends to her when she seems sad or sick, as Mother herself often feels, but she neglects the baby's states of joy or playfulness. She can only see the child when she is like Mother, in her unhappiness. The child's pleasure states may become paired with distress if the mother spoiled the child's pleasure or withdrew in the face of it. Later in life, such a child may discover that she can pursue, through inner feeling states, the sadness that attaches her to internal and transferential representations of Mother.

With specific regard to shame, we can conjecture that, if the caregiver's predominant, visible emotion is some variety of shame— for example, she is constantly self-effacing—the infant may seek closeness by attempting to feel what Mother seems to feel. Thus, she adds that identification-based shame to whatever shame-linked feeling comes directly from the experience of failing to engage the parent. In some cases, the baby may also learn that her own shame is precisely what engages the caregiver. For example, an infant may come to recognize that her depressed mother tends to her whenever she soils her diaper. Even as an older toddler, when the soiled state has become shameful, its associations to bringing Mother close may make it rewarding. As an adult, the

person soils herself through dirty speech or dirty business dealings and feels ashamed but also reassured and thus driven to
self-soiling. A variation on this theme would be the experience
of the baby whose irritable father becomes tender and sympathetic only when the child appears cowed and humbled. So we
see that shame feelings early on can have significance both as
statements of inefficacy (at engaging or pleasing a caregiver) and
as attempts at efficacy (in engaging, gratifying, or involving a
caregiver). Movement away from such feelings may engender the
loneliness, panic, and rage of isolation and may revive the original shame of inefficacy.

As already indicated, a depressed caregiver may produce motivation in an infant to share the parent's experience. Early
movement toward depression would have significance for later
shame experience because all states of self-diminution, including
depression, tend to be read as shameful once the self-judging
aspects of shame develop. A similar dynamic might appear around
parental anxiety.

Another early experience contributing to later masochism is
that of finding satisfaction in actively destroying one's own pleasure. Such gratification may occur for a child whose parent
sadistically attacks the child's joy or capriciously interrupts it,
so the child discovers that destroying her own pleasure negates
the parent's power. Pride is one important form of pleasure over
which a child may wish to take control. Under adverse circumstances, the child perversely may find pleasure in dashing her
own pride. The gratification in such self-abuse is significantly
enhanced if a perception exists that the former abuser has been
frustrated or distressed by the child's behavior.

A child whose caregiver constantly turns away from that child
to pursue other pleasures (an alcoholic parent, for example) also
may find solace in the undermining of good feeling, since the
parent's good feeling has led to helplessness and unhappiness for
the child. Such a child may develop a strongly antipleasure superego,
which then turns its fury on the child's own satisfactions, as well
as those of others. Such attacks on one's own and others' gratification can bring a sense of power and also bring pride over
moral superiority as long as the person's conscience continues
to offer admiration for her antilibidinal stance. If the conscience
withdraws such admiration, recognizing perhaps the person's
increasing human impairments or her destructiveness, the attacks

on pleasure likely will bring shame as the person struggles for normal enjoyment but cannot attain it, due to the persistence of a longstanding attachment to her antagonism to joy.

Thus, we begin to see that masochism is a final common path, and a number of roads may lead to it. The more pressing or numerous the developmental problems "solved" by adopting a suffering and deformed self, the more invested will be the solution. The specific roots of masochism may include the rejected or neglected child's direct experiences of shame (or other dysphoric emotion) over failing to engage the parent and may also involve early lessons that interpersonal connection and efficacy can be achieved or persuasively imagined through the experiencing and displaying of pain, disability, or feeling "bad." The pairing of the two sets of experiences may lead to extreme reservations about pursuing pleasure-based engagement and may also produce a person hellbent on preserving behaviors and self-appraisals that generate misery. Internally, the person's reservations about pleasure may take the form of feelings of stubborn refusal (e.g., "digging one's heels in"), anxiety, and fury, any of which may erupt when she is tempted by ordinary forms of pleasure.

LATER DEVELOPMENTAL CONTRIBUTIONS TO MASOCHISM

In later childhood, there may occur a number of shame-relevant family dynamics. Shame can be directly elicited; for example, the parent provokes a child into a rage through broken promises and then points to the enraged child and says, "Just look at you; you're a wild animal." Especially relevant to masochism is shame that follows from communications suggesting that some severe problem in the child's life or in the family system might be alleviated if the child experienced shame or depression or another form of pain. A mother's insecurity might be made less painful if her daughter also felt discomposed; a physically abused child might provoke less humiliation and abuse if she adopted an ashamed stance; an adolescent boy tempted by separation might reassure himself that he won't forget his sickly father if he shares in the father's shame and thus needs him for support; or a neglected son of a hypochondriacal parent might believe he finally will be attended to if he, like Mother, is sick and suffering. In these complex situations, a child moves further and further from the spontaneous expressions of the indwelling self, especially those oriented around pleasure and ordinary forms of success. Secondary gain attaches to the fantasy of saving the family from catastrophe.

If the child's appropriate expressions of aggression or her joyful, adaptive, or individuated action bring actual punishment, such penalty for health strongly reinforces reliance on misery as an effort to draw close to others, to avoid rebuke, and to achieve some satisfaction of needs. An example of such dynamics is Donald, a young man who spoils his own pleasures and turns ordinary adult burdens into sources of misery. Donald's memories of Catholic school feature nuns warning that he who jumps the highest falls the hardest. Paired with this overt discouragement of a child's exuberance and health was a truly burdensome home situation. Donald's parents had several disabled children and several healthy children. Perhaps due to guilt over bearing the ill children, the mother could only really see and accept disabled people. As an adult, Donald complained of his own "perfectionism." He abandoned many areas of capable, even outstanding, functioning out of frustration and shame over less than perfect performance. On the face of it, he looked like Jeremy, who demanded specialness in all that he did, or Fred, who could not stand defeat even in moving through an intersection ahead of the competing traffic. But closer attention to Donald's feelings suggested a need to abandon areas of competence in order to be disabled and, thus, acceptable to his mother. His need to be perfect (which led paradoxically to appearing disabled) had intensified after the death of a sibling. Recalling that painful loss, he stressed his need to huddle closer to the remaining family members (several by then had died) and his terror of being left on his own as the only healthy one, ultimately the only one alive. To be capable meant being disconnected from the group. Better to fail, even to die with the group than to be left all alone. A perfectionistic attitude toward the self meant a constant focusing of attention on his deviations from perfection, which were, symbolically, his disabilities. These shameful imperfections became the source of complaint and of chronic, amply displayed suffering.

Another form of emotional logic that can attend later childhood choices to immerse oneself in painful emotion is the reasoning that circumstances too painful to view from outside can be altered by fusing with them. We can consider, for example, a child who finds it intolerable to witness, time and again, her mother's crippling social shame and anxiety. By developing similarly anxious feelings herself, she shifts her attention from the mother's lonely suffering to her own struggles with feelings so vast they remove her from the position of helpless witness to her mother's pain. Entering into the experience, she can no longer see it, just as a person who dives into a large body of water no longer sees the water as a separate element, a thing apart, but experiences it as the medium in which she exists.

The notion of negative affect donned either to enhance connection with a caregiver or to manage various forms of trauma suggests a partially inauthentic nature to the emotion. That is, one's shame is not a simple and straightforward assessment of one's shortcomings. The shame signifies a need to notice, amplify, and communicate flaws (even to cultivate them) for some interpersonal and internal purpose. Though genuinely felt, this type of shame is not operating as a reliable self-assessment. The individual's feelings are not a dependable guide (certainly they are not a straightforward guide) to her strengths and weaknesses.

SHAME OVER MASOCHISTIC DESTRUCTIVENESS

Masochism interacts with shame in a number of additional ways. Shame is a predictable (and straightforward) response to the crippling of one's own spirit (Grinker, 1955) that masochism entails. This variety of shame is mediated by values; it is akin to the shame the obsessive-compulsive feels over the strangulation of her expressiveness. The logic of such shame is: "I destroy myself; I am ashamed of this act." A patient coming in for a first therapy session commented, "I don't jump into things. I'm like the swimmer inching into cold water; I draw out the pain and the misery." He had a history of addiction to many substances and experiences, including pain. All these addictions—not excepting the addiction to misery—shamed him.

Moral shame over harming the self is akin to the shame felt when one attacks the healthy aspects of another. When masochism leads to destructiveness toward others, there is occasion for deep shame and guilt, which may be felt directly, or the voice of conscience may be externalized onto another person who is experienced as critical of one's behavior. An example is Annette, discussed earlier, whose conflicts led to a need to experience much pain during sexual intercourse. She habitually berated her husband for his insensitivity to her difficulties, but as her conflicts were analyzed, she came to recognize shame and guilt over depriving her husband of a vigorous sexual life and pushing him into the role of abuser. She also felt shame and guilt regarding her wish to control their sexual interactions like a puppetmaster and shame about the rage she unleashed against her husband after he "abused" her. At times he in fact mistreated her because of his own externalizing tendencies (which originally attracted her), but she needed to amplify the worst in him and be his victim, and that brought shame and guilt.

A number of important contributions by Kinston (1980, 1982, 1983, 1987) are relevant to the idea that shame experience has links to the abandonment of the indwelling self and links to ultimately destructive efforts at increasing one's personal power. Calling his theory a theory of narcissism, Kinston talks of individuals whose investment in the healthy self has been severely thwarted by parental mistreatment, such that maintaining a natural experience of the self is linked with feeling "wrong" in the eyes of the parent and may be associated as well with feeling one has harmed (e.g., depressed) the parent. Kinston sees these individuals as having great difficulty maintaining the investment in and commitment to the ordinary self and ordinary others, since such commitment requires vulnerability and dependency. He calls the healthy state of commitment to self and others "self-narcissism" and talks about how such individuals regress at times to "object-narcissism," a state of self-negating submission to abusive others, which destroys the individuated self and eliminates ordinary human feelings of vulnerability. Object-narcissism is the state of "evil," in Kinston's moralistic lexicon; it is an omnipotent posture in which one imagines one controls all negative potentials through one's willingness to act as the abuser's zombie. Kinston's object-narcissism appears to be close kin to masochistic states of destroying all pleasure capability in the self and achieving a kind of grim satisfaction through self-subjugation and misery. Kinston (1983) states:

> Fundamentally, in the intersubjective reality, the child is all wrong. This is the origin for the child of a negative valuation of his core

self-images, and for the later adult manifestations of self-narcissism pathology. The child learns that fitting into the symbiosis, being what the parent wants, is rewarded by parental love, pleasure and approval, even though this requires self-destruction (i.e., destruction of his own experience). These fusion states are the precursors or adult manifestations of object-narcissism [p. 217].

Kinston's two conditions of narcissism are roughly equivalent to Novick and Novick's (1991) two "systems": one system characterized by a delusion of omnipotent control (and often of omnipotent destructiveness) and the other by mature acceptance of one's human limitations, which include the finite nature of one's power for good or evil. Novick and Novick go further than Kinston in exploring the secondary gain crucial to the masochistic experience of being overwhelmed or beaten by the abusive other. Kinston's emphasis remains on the abandonment of self and on the shame experience seen as signaling such surrender.

Kinston's (1983) formulation of shame as a transitional experience follows:

[S]hame appears in the state of self-narcissism associated with the urge to move to object-narcissism. . . . Shame is the signal experience that the individual, faced with painful self-awareness (similar to "identity" in Lichtenstein's terminology) and still with the capacity to relate meaningfully to another, wishes to abandon this and to adopt a state of mind which is essentially evil, that is to say, characterized by a denial of all that is human: need, dependency, conflicts, meaning, imperfection [p. 217].

Kinston's comments on self-narcissism and object-narcissism are astute and integrate well with others' observations; however, his view of shame as the "signal" of an imminent regressive shift seems too narrow to account for shame's various operations, even in the specific context that interests him. Shame can in fact play a number of different roles in dual-postured (masochistic) personality organizations such as Kinston describes. For example, intense shame in the self-narcissistic experience may represent a *motive* to escape to the object-narcissistic experience, where one imagines one will be shame-free since now the parent (or internal representative of such) is no longer displeased with the self. Kinston's comments imply a separation between shame—the signal of imminent regression—and other, self-esteem-related feelings that grow out of the child's "negative valuation of his core self-images" and presumably operate as a motive for regression.

It is true that, once in the object-narcissistic state, the person may be freed of the type of self-conscious shame that says, "You are ridiculous as you try to talk with others, laugh with others, sing songs, and be yourself," but generally, the person is *not* fully shame-free in the object-narcissistic state (unless it proceeds toward severe disorganization) since shame is a common, often profound, response to such self-destroying regression and may occur even in the midst of the retreat and certainly occurs following recovery. Such loss of individuality, or personhood, can be cause for some of the deepest shame experiences of which humans are capable. It is the variety of shame that attends schizophrenic loss of self-cohesion or the shame of abandoning humanness and becoming only flesh in response to child abuse or politically motivated torture. This is the shame referred to by Amery (1995), a holocaust survivor, who stated, "Whoever has succumbed to torture can no longer feel at home in the world. The shame of destruction cannot be erased" (p. 136). Grinker (1955) explored related terrain in considering certain suicides. Individuals who regress to object-narcissism may also intuit the destructive omnipotence of such regression and may feel ashamed of their refusal to live in the ordinary world.

Kinston (1983) argues that "completing the transition to object-narcissism will immediately extinguish shame" (p. 222), but that "the destructiveness of object-narcissism does, of course, commonly lead to experiences of guilt or failure" (p. 220). Again, he seems to be distinguishing experiences of failure from shame feelings, but he remains unclear about the distinction, except insofar as shame is defined by its signal function, not by the felt experience. I find it implausible that guilt persists in the object-narcissistic state, but shame cannot. The level of self-integration necessary to support guilt feelings surely would allow for shame feelings as well.

In some instances, people move from shame to self-understanding without regressing into object-narcissism; thus, shame in the self-narcissistic state may be a stimulus for enhanced integration, rather than a prelude to regression. Shame experienced within the self-narcissistic state is better understood as an experience of tension or conflict over being oneself (which, as indicated earlier, may be supported by complex motives), to which the individual may respond progressively or regressively: it is not invariably linked to regression. Goldberg's (1989) image of shame as a signal more accurately conveys the range of shame's operations than does Kinston's. Goldberg states that "shame may be viewed, metaphorically, as a traffic signal—sometimes red, but also yellow and green—telling us about the necessity of proceeding along an important and perilous avenue of our inner self" (p. 600).

In keeping with earlier comments on the power achieved through suffering, it is important to remember that shame experienced in the self-narcissistic state at times can be well understood as being itself a regression and not invariably a *prelude* to regression to object-narcissism. Such is the case if the shame represents a concession to an abusive parent's demeaning view of the self or signifies an effort to belittle the self in order to identify with an inadequate parent. To become ashamed may symbolize realigning with the parent, as the chapter to follow should demonstrate.

Kinston's theory of narcissism is stronger than his theory of shame. More important than his "shame as signal" hypothesis are his descriptions of the self-narcissistic and object-narcissistic states and his understanding of the relief from stress that may be obtained through regression to object-narcissism. He implies that, within the self-narcissistic state, shame may attend those core self-experiences that have displeased the parent, but he does not emphasis this aspect of shame nor does he emphasize the role of shame in preserving the link to the abusive parent; he principally explores shame's signal function.

I hope to have made clear in this chapter that shame plays a number of important roles in masochism. In some cases, it figures as one of the childhood emotions elicited too strongly or too frequently or in too stressful a context to be healthfully integrated. In these same cases and others, shame may be preferred as an adult posture since it defines a diminished and suffering self that is experienced, ironically, as a powerful antidote to early forms of helplessness. It is the adopting of shame or other painful emotions in adulthood, as an attempted solution to emotional problems, that distinguishes masochism. The chapter to follow aims to concretize these ideas by use of longer case examples that show the use of adult shame to manage early helplessness.

CHAPTER 7

Masochism

Case Examples

If it could just be a hell beyond that: the clean flame the two of us
more than dead. Then you will have only me then only me then the
two of us amid the pointing and the horror beyond the clean flame.
—William Faulkner *(The Sound and the Fury)*

Case examples can help us explore the role shame can play
in allowing a person to maintain a psychological organization the individual experiences as necessary for survival.
Painful adult shame experience is not always correlated with excess
childhood shaming, as Wurmser (1981) notes (p. 63), but is probably correlated with a surfeit of childhood pain and helplessness.
The pain that is managed through the pursuit of adult shame may
be childhood shame, but more likely it is a complex of interrelated
emotions. This observation has important treatment consequences
to be explored later. Here, suffice it to say that I think it a mistake
to assume that treatment for those presenting with painful adult
shame always should center on specific shame memories from childhood, as is implied in the work of some writers. David Shapiro's
(1965, 1981) work on character formation does a fine job demonstrating how adult character stances can generate affect. As one
such character formation, masochism of varying types and inten-
sities can be thought of as a set of structures by means of which
varieties of helplessness are managed through perpetuation of painful
relationships with others, as well as through painful self-reflection.

VIRGINIA

Virginia was a sensitive little girl in whom both parents found
a model of physical and spiritual purity and perfection that, if
kept unsullied, could compensate them for their human shortcomings, make tolerable their unsatisfying marriage, and serve

to deny destructive behavior in other areas of their lives. She was Snow White. She was expected to be her mother's polished reflection in the mirror and also her loving support and tireless confidante. Her father treated her as a charming little angel and his refuge from Mother's hystrionic demands and hypochondriasis. Virginia was led to understand that Mother was too weak to tolerate a child's real feelings and Father was too tired from all the demands Mother made.

Virginia grew into a young woman severely troubled by self-doubt, social insecurity, and social mortification. Anything she did that brought her public attention came in a tide of self-consciousness and self-criticism. At times, flooded with self-doubt, she locked herself in the bedroom and couldn't face the world. She regularly dreaded and restricted contact with people outside the family, even passing contact with neighbors. She couldn't acknowledge her physical attractiveness, and she regarded her body as sickly and disgusting. Often, she couldn't bear to make eye contact with others, including her therapist. If she saw me looking at her, she averted her eyes. Though it was apparent from the outset that Virginia had many personal gifts and areas of outstanding competence, therapy hours early on were filled with reports of her inadequacies and of the shame and social apprehension they brought.

Virginia was aware that her shame-laden self-images aligned her closely with Mother, who was also "insecure" and sickly, but she did not recognize that alignment as a *motive* for feeling ashamed or for retreating fearfully from life in ways that caused shame. As long as Virginia was ashamed of herself, she stayed at home with Mother, at first, physically, later, psychologically. By staying at Mother's side, she kept Mother sane and serene (at least in fantasy), thus protecting herself from great guilt over abandoning and thus destroying Mother. The familial model of the destroyed parent was Mother's own mother, who dropped dead one day after Mother had gone out against her wishes. By staying at Mother's side, Virginia also kept her mother from aggressively devaluing her like she devalued Virginia's headstrong younger brothers. Instead of facing Mother's anger and dismissal, she guaranteed her warm approval.

Virginia clung to highly distorted views of herself in order to remain in a shame state; for example, she believed she was stupid and ugly, though most people would see her as intelligent and unusually pretty. The negative ideas about herself brought various forms of shame, as did the socially retiring behavior that the ideas promoted. Shame also followed when she behaved in truly reprehensible ways that made her appear indistinguishable from Mother. For example, she mimicked her mother's temper tantrums and emotionally abused her boyfriend as Mother had abused Father.

Very few memories of childhood shaming (except by her brothers) came to light in years of treatment. Virginia's shame did not seem to be a response to being shamed, in the present or the past. Shame first seems to have become a reality for Virginia as something her mother felt and also as the natural antidote to pride, an emotion promoted in her by parental admiration and objective success. She appears to have taken on shame as her own burden in order to inhabit the self she felt her mother needed her to inhabit.

To put aside shame, to look the world in the eye and be herself, was viewed as having enormous significance, much of it destructive. For example, if she faced the world, her attractiveness and creative intelligence would be seen, and she would move ahead in pursuing her professional goals. Then Mother would be alone with her own sense of unattractiveness and failure, and Mother might die or lose her mind or become enraged. Among Virginia's earliest memories were those of her mother fleeing to the bedroom in hysterics, begging her young daughter (of about five) to "help me." Thus, for Virginia to enjoy her own, separate, capable self meant facing the overwhelming helplessness of watching her mother fall apart. In fantasy, she could prevent Mother's crises by restricting her own social competence.

Virginia had to achieve a difficult balancing act composed of sharing Mother's insecurities while also embodying Mother's lost perfection. Thus she had to find ways of being beautiful and capable so that her mother could delight in her, but she needed also to deny these traits and suffer shame over herself in order to be insecure along with Mother. As an example of her need to compensate her mother for some of Mother's own narcissistic losses, Virginia had to keep her red hair silky and straight because Mother always regretted the rough texture and curls in her own hair. Later in treatment, when she had a sense of humor about such things, Virginia said, "My mother had to go into the hospital and I thought, 'If she dies, at least I can curl my hair!'"

Giving up personal suffering and vulnerability meant loss of the power to control others by eliciting their concern. If she missed several appointments in a row, without giving notice, and spent the time in an anxious state of insecurity or "hiding out," she was blameless because she was impaired; thus, she could express her aggression and her wishes for independence but take no responsibility either for the core feelings or for the hostile manner of their expression. She made of herself a helpless, suffering child, who could then behave with a child's abandon.

Giving up shame also meant loss of the secondary gain associated with being Mother's partner in misery, and it meant surrendering burdensome, but also gratifying, fantasies of having great power over her parents' happiness. The thought that her mother could have a pleasant day even if Virginia didn't visit or that her mother actually might refuse Virginia's dinner invitation in order to spend time with a friend initially was frightening to Virginia and represented a significant loss. She wasn't certain how she would remain close to her parents if she were no longer indispensable to them. She experienced her mother's love as conditional, and clearly one condition was Virginia's neurotic crippling of herself, which led Mother to histrionic expressions of worry.

A characteristic story of Virginia's childhood demonstrated the pressures toward incompetence and dependence that led her increasingly to adopt shame-generative stances as the way to manage her relationship with her mother. The story centered on her mother's insistence on driving her daughter the few blocks to her summer camp because of a "very dangerous" field Virginia would have to cross were she to walk. Though Virginia wanted to walk to camp, she complied with her mother's wishes, and she accepted, at least superficially, the notion that Mother was driving her only to protect her since she was so well loved. One morning, she and Mother had a fight, and Virginia "punished" her mother by storming out of the house with the announcement that she would walk to camp. It was clear from the language of the story that ordinary independent action had come to be understood as an attack on Mother. Crossing the dreaded field, Virginia was quaking. Soon she encountered an intimidating dog and was "forced" to run home, where Mother greeted her tearfully and drove her to camp, their harmony restored. In all likelihood, Virginia needed to find a scary dog in the field; otherwise, she would have felt too guilty about hurting her mother and too frightened about the possibility that Mother would abandon her emotionally for not restoring their relationship of shared debility. The fearful retreat from the dog was analogous to the many frightened and ashamed retreats from the outer world that came in later years. She positioned a dog internally that said, "You cannot handle this situation; you are not strong enough, smart enough, worthy enough." All the feelings of weakness the inner dog created constituted shame.

As already stated, Virginia recalled little shaming by either parent. In fact, she was idealized. Broucek (1991) argues that idealized children feel ashamed because they are objectified— that is, the true inner self is not a source of interest to the caregiver. It was not clear from Virginia's report whether she felt ashamed when her inner reality was denied by her idealizing parents; it *was* evident that she felt trapped and felt bound to maintain the parents' illusions, a situation that angered her. Since the idealizing parent's need to make the child other than what she is suggests to the child that the real self is not sufficient, it is easy to imagine that persistant idealization might become an indirect source for shame. It may also be the case that whatever shame occurs in response to objectification may get obscured by the idealized child's move to inhabit the temptingly fine, though false, self-images dangled in front of her. Once adopting such images, there exists an ongoing potential for shame if one acknowledges or others recognize that one is not, in fact, the perfect angel or saint or beauty the idealizing parent has taken one for.

Virginia clearly illustrates another variety of shame, the shame that follows from abandoning personal growth potential. She felt ashamed, angry, and grieved over not experiencing the social life normal for someone her age. She had became extremely compliant and blind to her own needs and wishes, while concurrently indulging in histrionic displays of dramatic dysfunction and demandingness. These ways of defining the self had interfered greatly with normal social activities. When no longer straitjacketed by the need to appear impaired, Virginia felt elated by age-appropriate experiences or those representing a belated chance at normal life.

BETTY

The obsessive-compulsive person says, "I become mechanical and without feeling, like a perfectly operating machine: I cease to be myself." The masochistic person says, "I become your angel, your perfect one who has no needs of his own; I take over your shame and wear it as a mark of our loving connection: I cease to be myself." Alternatively, the masochistic person says, "I take in your crap; I become the bad, worthless stuff you want to be rid of: I cease to be myself but find my pleasure in this suffering." The obsessional, the masochistic, and the narcissistically disordered person all say, "Though I give up my indwelling self, I make myself anew; I fashion myself to a standard of perfection, and I control pain and helplessness."

Betty's case is more complex than Virginia's with regard to shame issues since Betty was repeatedly and cruelly shamed through many years of childhood. She was verbally shamed by her mother, who raged at her for being stupid and berated and beat her in insane, middle-of-the-night scenes for not cleaning undetectable dirt from her room or the kitchen. At other times, her mother idealized her as superbly smart, capable, and responsible, and she publically broadcast these views. She depended on the child as if the child were an adult and the mother a child; for example, she had her daughter help her dress for work and follow her around like a lady in waiting or a nursemaid, even into the bathroom or the mother's bed.

In addition to the alternating shame and idealization inflicted by her mother from earliest childhood, Betty suffered from years of sexual abuse by her mother's boyfriend. While her mother told her in words that she was no good, the boyfriend's actions told her she was someone of no independent worth. Constant violation of Betty's ordinary sense of privacy, a shame-related experience discussed by Schneider (1977) and Wurmser (1981), and by S. Miller (1993) in relation to the boundary-maintaining functions of disgust, led to acute shame and humiliation, some of which occurred as a delayed response, since during the abuse episode, terror and the determination simply to survive prevailed over other emotions.

Abuse frequently occurred when the boyfriend, who had been Betty's deceased father's coworker, was drunk. Often, the abuse was extraordinarily sadistic in nature, such that just listening to Betty's memories was stressful. The boyfriend subjected her to degrading, frightening behavior and laughed at her misery. Verbally, he represented her in idealized fashion by focusing on her beauty and sexiness and his fantasy that she and he would marry when she grew up. Thus, contrasted with Virginia, Betty had a childhood filled with verbal and behavioral shaming, intermingled with idealization. The idealization served as a justification for treating her like an adult in ways that, for a child, constituted extreme abuse.

In therapy, Betty struggled for years with inexpressably painful feelings, among them profound feelings of being dirty and worthless. Her shame had many levels but included self-loathing for being Mother's boyfriend's lover and a profound sense of being, at her core, nothing other than what she was treated as: garbage, a slut, a temptress, a plaything, her mother's ugly, dirty, stupid child. Her shame said she *was* all of these things. Association with the disgusting had made her disgusting and, thus, ashamed.

Clearly, with Betty, we are in the province of Wurmser's "unlovability" feelings. This case allows us another look at that concept and how it manifests in an actual therapy relationship, where it may be meaningful to the patient or the therapist or both. The patient's terror is of being fundamentally unlovable, thus condemned to a condition that is beyond remedy. An additional fear the patient holds, which the therapist may as well, is that the patient's *feeling* of being unlovable is fundamental and beyond relief, even if the feeling is not based on real deficiency. Psychoanalytic ideas about layers of the psyche, which place "unlovability feelings" at the bottom as the fundamental level or "core," contain in their form and language the horrible sense of irreparable damage that terrifies the patient. In therapy, it is important to maintain a view of the psyche as dynamic, which means that choices of belief and feeling are always being made and remade and are able to be influenced by thinking and by new experience, even though resistance to such change may be formidable and the courage and persistence needed to pursue it may be great.

With Betty, I encouraged her to explore why she maintained the astoundingly painful views of herself as dirty, bad, stupid, and sinful—in effect unlovable to herself or anyone else—rather than discarding such views as not truly descriptive of her, which would allow her to live from within other, better, more realistic images of herself that also were available to her. What emerged over and over was a profound, many layered sense of extraordinary danger and remarkable guilt associated with rejecting the shame-laced views of self her mother had assigned her, both directly and by putting a sexually sadistic man in her path. It is at this point, in exploring Betty's motives to maintain in the present the sense of herself as a shamefully soiled or diminished, incomparably miserable victim, that we enter the domain of masochism. Given the insistency of real, embodied voices telling Betty she was worthless, it seems almost absurd to consider her own activity in maintaining such beliefs, yet understanding whatever forces within her led to perpetuation of imposed suffering would seem crucial to searching out pathways for therapy.

The ashamed, dirtied self was profoundly interdependent with Mother at a number of levels and satisfied many needs of the mother. Mother was acutely abandonment sensitive and needed her daughter to be absolutely dependent on her and, thus, incapable of leaving her. The more battered Betty felt by her mother's and her mother's boyfriend's insults, the less she could function independently and the less likely she was to separate. Needing to hide in shame from the world, Betty often remained home from school, and while Mother was at work, she donned Mother's nightclothes and cabined herself in Mother's bedroom. At night, they often shared the bed. Being too bad for the rest of the world meant Betty stayed close to Mother, meeting Mother's needs for symbiosis.

During a period of Betty's increasing independence and self-confidence during adolescence, her mother had a terrible accident at work, arguably a suicide attempt, that further invigorated Betty's already great guilt and anxiety over impulses to jettison Mother's degrading views of her. Later in life, for the adult Betty to give up the self-concepts forged out of shame meant to risk guilt over abandoning Mother and to risk the internal mother's rage, which literally meant to risk annihilation, given the history of terrifying abuse.

Abandonment was another major danger associated with jettisoning the shame-based false self. Mother had repeatedly, dramatically deserted her children, both psychologically and physically—at times leaving them hungry and without a decent place to live. Among other things, wearing shame all over her was Betty's advertisement of being unattractive, and it was her repudiation of sexual wishes. Such advertisement and renunciation worked to counter her sexual guilt but also to reassure Mother that Betty had no desire to steal her man. This reassurance was necessary to forestall abandonment, which was seen, in part, as the inexorable punishment for Betty's sexual involvement. In therapy, her sense of being offensive, unattractive, uniquely needy, indebted, and incompetent represented her assurance that I would not abandon her.

The following note, which I made after a therapy hour seven months into treatment, demonstrates the vast dangers Betty associated with abandoning the shameful self:

> Betty called me last Friday A.M. to tell me I'd made a mistake on the diagnosis code on her bill. After the call, she needed to punish herself for not staying "in her place" in relation to a "higher-up" person. She can be outspoken with the church elders, she says, because they're men. But she can't with me, a woman. It was hard for her to talk about what she did to punish herself (painful, dangerous physical punishments that reenact her sexual abuse as a young child). She says she's always had to do these things, she's had to punish herself some way if she's out of her "position." Mother would treat her badly: beat her, force her to clean her room ten times and she never questioned it, just felt she must be "wrong." Yet when Mother talked about her to others, she portrayed Betty as perfect, superior, "above" other children, like an adult. If she gets out of the place Mother put her in, she must put herself back. Otherwise, God will punish her with something worse, with a terrible loss. When she played sexually with another 12 year old girl, the girl's mother died a few months later and then Betty's mother had her accident. She feels these events were related to her sins. First, she thought my bill error was not an error but was a deliberate (punitive) change of the diagnosis. Then she woke up in the morning "in a joking mood" and called me to tell me my mistake and was joking with me (putting me down, putting me in my place for my error). Afterwards, she felt that was wrong to do. The only reason she feels better now is because she punished herself.

The sequence described in the note shows Betty's profound sense of needing to live within the degraded, enslaved self Mother allowed her; otherwise, she would face terrible punishment, such as catastrophic loss and the guilt associated with feeling responsible for a parent's death. Her self-abuse is a massive passive-to-active defense. If she hurts herself, she may have some chance of escaping further injury from her mother, from God, and from her conscience. At the same time, she can reap some benefit from her pain because her long record of suffering entitles her to rage against all pain, including ordinary discomfort, and to demand exemption from it.

Also prominent among Betty's shame-maintaining fears was the terror of losing any experience of a good mother. To reject Mother's shaming meant to doubt and discredit Mother and to confront her profound deficiencies as a parent. It was safer to idealize Mother and accept her shaming as deserved, rather than risk a world without a good mother in it. This fear of a world without goodness played out in therapy through her attaching herself to a second therapist, whom she seldom saw, whom she maintained in her mind as pure and good, thus allowing a freer play of emotions in relation to me. Any threat to the image of the pure second therapist, who stood removed and protectively hovering like an angel, brought enormous distress over a period of many years.

Shame also linked Betty to Victor, the abusive man who thrived on humiliating the child sexually. Sadly, she had lost her reportedly devoted biological father at a young age and was invested in finding a substitute in the man who had been her father's partner. Many dangers attended the refusing of shamefulness in that relationship. If she declined to be the defiled thing he needed her to be, he might go crazy and hurt them all; he might tell Mother about the sexual relationship he had with her slut-daughter, and Mother would kill or abandon her; he might leave them all; he might tell her father she's a wicked person; she might see *him,* Victor, as bad and lose all sense of finding a father in him. She imagined that, by accepting the debasement he wanted her to wear, she could soothe the savage beast in him and keep him from hurting her brother and sister and from exposing to others her mortifying activities with him. In her fantasy life, she could control him by offering him a modicum of humiliation and distress.

Within her current space and time, Betty's terrible shame experience served as a continual effort to prevent retraumatization, and it operated as well to extract some interpersonal benefit or some advantage in her internal world of objects. The violently demeaning superego that told her she is dirty, she is stupid, she is garbage kept her from presenting herself to others, most importantly now, to her therapist, in confident, hopeful ways that would leave her open to disappointments or reinjury. So, for example, she dared not say openly that she had been hurt and misused and inexcusably mistreated as a child, lest I traumatize her anew by claiming, "It wasn't so bad," or "Your mother didn't know," or "You must have asked for it; you must have seduced that man," any of which she would have found intolerable. So, initially, she shared her awful memories and then faulted herself, making all of the above claims herself or saying, "It couldn't have happened like that; I'm probably making it up" (i.e., she's the bad one who makes up ugly things; she isn't the victim of ugly things). She also maintained a physical presentation that alienated potential male partners, thus keeping her free of sexual danger and the danger of maternal fury.

Betty's trauma was in being forced to absorb awful ideas about herself (in order to maintain a connection to a vital object), but also in the other's failure to respond to her good aspects and good feeling. Such affirming response would have allowed for easier integration of pleasurable thoughts and feelings into the self-structure. This latter point is addressed well by Socarides and Stolorow (1984/1985) who state:

> As we have stressed, the need to disavow, dissociate, or otherwise defensively encapsulate affect arises originally in consequence of the failure of the early selfobject milieu to provide the requisite, phase-appropriate attunement and responsiveness to the child's emotional states. When such defenses against affect arise in treatment, they must be understood as being rooted in the patient's expectation or fear in the transference that his emerging feeling states will meet with the same faulty responsiveness that they received from the original caregivers [p. 111].

The authors go on to direct the therapist's attention to his own communications, which may trigger anxious retreat in the patient:

> Furthermore, these resistances against affect cannot be interpreted as resulting solely from intrapsychic processes within the patient. Such resistances are most often evoked by events occurring within the analytic situation which for the patient signal a lack of receptivity on the analyst's part to the patient's emerging feeling states and which therefore herald a traumatic recurrence of early selfobject failure [p. 111].

To Socarides's and Stolorow's comments, I would add that the appearance of painful ideas and feelings, such as shame, also can be seen as an effort to disavow good feelings that the caregiver has failed to mirror or, as with Betty, has actively attacked. In that way, the individual maintains the fantasy of control over traumatization.

In Betty's case, the need to avoid retraumatization by preserving shamefulness paired with a fantasy that her special badness could bring her some advantage that otherwise would be lost to her. So her debased, destroyed condition became the explanation for my interest in her: she would be my specially needy patient, unlike all others. She also believed that she possessed evil sexual powers; these mysterious powers brought shame and guilt but also a sense of distinction.

Betty's capacity for profound pain at times was brought into play psychologically as a means to escape the strains of ordinary reality. She had become accustomed to such extraordinary, intolerable events that flight from reality became a ready recourse whenever trouble loomed. In adulthood, such flight had to be justified by deep pain and suicidal longings. A relatively small disappointment or frustration might bring terrible suffering and suicidality, in part due to Betty's wish to pursue an enraged refusal of any further suffering. New forms of pain were equated with past abuse too readily, and escape through assertions of overwhelming pain was pursued.

Betty's story allows us opportunity for a final look at Kinston's (1983, 1987) idea that shame is the signal for imminent regression from self-narcissism to object-narcissism. Betty experienced regressive shifts that were consistent with Kinston's descriptions of omnipotent states that defend against the risks of relatedness (for example, dissociative states accompanied by acts of self-injury). Shame for Betty seemed a frequent accompaniment of object-narcissistic states, of which there was a great range, not simply one. In fact, many of the shame-dominated states Betty experienced seemed object-narcissistic in nature, using Kinston's definitions. For example, she succumbed to feeling like she did not exist except as Victor's degraded, enslaved, sexual object; that identity was permeated with shame. Shame generally did not operate as a signal of imminent regression and then turn off. It was an ongoing feature of the regressed states, except in certain highly dissociated conditions that nearly obliterated self-awareness and, thus, shame.

In dire circumstances, a person may be poised between the vulnerability of remaining himself and the shame of abandoning the self. For example, a traumatized individual experiences "flashbacks" in which traumatic events or the affects linked to them are reexperienced without present-day perspective. The past becomes the present and supplants any other present-day reality. The loss of self-control and self-integration such experience entails often brings deep shame over the collapse of the self. But flashback may be preferred to memory, because once horrendous experience takes the status of memory, the experience cannot be refused: it is completed and inalterable; it is forever a part of one's history, which one has permitted to become real.

An example would be Clarisse, who reeled under the disgrace of being the "town crazy lady" but preferred, for a long time, to maintain publically mortifying signs of disintegration, rather than face that she was helpless to revise her abusive childhood. The first time she experienced a flashback of sexual abuse in my office, she emerged from the odd, inaccessible state, looked up at me and muttered, "I made Lucy do it, and I watched." "Because you didn't want to go through it?" I asked, guessing at her meaning, and she said, "Yes." Though she had relived an awful experience, she had reformatted it as one in which she was watching the abuse, even directing it.

Thus, the intact ego, with its coherent sense of self, is vulnerable to dangers that can be relieved by incoherence. Shame, by its very nature, opposes the experience of an intact self and promotes a confused, disorganized, degraded self. Allowing shame to disorder one's self-experience can operate as a protection against the reality of trauma, though it establishes the new psychic burden of living with an ashamed self. Allowing shame to diminish the self also can work as an effective counter to guilt. The profoundly ashamed self is, almost by definition, not guilty, since the ashamed person is too weak and impaired to have done anything powerfully bad and is so deeply hurt that any conceivable sins would be requited by such suffering.

More could be said about Betty before moving on, but the primary point to be made is that this courageous young woman long needed to spend much of her time within the shame-organized self in order to manage a relationship with her psychological mother and to find disguised sources of power. Remarkable relief from shame coincided with Betty's progressive disidentification with the person her mother and her mother's boyfriend saw in her. She no longer took that person to be her; instead, that person was part of them, and she was someone who was funny, warm, a bit bossy and at times ballsy, talented artistically, angry, conscientious, often frightened, a good provider, and so forth. Incidentally, the huge gain in self-esteem Betty experienced when she risked jettisoning those externalizations highlights the problem with conventional usage of "self-esteem" as if it is a measurable substance one gets more or less of, often depending on whether people do or don't say nice, "self-esteem boosting" things about one. Self-esteem is a summary term for a whole array of feelings and thoughts that represent the endpoint of dynamic forces, including, for example, one's sense of safety about feeling proud. It is not some quantifiable stuff to be pumped into a person through nice words or stolen away with nasty ones. Using "low self-esteem" as an explanation for behavior generally does little to advance understanding, though the term is serviceable as a description of a person's predominant feelings about the self. Discussing those emotions that relate to ego ideals and superego ideals, Schafer (1967) states, "It may be that shame and pride are prototypes of mixed affects of this sort, and that what we call self-esteem, on the most general level, involves a blend or composite of such affects" (p. 139).

EFFECTS OF ABUSE ON GROUPS

Some of the dynamics Betty displays also appear in groups of people who have been mistreated over a long period of time. Minorities abused by a dominant social group will have difficulty jettisoning shame-based identities. Dynamics of masochism offer a partial explanation for the perpetuation of shame experience in situations where ongoing shaming no longer occurs.

The effort to discard a shame-based identity likely will provoke feelings of danger in those accustomed to a demeaned experience of self. The sense of danger initially relates to real and present dangers but may outlive those dangers due to an awareness of a terrifying, warning part of the historical record.

The story of Coalhouse Walker, introduced in discussing narcissistic rage, demonstrates the cost of refusing shame in a situation of ongoing racial oppression. Coalhouse's visible insistence on his own importance and dignity operated like an irritant and insult to the surrounding white society and put him in peril. Were Coalhouse Walker to have accepted the policeman's assertion that no real damage had been done and his suggestion that Coalhouse scrape the feces off his car seat and be on his way, he would have exchanged his narcissistic rage for shame and disgrace and would have remained safe. He also would have returned to acceptance by white society, though the inclusion would have been predicated on their terms, which were terms of debasement. Refusing the moment of shame and the broader, shame-based identity, Coalhouse is arrested, which signifies his helplessness at the hands of a malevolent and powerful other.

A similar story is that of the young black man, Tom, in *To Kill a Mockingbird* (Lee, 1960). Tom refuses to plead guilty to the rape of a lonely, seductive young white woman. He argues his innocence by asserting that he visited and assisted the young woman because he "felt right sorry for her." The notion that he, a black man, would feel sorry for a white woman—bespeaking his equality with her, perhaps even his superiority—had an incendiary effect in the southern courtroom and contributed to Tom's conviction and, indirectly, to his violent death. The defense lawyer explained his client's predicament by saying he "had the unmitigated temerity to 'feel sorry' for a white woman." The message for the oppressed group is similar to that for the individual abused within a family: You put aside the debased sense of self at great peril to your safety; it is safer to find power within the degraded identity than to attempt to discard it.

Jamaica Kincaid's character Xuela, quoted in the opening passage of the previous chapter, offers an important variation on this theme by suggesting one can wear an identity without internalizing it; one can make a show of an identity in order to fend off danger. For example, one can pretend to modesty or diffidence in order to deflect aggressive envy and achieve some security, as Kincaid's (1994) Xuela does in her stepmother's house; then her identity may be that of a pretender, not of one ashamed. But the safer route may be the internalization of the degraded identity, so that one is not even tempted out of hiding. The person who becomes truly insecure and ashamed is less inclined toward open fury or outrage over mistreatment, nor is that person moved to attempt mutually respectful relationships between equals, which may prove dangerous.

THE BAD SELF AND THE WEAK SELF

Betty's and Virginia's shames at times differ from each other phenomenologically. Betty feels "bad," meaning wicked, sinful, and dirty. Shame follows when she takes stock of the self and sees it as wholly bad. Virginia feels bad at times, but more often she feels weak and deficient, especially when venturing out in the world. Both experiences are a basis for shame, which responds to any view of the self as flawed. But the phenomenological difference remains important. Feeling bad points to images of abuse in which the person takes into the self bad qualities others assign to him. Feeling bad also contributes to guilt because it brings wishful fantasies of being powerfully destructive.

Feeling insignificant or weak is more closely allied with images of neglect, of being unworthy of notice, although these alliances must be investigated carefully because Virginia's feelings of insignificance did not, in my estimation, refer to actual neglect, but to her defensive need to appear insignificant (neglect-worthy) so that she would not outperform Mother and so that she could find a respite from the pressures of being an overvalued, parental child. Her behaviorally conveyed statement, "I am nothing," was as much a wish as a fear. While Betty's feelings of being bad brought guilt over imagined destructive power, Virginia's feelings of insignificance worked to counter guilt by arguing that she lacked power and, thus, could threaten no one.

Relevant here are Nathanson's (1992) ideas about dissmell and disgust; he suggests that feeling "bad" relates to the experience of being the object of another's disgust, which is different from the experience of incompetence that Broucek and others describe, the latter linked with the inability to arouse a response from the other, which is thematically connected with the experience of being inferior or powerless, not bad. As discussed previously, Nathanson, in an earlier writing, connected "the bad self" with a defensive need to disavow badness in the caregiver. His more recent discussion of feeling "bad" as a response to parental disgust suggests a simpler origin to the feeling, which rests on an assessment of the caregiver's emotion and does not utilize a notion of defense.

The literature contains numerous references both to parental disgust (or contempt) as a stimulus for a child's shame and to parental unresponsiveness as a shame stimulus. Kohut's work, and that of many followers, speaks to feelings of inadequacy that result from structural damage resulting from parental failure of responsiveness, rather than to feelings of badness associated with the disgusted or hostile caregiver, whose aggressiveness gives shape to the superego. Though Broucek's theoretical emphasis is closer to Kohut's in its primary concern with the unresponsive, objectifying parent, Broucek also sees disgust and contempt as shame stimuli. In reanalyzing a clinical episode of "contempt/disgust" that Lewis presented, Broucek (unpublished chapter) says, "Lewis comments that '[t]he mother's disgusted face has shamed the child . . .' an observation with which I would agree." In careful discussion, disgust should be differentiated from contempt (S. Miller, 1993).

PSYCHOTHERAPEUTIC ATTENTION
TO SHAME IN MASOCHISTIC CONTEXTS

From the discussion of masochism to this point, I hope to have demonstrated shame operating in a number of different ways. It operates as a set of self-perceptions about deficiencies, for example, deficiencies in "lovability"; these perceptions are disturbing, interfere with relatedness, and need reworking in treatment. It operates as conflict-based superego judgment about bad parts of the self that need to be stopped and as healthy superego judgment about destructive aspects of the self that need amendment, and it operates as an experience and presentation of the self meant to elicit needed complementary responses from others or to demonstrate one's power to destroy pleasure and goodness when such states have been perverted in their significance due to abuse.

The last two types, as well as shame derivable from superego conflict, are the shame experiences most defining of masochism. All three are associated with strong motives to feel pain and with rewards for feeling pain. At times, they interact; for example, the desire to demonstrate power to defeat pleasure may take the guise of superego-generated shame. The need to demonstrate such power may derive from a number of sources, one of which is early experience of being traumatized by another's mindless misuse of pleasure.

An example would be Betty's victimization by her abuser's indulgence of his sexual pleasure. Her pain was riveted to his pleasure, which made her furious at his capacity to enjoy himself sexually. Superego hostility toward sexual pleasure then provided her with a sense of authority in relation to her abuser's hated sexuality. Her hostile superego turned against her own sexual pleasure, in part out of guilt over indulging in the pleasures she condemned in another and, additionally, out of satisfaction over the newfound ability to arrest hated sexual expression, even within the self. Once her vengeful satisfaction and her power over abuse became attached to the authority to curtail her own sexual plea- sure, allowing herself sexual pleasure paradoxically brought fury and depression, as well as guilt, since yielding to pleasure signi- fied defeat. Shame was one of several mechanisms that enabled her to become a powerful destroyer of sexual pleasure. Questioning her attachment to shame could be expected to stir anxiety, anger, and stubborn entrenchment.

It is in masochistic contexts that the patient is most likely to wear shame on his sleeve. It is likewise in these contexts that the therapist needs to be most attuned to the complex roles shame plays within the personality structure. It is here that a person marshalls the most painful past realities (including shaming) in the fight against memory and current vulnerability and greatly resists the exposure of the mechanism, which shows the person himself as creator of the current madness.

In cases where shame is well hidden behind visible defenses (e.g., behind perfectionism and arrogance), seeing the sense of weakness that is obscured may take the therapist a long way in helping the patient. But when overt shame complaints dominate the early phase of therapy, we are likely in the realm of that type of psychopathology for which the notion of present-day shame as a simple residuum of unrecognized instances of childhood shaming can be most problematic, since such a theory neglects the role of self-protection in contributing to what is experienced, presented to the world, and offered to the therapist. In dictating strategies of treatment that mainly involve mirroring, those shame theo- ries focused exclusively on early, traumatic shame neglect the power of resistance to change.

Morrison (1989) generously makes available his clinical work in sufficient detail to allow for discussion of his treatment approaches. Lily's treatment is an example of a therapy that is dominated by a patient's communications about her deficiencies and low self-esteem. Morrison describes Lily, a young college student, as initially "extremely diffident, speaking in a barely audible voice as she described her great pain and self-doubts with regard to her studies" (p. 135). Her self-presentation emphasized suffering and personal doubt, and she quickly developed an ideal- izing attitude toward her therapist. Whenever Morrison attempted to point out to Lily her significant strengths, she "became hurt or angry, claiming I was doubting her experience: 'You are just wrong'" (p. 138). Morrison backed off, though feeling angry, misunderstood, and personally unrecognized, and he returned to his predominant stance, which was that of acknowledging Lily's feelings of deficiency, her "psychic reality," in order to show that he understood and appreciated the painfulness and significance of what Lily felt about herself. Increasingly, he concluded that any addressing of her strengths was unempathic, even bullying, and that he must hold to the mirroring-of-deficiency posture. Morrison indicates that other tasks of the treatment—recognizing her hostility, recognizing her assets—would "have to await belief and improvement in, and understanding of the source of, her distressed self-image and her concern about others' ability to tolerate her needs" (p. 139). Morrison's statements raise questions as to whether such improvement can, in fact, occur without first addressing specific areas of conflict.

Morrison dismisses the idea of masochism, referring to Lily's "so-called masochism," but this case strikes me as one in which the patient is profoundly invested in her masochism (more specifically, her suffering based on negative, shame-filled views of the self) as a way to obviate various forms of dreaded vulnerability and to maintain interpersonal power, however obliquely. My usage here corresponds to Novick and Novick (1987) who state, "Masochism is the active pursuit of psychic or physical pain, suffering, or humiliation in the service of adaptation, defense, and instinctual gratification at oral, anal, and phallic levels" (p. 381). They further explain that masochism will be "figured forth" in the transference–counterreaction situation (p. 382).

Lily becomes angry and panicked when Morrison identifies her strengths. One can conjecture that she reacts in that fashion not so much because she feels misunderstood (after all, we know Morrison repeatedly acknowledged her pain and shame, not just her strengths), but because her therapist is undermining the deeply invested mechanism she uses to control current experience so that it will not become traumatic—narcissistically or otherwise—in the ways past experience was and because he threatens established ways of securing gratification. She is not being misunderstood; she is being asked to acknowledge parts of herself she disavows because they are frightening.

I share Morrison's conviction that maintaining empathic contact with a patient by recognizing her "psychic reality" is crucial, and I agree that, with Lily, he could not proceed far without communicating to her his appreciation of the intensity of her suffering, which was real and likely did represent, *among other things,* a communication about devaluation conveyed by the caregiving environment. The problem for the treatment comes when mirroring Lily's shame and misery becomes the only activity of the analyst, who is paralyzed or tied up (i.e., victimized) by the patient's angry, hurt, or panicky insistence that he address nothing else. Now the patient is assuming a grandiose and destructive posture in which she essentially commands the therapist to be what she feels she needs, and he submits, presumably leading to heightened anxiety on her part about her sadistic controllingness. The patient says, "Don't you dare give those other attributes and activities of mine reality status, or I will attack you for your insensitive transgression and tell you you are powerfully destructive: I control the drama here." The silenced therapist colludes not only with a sadomasochistic enactment, in which the patient is all-powerful; he also colludes with her fearful refusal to attempt integration of major pieces of reality, the most important one of which Morrison identifies: her own strengths.

An alternative therapeutic stance would be to acknowledge the reality of Lily's suffering, while at the same time continuing to represent other realities she denies (e.g., her strengths, her anger). The denied realities could be addressed in the context of exploring how her defenses operate and exploring the frightening possibilities from which she protects herself. Her defensive denial of strengths and her attachment to new forms of old suffering should also be identified as crucial impediments to achieving desired pleasures.

In responding to Lily's distress about his mirroring "lapses," the therapist must find a way to communicate that she is requiring him to be a broken or distorting mirror that reflects only her damaged self and does not see and help her to claim her undamaged self. He must find ways to ask, "Why are you so frightened of having us look at your strengths and abilities? What guilt or aloneness or loss of power do you imagine the ownership of such strengths will entail?" In Lily's case and others, the intensity of the patient's pain and its traumatic origins are used to control interpretations. Morrison gives voice to a particular strength of Lily's, and she mobilizes her whole capacity to remember feeling assaulted and belittled, to import that into the present, in order to fend off the interpretation, which threatens an inner world where she is in control, does not risk attachment and loss, and does not risk retraumatization. Rather than back off entirely, he might look with her at the eruption of hurt and angry feeling and help her examine its purposes. He need not question the relationship between her pain state and earlier stresses but should question the need to keep the pain alive in the present, between him and her, and the need to keep other aspects of herself unreal. He can help her consider what happens if she lets the suffering go, if she moves toward fuller identification with stronger self-aspects. If these concerns are not addressed, the therapist will remain forever an overcontrolled selfobject who is restricted to empathizing with his patient's damaged state.

Lily acts as if her analyst is performing some essential mirroring function for her, but I wonder if his empathy really is what relieves her of distress or if she is relieved that her analyst does not threaten her inhabitance of a world in which she controls his responses and compromises her own strengths and pleasures. Perhaps she is afraid that remaining in such a world means being alone in an objectless state; he reassures her that she can stay where she is without feeling objectless, since he will join her there. She need not get anxious about being forced out by aloneness.

Sidney, discussed earlier, had a personality organization more obsessive-compulsive and narcissistic than masochistic, but his strategy for pain management bears an interesting relationship of opposites to Lily's. He described circumstances in which his relations with others were strained; in doing so, he made clear his unwillingness to identify any of the shortcomings in himself that might contribute to bad relations with others. Sidney insisted that all fault lay outside the self, and he constantly told cautionary tales about a previous therapist who focused on Sidney's role in difficult situations, including the therapy itself. When I would simply empathize with the real difficulties of the situations he encountered, Sidney soon enough would let me know our exchanges were pointless, seemed patronizing, and told him nothing he didn't already know; his criticism was one part rejection of empathy and one part accurate reflection. But if I would try to address his own role in tangled interactions, including our own, he became testy and informed me that I sounded exactly like the last, now discarded, therapist. When I began to articulate for him this dilemma he and I were in, where attention to external reality alone left him unenlightened and dissatisfied, but where attempts to study his inner life angered him, he was able to step back from the situation and share a number of past experiences in which he felt his inner life and self had been treated dismissively and hurtfully. In these exchanges, he felt he had been held responsible for *all* the communication difficulty that arose between himself and another. He recognized that he had subsequently adopted a rigid policy of refusing to take "blame" and of insisting that attention be focused on the other person's responsibility, even when such emphasis ultimately was unsatisfying. His recognition represented a small opening for more honest exploration within the therapy.

As indicated earlier, Sidney's and Lily's stances were opposite, in that Lily insisted that her inner self was entirely deficient and blameworthy, whereas Sidney wanted no fault assigned to him. But these opposite stances had a similar effect in tying up the therapy: exploration of the person's active role in establishing the character of his or her relationships was stymied.

MASOCHISM, SADISM, AND SHAME

Using Annette's life story, I will briefly examine anxiety about sadism in a person whose presentation combines masochistic and obsessive-compulsive elements. Since my primary interest is in shame, I wish to highlight the ways in wish the shameful and suffering self represents a denial of sadism, which, if acknowledged, would occasion guilt and the specific form of shame—moral shame—that regularly co-occurs with guilt.

Annette often feels insecure, stupid, self-doubting, and socially rejected, all of which are feelings in the shame domain. She suffers from a generalized sense of deficiency but also from feelings of worthlessness she experiences as forced on her from outside, often by others seen as humiliating her. When her insecurity or humiliation feels inflicted from outside, she complains angrily. Sometimes, she arranges to be victimized and then seems to take to the air with the pleasure of articulate complaint, as if such grievance has a significant discharge function that relieves anxiety. In her sexual fantasy, abuse and humiliation are the most reliable routes to arousal. Thus, in Annette, we see both the ashamed self and the victimized, suffering self as prominent, intertwined presentations.

Though some of the masochistic dynamics discussed earlier apply as well in Annette's case, for her, an equally compelling reason to emphasize both victimization and an inept, embarrassed self appears to be her need to disguise specific sadistic impulses. Given her Catholic upbringing, her mother's anxious devotion to peace and quiet, and Annette's own early condemnation of her father's aggressiveness, Annette found her sadistic impulses intolerable. Her conscience could not abide them. They brought intense moral shame, as well as guilt and fear of abandonment, and also a frightening feeling of being an essentially bad person who could not be loved by Mother. As an example of these conflicts made manifest in daily life, consider her at her job, where she is asked one day not to sit on a chair passively while she monitors the other workers, but to walk around and make her presence felt. At first, she complains about the burden of having to leave her comfortable perch. But then she follows instructions because she is dutiful. She actually perambulates the grounds in bosslike fashion, at which point she begins to worry that she is "power hungry" because she notes some pleasure in reprimanding and disciplining others.

An important logic of her self-presentation is: "If I am hurt, humiliated, and intimidated by powerful others, I cannot be hurting or humiliating anyone myself." Similarly, she feels: "If I am a sickly and incompetent person who feels insecure and foolish, I cannot possibly be a powerful, angry person who gets pleasure from thoughts of hurting others."

Annette appeared to have responded with sadistic feeling and fantasy to three brothers who competed with her for the attention of her dolorous, yet doting, mother. A vivid dream life and a number of recollections of childhood fantasy suggested that she entertained sadistic feeling about her brothers' genitals, though she tried as a child to manage the sadism through dismissive contempt for such a silly, apparently useless apparatus. Sadistic impulses toward her mother also were problematic, especially so given Mother's appearance of vulnerability and her unwillingness to defend herself against aggression. Sadistic impulses were denied by asserting shameful helplessness; they were also managed through the obsessive-compulsive rigidity that both controlled and obscured sadism.

Annette's sexual life was dominated by fear of penetration and by physical pain, body shame, and rage at her partner for inflicting suffering on her. While her actual sexual relations seldom proceeded toward much excitement, her fantasy life—when tolerated— provided excitement through sadomasochistic scenes of which she was much ashamed. In treatment, she often became suddenly and irresistably sleepy when I commented on sexual matters. Only after years of work did she reveal that, in her fantasies of being tied up and raped, she frequently experienced the action from the point of view of the abuser, whose "dominance" she vividly represented in her mind's eye. With much embarrassment and with anxiety about being weird or perverse, she revealed specific sadistic fantasies of childhood.

Wurmser (1981) asserts that shame over anal-masochistic pleasure is one of the recurrent, problematic forms of deep shame (see his case of Anne). Annette unquestionably felt ashamed of the excitement derived from fantasies of being beaten, tied up, humiliated, and raped, but her moral shame, guilt, and sense of embarrassing perversity over sadistic impulses to rape and torture seemed equally or more profound. Acknowledging wishes to hurt others threatened to remove her very right to be and, certainly, her right to be loved by her pacifistic mother. Admission of such self-aspects also disrupted her identification with her mother, which she saw as her foundation and sustenence. In therapy, gradual exploration of not-so-nice feelings and of her utilization of victimhood was associated with newfound energy, humor, and a greatly enhanced sense of control over her own future.

In concluding the remarks on Annette, let me note that Annette's masochism within specific relationships not only allowed her to escape her sadism; it also permitted her to eschew the relationship itself, in order to retreat to a conflict-free plain where she was magically in control. If she could see herself as her husband's victim when he complained about their compromised sex life, she soon began to imagine leaving him and finding some other partner who would be perfect and adoring and treat her like a queen. She exited the actuality of their relationship, which included, among other things, some unpalatable realities about the destructiveness of her masochism; she retreated to a gratifying fantasy world of her own making. Similarly, at work, she exaggerated dangers from disgruntled coworkers and building engineers and then used the hyperbolic interpretation of danger to justify ceasing all interactions with any person she could not control.

As treatment progressed, she became increasingly aware of her attachment to perfect control. She knew, for example, that there was something worth examining in her rage at traffic tie-ups or minor criticisms of her work. She would say that she "needs to be perfect" but also that she "*wants* to be perfect" and resents being told she is anything less. Thus, she began to see how her attachment to being a humiliated, self-doubting victim of abuse served to disguise the sadism that terrified her and also to facilitate her escape to the fantasy land where she could be perfect, a need and longing that had been promoted by too much pain of childhood criticism by Father, too little help modulating her aggression, and too much affirmation by Mother that anything Annette did was beyond reproach.

She developed a sense of humor about her own escapist and sadistic wishes. After a number of years of treatment, if I put into words her passionate insistence on control in one arena or another, she would respond with a hearty laugh of affirmation, the laugh signifying her awareness of the pleasure she derived from omnipotent fantasy. Once she related a memory of adopting a fantasy role of "goddess of winds and oceans" in a group of student mythology buffs and, within that role, delighting in the fantasy of elemental power.

Andrew, discussed earlier with respect to his grandiosity, was attached to detecting, often creating, scenarios in which his worthlessness or oppression entitled him to require another person to do something for him against that person's will. He might arrive for therapy at the wrong hour and pound on the therapist's closed door, entitled, he felt, to admission because of his conviction that the time was his. He then would take pleasure in the discomfort he caused the therapist and the patient whose hour he had disturbed. His sadistic behavior later would be excused by his notion that the confused condition of his poor, pathetic mind rendered such errors inevitable, even pitiable. He was the victim of his disorder, not the perpetrator of an aggressive act. His attraction to veiled coercion also led to rape fantasies in which sexual contact was achieved not through physical violence, but through mental manipulation of the other person's will and wishes. He felt guilty and ashamed about his sadistic "forcing" fantasies, which violated his own moral code; nevertheless, he found them intensely gratifying. In Andrew's case, shameful weakness and victimization hid his sadism while also allowing him to enact it.

Once Andrew had established a victim status, his sadism seemed justified and could be revealed, usually through fantasies of revenge in which he would gleefully "stick it to" the supposed abuser. Discussing Marlon Brando's adaptation to an abusive, humiliating father, Harold Brodkey (1994) said, "We can guess at the son's rabid and contemptuous ambition to escape from humiliation into the topmost stratospherics of triumph—to become the greatest of all time, as it were" (p. 80). This comment describes well Andrew's joyful attachment (despite moral shame and guilt) to grandiose fantasies of forcing others into submission.

Looking from a different perspective, we can also see that Andrew used sadism to deny vulnerable aspects of the self that seemed shameful. One day, he complained he was just stringing together meaningless ideas in an intellectualized fashion. I suggested he let his mind be open to whatever feelings or images might come. A second later he said, "Well, I just had an image of you dancing naked across the room. You're not very happy. I'm telling you, 'Do this, do that' and you're doing whatever silly [sexual] thing I tell you to do." Then came an eruptive laugh. Andrew's image seemed to contain at least the following strands: (1) He will feel relieved of his usual feelings that I shut him out and am impervious to him since, in the fantasy, I am utterly responsive to him, like a puppet would be. (2) He will humiliate me in revenge for the humiliation he feels, which follows from lacking power over me. (3) Instead of his exposing himself to me by doing silly things I suggest (like free associating, which had just been recommended to him), he will have me expose and humiliate myself. Thus, his sadistic fantasy, where indulged, works to counter his shame over being vulnerable to others and vulnerable to his need for others. In the session prior to this one, he had talked of feelings of failure and shame connected with a visit to a massage parlor where an Asian girl in her twenties "let me manhandle her." The shame over his behavior seemed connected to his need to pay money for sexual and emotional satisfaction. The shame was mitigated somewhat by sadistic images of the young woman being even more shamed than he.

Maxine Hong Kingston (1977) offers a stunning fictional description of sadism stimulated by projective identification with a shameful other. The projective identification provokes the wish to eradicate in the other what one despises in the self. She portrays a tongue-tied Chinese girl who finds another young girl even more intimidated and silent than she. I will quote only a small portion of her lengthy passage:

> "You're going to talk," I said, my voice steady and normal, as it is when talking to the familiar, the weak, and the small. "I am going to make you talk, you sissy-girl." She stopped backing away and stood fixed.
>
> I looked into her face so I could hate it close up. She wore black bangs, and her cheeks were pink and white. She was baby-soft. I thought that I could put my thumb on her nose and push it bonelessly in, indent her face. I could poke dimples into her cheeks. I could work her face around like dough. She stood still, and I did not want to look at her face anymore; I hated fragility. . . . I reached up and took the fatty part of her cheek, not dough, but meat, between my thumb and finger. This close, and I saw no pores. "Talk," I said. "are you going to talk?" Her skin was fleshy, like squid out of which the glassy blades of bones had been pulled. I wanted tough skin, hard brown skin [pp. 204–205].

Like Jeremy's "play world" and Annette's world of victimization, Andrew's retreat to sadism and masochism kept him at safe remove from ordinary relatedness. He had created a domain that he mentally manipulated like a god, in which one character, sometimes Andrew, sometimes his antagonist, coerced another into perverted relatedness. As treatment progressed, his attachment to this world, for which he had many names and vivid images, became starkly apparent to him, and his resistance to quitting it became more and more palpable.

His explorations led to what, for him, were startling recognitions of the ways in which acts of self-debasement guaranteed him safe haven in this world of fantasy. He was amazed to see how his shame and sense of worthlessness served to keep him in a world he wanted to inhabit, though he also sought desperately to leave it in order to taste the ordinary pleasures he had long denied himself. The recurring sequence he came to recognize and vividly to convey due to a talent for metaphor consisted of his experiencing wishes for ordinary pleasure and then humiliating himself through some real or fantasied acting out (often, sexually sadistic or sadomasochistic in form), at which point he reviled himself as a disgusting person unsuited for normal company, who needed to go into a state of retreat, to return to "his hole." The idea of being in his hole or staying "with the crap" occurred again and again as the representation of the safe sewer in which he lived and to which he felt suited because he was dirty and offensive. There he found obscure pleasure by means of sexually exploitative fantasy, which then brought punishment that excited but also terrified him.

But his greater fear, and his most angrily repudiated temptation, was movement into the world of ordinary pain and pleasure, which was the world in which, as a child, he experienced chronic emotional neglect. Though he ruminated about the possibility he had been physically assaulted as a youngster, the images of abuse seemed likely to have been his own childhood fantasies of finally getting down in the mud, in enlivening, terrifying conflict with the unengageable parents who infuriated him with their detachment. He had had so little power to draw people close for good and loving exchanges that he seemed to have shifted his efforts toward the destruction of relatedness. Though, as a child, he could not force human connections or make himself memorable to others, he could spoil any budding relationship at will by behaving in a dirty fashion that made him unworthy of relatedness, at which point he "had to" retreat from the other.

SHAME INTENSITY

I have talked thus far, in chapter and book, about the *content* of shame feelings, about how one can feel ashamed over being oneself or not being oneself or betraying another. And I have talked about *circumstances* that occasion shame feelings, which include times of being treated like an object or treated as vile but also include occasions in which self-reflection leads to negative judgment about the self and instances when maintaining a strong and confident self seems risky or leaves one disquietingly responsible for one's aggression. There also are questions to pose about determinants of *intensity* in shame experience. I have chosen to place this discussion in a chapter on masochism because intensity of painful feeling, including shame, often is a hallmark of masochism, though, certainly, it is seen in other contexts.

Some people are subject to shame feelings that are remarkable for their intensity. Feelings may occur that have the character of explosions within the self or terrible attacks or blows to be fended off with life-preserving aggression. Such shame feelings threaten the person's right and reason to continue living. They say, "You are so fundamentally bad, or worthless, or deficient, you ought not to exist." They may bring dissociative responses and a sense of psychic catastrophe. Shame feelings with this devastating character control relationships, including the therapy relationship, because explorations that evoke such emotion must be barred, and the therapist or whoever else wants to violate that injunction becomes a threat to combat.

Here, I am interested in exploring what forces in development might lead to shame feelings of such potency. There are a number of contributory factors I have considered, some of them related to masochism. One factor appears to be a broad tendency within the personality toward severe judgment, both of self and others. Stated differently, the superego has a stringent and aggressive quality. Judgment is frequent and harsh. Historically, such a development is often linked with extreme, hostile rejection of the child's indwelling self, to which the child responds with rage and hate that colors superego development. In some cases, the child may overvalue his hard-hearted superego as the only source of moral order and judgment in a chaotic home or as a respected voice of authority. Judgments made about "badness"—bad self, bad others—may be intensified by defensive splitting aimed at preserving some area of reliable goodness.

For the patient in therapy, there is often a specific, defined set of ideas that precipitates overwhelming shame, not an endless range of such instigators. Present in many instances is a historical pairing of a particular idea or idea-cluster with the notion of being fully bad or fully defective, thus not entitled to participate in society, perhaps needing to be destroyed or expelled. The history of the dangerous idea frequently includes a parent's aggressive wielding of a damning idea against a still immature child, who hears his angry parent condemning him as selfish, hateful, sick, a juvenile delinquent, or a slut. For one man I recall, it was the idea of being "a sissy." The parent's judgment seems "global," to use Lewis's term. The child is cast out, wholly and permanently, and he constructs internally a stunning idea, such as, "You are no good," or "You are unlovable." The therapist can look to the nuances of the adult's intense feeling for clues about its history. One person experiences his acute shame as a shock, a stunning surprise, usually in the context of wishes; the shock quality may speak to infantile experiences of exhibitionism surprised by fierce censure. Another person associates her shame with a black feeling about herself, a "punishment place" she cannot tolerate, which speaks to her mother's periods of icy shunning.

In some cases, the terrible judgment has been made not against the child, but against someone important to that child, and the judgment has been made by someone the child respects. A young boy hears his mother indict Father as a worthless philanderer whom she plans to kick out of the house. A girl hears her older sister demeaned as retarded, as too stupid to live. The danger looms that I, myself, could be like that, could be extruded like that. The superego may become one's protection. If the developing child can say to himself, "You, too, are becoming bad; you must stop yourself or control yourself," he may keep himself from being attacked or extruded. In other cases, denial is the only defense. One acts as if one does not know or care about the danger. Drugs can facilitate such denial.

The danger of wholly condemning ideas is often compounded by judgments the child himself has made in similarly polarized terms. For example, a young girl sexually abused by a neighbor feels "bad" or "dirty" because of the activities in which she engages. Years later, entering puberty, she acts out sexually, and her furious father condemns her as a "slut." The horrible power of Father's disapprobation is intensified by her superego's agreement, rooted in longstanding feelings, that she *is* a slut, *is* bad, *is* dirty. The powerful shame idea may be disguised, such that the shame trigger evident in treatment bears only an oblique relationship to the history of shaming. For example, the shame history points to sexual activity as the core, shame-linked behavior, but the shame trigger in treatment is something as apparently innocuous as a reference to the patient's "casual clothes" or "open purse," which are associatively linked to sexual activity.

Judgments the child has made about another also contribute to shame intensity. Take, for example, the same sexually abused child. She detests her abuser and continually describes him in her private thoughts as a "bad" person whose badness is defined by his sadism. Internally, she dwells on her hatred. He deserves mutilation, he deserves death, she tells herself. She uses her condemnation to separate herself from him and to establish an identity for herself that is apart from his. Years later, in treatment, this woman is asked by her therapist to look at some of her own sadistic feelings. No matter how commonplace her sadism might be, she immediately links her feelings with the cruelty of her abuser, for which she felt he deserved damnation. She panics as the distance between her and him, her goodness and his badness, collapses. She cannot preserve her old, self-protective hatred toward him without now hating herself. Any time a child needs to establish a highly defined set of moral indictments of some person or group, the risk is great that such judgment will be wielded against the self.

Masochistic postures that are secondary to abuse leave a person in a position in which an attacking, overpowering shame feeling serves as the present-day reenstatement of the abusive parent's life and death power. To succumb to the deadly feeling is to accept and validate the parent's power, thus preserving the old relationship. To refuse the overpowering shame is to separate from the parent, to say, "You cannot make me feel deeply bad and unworthy of living." In these situations, the punishing superego attack generally comes as a response to an attempt to be oneself, to move outside the masochistic framework in which power is achievable only through victimization. The shame feeling says that one must reenter the framework in order for the abuser to call off the dogs.

Adaptation to the victim position leads to secondary gain from power that is ascribed to the experience of being attacked, degraded, or deprived; thus, the person becomes loath to give up that experience, which can be represented through attacks of terrible shame. A physically abused child may fly away to a place in which he is all-powerful or is ready to receive rescue from a dead, idealized parent. The license to escape to such a magical place depends on the continued experience of assault; therefore, victimization may be preserved in adulthood.

In therapy, confronting a person with his active role in maintaining situations of deprivation or victimization may lead to shame of great intensity, accompanied by rage at the therapist who is seen as inflicting such humiliation. A vicious cycle may be established in which shame plays a pivotal role: the person needs to feel victimized in order to justify withdrawal to an omnipotent state; if he is confronted about those needs, he feels intensely shamed, which he construes as an attack, which justifies the very withdrawal about which he has been confronted. Attachment to such withdrawal comes, in part, from the severity of the stresses that have been escaped and, in part, from the magical sense of relief that is attained. On a radio report, a young man left quadraplegic after an automobile accident told of lying in his totalled vehicle, unable to move his legs, thinking in a state of dissociative tranquility, "Why didn't I think of doing this before? No more worries about algebra, no need to put gas in the car, no arguments with parents. Everything is solved."

THEMES OF LOOKING AND BEING SEEN:
LINKS TO SHAME AND GUILT

The wish to hide from sight is a defining aspect of the shame experience, whatever the clinical or nonclinical context. But in some individuals, concerns about being seen and about looking extend beyond moments of shame and become broad preoccupations. This topic could be addressed under a number of headings. I include it here because concerns about looking at others or about presenting the self for visual attention existed for several of the masochistic individuals already introduced and seemed linked with the disposition to suffer. I would like to examine these concerns and assess their relationship to Wurmser's (1981) ideas about the early instinct to connect with others through curiosity and self-display, urges that accrue aggressiveness when impeded. Also relevant will be Wurmser's idea that the stressed infant develops notions that his looking and self-exhibition are magically powerful in creating and reorganizing reality. Wurmser reminds us that for a clinician to explore looking themes with attention only to the content that is perceived (e.g., a primal scene) neglects the broad significance of looking as a core aspect of one's activity in the world. A parallel argument exists with respect to showing the self. In the material to follow, interactions between guilt and shame abound and will be identified as they appear.

From my case material, it was not possible for me to make any clear determination about the earliest roots of Betty's and Virginia's experiences of looking; thus, I do not know whether their earliest curiosity met with the punishing responses (which include unresponsiveness) Wurmser assumes. But in both cases, the notion of powerful eyes is present for the adult. Betty thinks of her eyes as powerful in their physical attractiveness: they are irresistible; they tantalize by their shape and color. Thus, she seems to be talking more about what Wurmser calls "delophilia"— showing the self and entrancing the other—than about looking per se, but it is of interest that it is her eyes that overwhelm others with their beauty, since it is hard to think of eyes without considering their perceptual function. Thus, it remains a possibility that the distorted idea, "powerful eyes," conflates concerns about showing one's self powerfully and looking powerfully.

The notion of having a bad or destructive power to attract is also interesting in that Wurmser's ideas about delophilia likely would point to a profoundly shaming sense of impotence to attract, which might, however, lead to compensatory fantasies of all-powerful attractiveness, a line of argument consistent with Novick and Novick's (1991) pairing of early helplessness and delusions of destructive omnipotence. Betty associates her powerful eyes primarily with guilt, not shame (except for moral shame), since they attract forbidden men. If shame over interpersonal helplessness is important to her dynamics around powerful eyes, it belongs to the prehistory of her symptomatic complaint.

As indicated earlier, Virginia experienced an inhibition of looking, which seemed related both to looking and to being the object of others' visual attention, the latter concern implied by an ostrich logic that said, "If I don't look at you, you won't see me." In Virginia's case, the surface concern was clearly a shame experience: she felt acutely self-conscious and embarrassed about looking and being seen. If we consider the dynamics producing these moments of shame, the power to use one's looking and showing in highly destructive fashion seemed very much at issue. Developmental contributions included the fear that Virginia's attractiveness would generate depression, hysteria, and rage in her mother. Thus, she could not allow herself to be seen if to be seen meant having her beauty recognized. Also prohibited was any discriminating form of looking, which might lead Virginia to make judgments such as, "I look better than she," or "I'm glad that homely dress isn't mine," or "Something must be wrong with her if she acts that way." Such judgments were seen as highly dangerous, even when the impulse that powered them was not sadistic. One simply shouldn't see such things or speak of them. One shouldn't notice such differences between oneself and one's mother. An associated fantasy was that, if she failed to see, if she denied the other person's shortcomings, she could protect that person from any consequences those limitations might have. Thus, to curtail one's own looking and showing through shame-faced withdrawal protected the vulnerable partner.

For several sessions, Virginia discussed a rotating committee chairpersonship that would require her to stand up in front of a group and lead a discussion. Past experience had led her to believe she would excel at this assignment, but she felt terrified and insecure, and the risk of humiliating herself felt great. Before her turn came to speak, she focused her visual attention on one member of the group and decided that particular woman was highly critical; she determined not to look at her during the discussion. Virginia's performance was flawless and brought much praise, as well as expressions of anxiety from those to assume leadership at the following weeks' meetings. Virginia skipped the next two meetings, with weather as her justification.

In exploring her fantasy of the critical group member, it came to light that Virginia had had some negative thoughts about the woman's hairdo, thoughts she judged to be horrid, though they were rather benign by most people's standards. She seemed to have projected her own critical looking onto the other woman and made herself its potential victim, which helped her sustain the image of her own unworthiness, an image she needed in order to remain free of guilt. She started the hour in which this story unfolded by admiring my haircut.

Over a long period of time, Virginia presented herself as consistently accepting of me and often admiring. Frequently, she would listen to my comments and then privately fault herself for being inarticulate. The comparison with me constituted the context for her self-criticism, which led to inhibition of self-expression. As this process came to light, we could conjecture that her self-criticism represented, in part, a denial of more discriminating perceptions about me, which would include not only recognition of my moments of articulateness, but also observations of inarticulateness and other imperfections.

With a third woman, Adrianna, inhibition of looking and showing centered on fears, similar to Betty's, of having an irresistable sexual authority over a man she would "leer at" or to whom she might display her fine figure. Like Betty, she would hold herself responsible if an inappropriate man responded to her sexually, which meant she had failed to keep her powerful weapon sheathed. To look (leer) and to show were equally powerful provocations. Her focus was as much on shame as guilt, since she saw her leering and her sexual exhibition as something uncontrolled, provocative, and disgusting to others.

In all three of these cases, there is a fantasy of highly powerful looking and showing, especially active within the sexual-exhibitionistic sphere, which defines the immorality of one's activities. To some extent, the fantasies of power seem to be direct consequences of a caregiver's attribution of destructive force to a child. Betty, for example, was told explicitly that she was irresistibly sexy and had gorgeous eyes. She experienced the damaging coalescence of (a) a child's wishful sexual fantasies with (b) real, inappropriate sexual activity. She drew the conclusion that her inner feelings and thoughts were very powerful. If her abuser's activity corresponded in some way with her fantasy, it must be that she caused the activity. The overall powerlessness of the abused child likely makes this circumscribed attribution of power something to adopt and cling to, even exult over, though one then bears its heavy responsibilities.

I am not able to say from the case material whether these individuals experienced the specific forms of early helplessness Wurmser discusses (i.e., helplessness in engaging the caretaker through looking and showing) or whether such experience contributed to the overinvestment in vision as a mode of contact, and the strengthened sense of destructive power in looking and showing. It may be that, for Adrianna, who experienced maternal neglect, in back of the fantasy of power to move the penis (and its possessor) through her eyes is the wishful fantasy of moving the mother and breast through searching, wishful visual contact. What *is* apparent is that in none of the three cases could looking be integrated as a valued capability associated, for example, with discriminating perception or acceptable sexual power. The primary link to masochism was the women's needs to degrade their functioning (by concealing personal assets and by inhibiting vision in embarrassment) in order to protect relationships with those they imagined would be threatened by more active use of vision and self-display.

Andrew's case offers stronger evidence for Wurmser's ideas about early helplessness to engage caretakers through looking and showing. In treatment, Andrew, like the women discussed, insisted on his special powers of looking. Though his actual gazing at others was inhibited by self-consciousness, he imagined he could magically penetrate others with his vision in order to detect their concealed motives. This presumed power brought him sadistic pleasure and seemed to work counter to fears that others could, at will, shut him out emotionally. Thus, to penetrate visually was to gain access to the person's subjectivity. In the transference, Andrew was angered by my closed door, by my freedom to keep him waiting until the agreed-upon time of the appointment, and by my vision, which supposedly left me unable to see him due to defective eyes. His fantasies of visually penetrating others occasionally brought guilt but, more regularly, brought a triumphant feeling accompanied by anxiety about enraged retaliation by the other person, who was seen as intent on protecting his boundaries.

For Andrew, shame was not in the fantasied looking (which was highly aggressive and therefore brought more guilt than shame), but in a group of associated images of being looked at or looked into and seen to be "nothing," to be not worth steadying one's eyes upon, experiences like those Wurmser discusses. He judged his own inner life as "nothing," in part to eliminate the possibility of showing his best self, with hopeful attitude, only to find the other pronouncing it worthless. One rageful defense against the pain of not being seen was not to see or remember others, thus generating in them the fury Andrew once felt over being denied acknowledgment.

As is often the case, shame played multiple roles within the particular segment of Andrew's personality I have been considering. It operated as a current-day means for him to withdraw from a visually active approach to others. Such approaches were allowed in fantasy but restricted in reality, in part because of their sadistic content, in part because, if pursued without sadism, they would connect him with others in commonplace ways. Shame also had importance as part of the feared, infantile experience of being insignificant to those he loved and needed.

ADOLESCENT ONSET OF SELF-CONSCIOUSNESS,
DREAD OF BLUSHING, AND MASOCHISTIC FANTASY,
ALL ASSOCIATED WITH SEPARATION STRESS

Patricia was in her early twenties when she sought treatment for periods of painful depression, as well as for chronic self-consciousness, self-doubt, social anxiety and dreaded episodes of blushing. She quickly impressed me with her critically oriented, subtle intelligence. Her overall demeanor was polite but reserved, her sense of enjoyment restricted. Patricia had developed a cluster of shame complaints in mid-adolescence; these became increasingly severe in her early twenties.

Patricia recalled episodic shame in earlier childhood, but shame's ascendance as a chronic burden, taking the several forms already noted, did not occur until mid-adolescence and beyond. It appeared to be part of a broader movement toward intensification of the masochistic elements in her personality, through which she tormented herself with miserable feelings, some of which had occurred earlier in life as transient, situationally appropriate responses to difficult situations. An example was her relationship to blushing. She recalled blushing in the presence of boys she liked around the age of puberty. Those experiences did not seem especially painful; in fact, they appeared to be dominated by pleasure. But later in adolescence, she began to dread episodes of blushing as if they represented terrible public mortification. A new significance had been assigned to an old experience.

Her depressions also had a masochistic organization in that they occurred in response to situations she interpreted as indications of terrible oppression of the weak (often female) by the strong (often male). Her views of societal events could be astute, but her attention was selectively tuned to episodes of exploitation and dominance, which mirrored the worst elements in her parents' treatment of her. Pleasurable aspects of male–female sexual interactions were lost to predictable images of female victimization.

Patricia's childhood experiences included many examples of both parents displaying harsh criticism of her expressive nature and tendency toward social leadership. One memory placed her at a Hannukah party at her home, surrounded by children and the gifts she was opening. She joked to the assembled guests that she should have invited more kids so she could get more presents. Rather than appreciate her daughter's cleverness and charming bluntness, her mother became angry at the child and berated her for selfishness and bad manners. Exhibitionism regularly brought such punishing, humorless responses from both parents.

Patricia appears to have retained pleasure in her outgoing self until mid-adolescence, despite heavy pressures from her parents. In middle adolescence, clashes with her mother and father around dating became intense, and Mother threatened to evict her from the house. Overt abandonment threats, combined with normative adolescent fears about separation from parents, seem to have been the forces that ushered in Patricia's gradually more severe experiences of self-consciousness, social anxiety, blushing fear, and performance fear, all of which contributed to her eventually alienating herself entirely from the outgoing, happily exhibitionistic ways of her earlier years. Her constant self-consciousness, which judged her to be stupid, ridiculous, and deficient, was very effective in echoing the voice of parental hostility to her indwelling self, especially in its exhibitionistic aspects. The symptomatic nature of Patricia's self-consciousness was suggested by the ascending curve it followed as she moved into early adulthood and by its strikingly harsh character.

Many discussions of self-consciousness include it as part of the phenomenology of shame. For example, Kaufman (1989) states:

> Self-consciousness is usually mistaken for anxiety, which, of course, often *accompanies* it. However, the two are quite different affects. Anxiety is a manifestation of fear affect, while self-consciousness is a manifestation of shame [p. 23].

> The affect of shame calls attention to the self, exposing it to view, and the self lives in the face. We become suddenly aware of being seen, and unexpectedly aware of our face. We become *self-conscious,* as if the self suddenly were impaled under a magnifying glass. The shame response of hanging the head or lowering the eyes is one that reduces that agonizing facial visibility [p. 23].

Although self-consciousness does often appear as part of the shame family of emotions (because it involves an uncomfortable awareness of the self's or body's deficits), it is worth holding in mind that the term *self-conscious* also implies an activity, which may or may not involve great discomfort and a negative sense of self. In another context, I (Miller, 1985) state:

> Self-consciousness can be conceptualized as an activity that may be attended by a variety of feeling tones. The activity of maintaining consciousness of a mental representation of one's self has significance both as an indicator of ego strength and as an indicator of ego strain. . . . Self-consciousness as an indicator of ego strain generally is experienced as something plaguing the person, not as an activity voluntarily undertaken. The person is unable fully to engage the self in any activity requiring that the greater part of attention be directed away from the image of the self. One finds oneself simultaneously engaging and watching oneself engage. The inability to relinquish self-consciousness can occur in any situation that leaves a person feeling unable to trust his or her spontaneous behavior [pp. 45–46].

Fenigstein, Scheier, and Buss (1975) get at some similar points when they state:

> There appear to be two separate aspects of self-consciousness: One deals with a cognitive, private mulling over the self, and the other emphasizes an awareness and concern over the self as a social stimulus. . . . The thrust of private self-consciousness is more specific: Its focus is on thoughts and reflections that deal solely with the self.

> Public self-consciousness is related to the conceptions of Mead (1934). Mead argued that consciousness of self comes about when the person becomes aware of another's perspective; then he can view himself as a social object. The emphasis here is clearly on the reactions of others to the self. Similarly, the essence of public self-consciousness is the self as a social object.

> The relationship of social anxiety to public self-consciousnesss may be of some theoretical importance. Although the items comprising these two factors appear to be similar, social anxiety and public self-consciousness repeatedly emerge as separate factors. Moreover, the correlation between them is consistently low; but there is a correlation. Why? In our view, the sequence is as follows: First a person becomes aware of himself as a social object. Given this public self-consciousness, he may then evaluate himself and become apprehensive; that is, public self-consciousness may be a necessary antecedent of social anxiety. However, self-awareness does not automatically imply social anxiety; a person may focus attention on himself without experiencing discomfort [pp. 525–526].

It seems reasonable to argue that some increase in self-consciousness is normative in adolescence; it is a predictable response to a changing self and to an expanding capability for self-awareness and discriminating awareness of others. But the highly critical self-consciousness that Patricia experienced, which intensified in young adulthood, appeared to be associated with exceptional developmental strain. This young woman's normal adolescent need to maintain the love of her parents seemed to have brought with it great anxiety about following her own strong impulses toward pleasurable social exhibitionism and other forms of individuated, adult expression.

Her self-consciousness worked in concert with her masochism. Through self-consciousness and associated shame states, she restricted ordinary self-expression. She then identified with oppressed groups and gained some pleasure from the aggression and self-righteousness such an identification justified. That identification was supported by many childhood experiences of actual victimization at the hands of unempathic, autocratic parents and a tormenting sibling. The defensive amplification of such an identification cost her dearly since it produced a demoralizing, depressive sense of the world overrun by oppression and abuse, and it required that she give up pleasures associated with ordinary competence and attractiveness.

CHAPTER 8

Giving and Receiving

Gift Commerce, Shame, and Pride

Giving, itself, is one of the strongest sociological functions. Without constant giving and taking within society—outside of exchange, too—society would not come about. For, giving is by no means only a simple effect that one individual has upon another: it is precisely what is required of all sociological functions, namely, interaction. By either accepting or rejecting a gift, the receiver has a highly specific effect upon the giver. . . . Every act of giving is, thus, an interaction between giver and receiver.

—Georg Simmel (1950)

In drawing this book to a close, I turn my attention to shame and its counterpoint, pride, as part of the fabric of ordinary social interactions. I hope, by so doing, to stress a point heretofore neglected in my presentation, which is the notion that the shame family of emotions is by no means restricted to pathology but has a place in the current of ordinary emotional life. In looking at some of the day-to-day situations that promote pride and other feelings of well being or that provoke shame, I will examine various settings, including the two-person psychoanalytic situation. My emphasis here will be more on the predictable interpersonal elicitors of shame and pride and less on idiosyncratic interpretations of situations, sometimes suggestive of pathology, that elicit shame or self-satisfaction.

One frame of reference I will introduce is that of gift-giving, a construct that has been much used by sociologists and anthropologists for considering human exchanges, usually of goods, that generate feelings of pride or shame. Since the giving and receiving of gifts, both material and intangible, constitutes an important aspect of daily life in society, it seems reasonable to examine that large segment of human interactions as one that creates many opportunities for shame and pride.

I begin with some work by William Miller, a law professor and expert on Icelandic sagas. Miller (1993) explicitly ties gift-giving and "honor," a concept with clear implications for shame and pride experience. I will move from Miller's framework into Hyde's (1979) consideration of gift giving and on to a discussion of nonmaterial gifts. The psychoanalytic situation will also be examined from the point of view of giving and receiving, as will creativity, both within and outside of psychotherapy.

GIVING AND RECEIVING IN HONOR-BASED SOCIETIES

William Miller (1993) explores the dynamics of gift exchange in the "heroic cultures," such as saga Iceland, in which preserving and augmenting one's honor was a major preoccupation, and experiences with gift exchange were major sources of pride or humiliation. Of honor, Miller says, "[It] is above all the keen sensitivity to the experience of humiliation and shame, a sensitivity manifested by the desire to be envied by others and the propensity to envy the successes of others" (p. 84). He argues that our own society sees gift-giving and receiving in terms that are closer than we might imagine to those of the heroic cultures.

Miller is most concerned with shame as it occurs publically, precipitated by social interchange. He is less concerned with more private, internal "I feel ashamed" experiences, except when they follow directly from a social humiliation. Of the shame-group emotions, humiliation and embarrassment especially interest him; these are more social emotions than the forms of shame that are essentially private reflections on the self.

Miller redresses an imbalance created by some of the recent shame literature in which the role the shame emotions play in public interchange is almost lost due to the emphasis on inner pain and individual pathology. Like Lasch (1992), Miller grounds his resurrection of societal shame in a disdainful dismissal of studies of internal experience, as if one area of inquiry or the other can be worthy, but not both. Though he and Lasch both have reason to grumble about studies of shame emotion that portray shame as invariably a pathology and never an individual's registration of her shortcomings, the notion that private experience is necessarily trivial I find problematic. Here is Miller (1993), on this point:

> The new shame psychologists privatize and trivialize it by making it less an emotion whose paradigmatic context is one of losing or maintaining face against challenges to reputation than the emotion

of simply not feeling good about oneself, the feeling of low self-esteem. The social has a very small role in this kind of shame, if any at all. The new shame might even be seen as the linchpin of a new politics of the antisocial, in which it is nearly supposed that a person should maintain self-esteem no matter how inept or offensive he or she might be [p. 135].

One might as easily complain of Miller's approach that it implies a person merits high self-esteem so long as she is honored within her society.

Miller's notion that privatizing equates with trivializing distinguishes his experience of the world from that of someone like Wurmser, who sees the private as nontrivial and recognizes self-reflective shame as, at times, a profound experience. Wurmser (1981) states:

Such stress on social interaction and group psychology has great intrinsic value, especially for research, but it once again tends to obfuscate the centrality of inner conflict. It is understandable that the shame affects are particularly predisposed to be reduced to power conflicts, to deviances in the vicissitudes of shared focal attention and to other more observable and formal characteristics of interaction. Their value as affect gets lost on the way [p. 14].

Wurmser's comment that shame can be "reduced to power conflicts" is particularly relevant to Miller's study of gift exchange and humiliation. In Miller's analysis, the gift is almost entirely about power—the wish to acquire it, the fear of losing it. Miller is fully occupied with the dangers we, as social creatures, encounter. Social life is a minefield, studded with hazards to honor and self-esteem. While often astute and amusing, his analyses of present-day social encounters can overplay the competitive, status-related, heavily scripted elements at work. The cooking of dinners for guests becomes a competitive sport in which one hostess vies with another for honors or at least seeks to avoid the dreaded state of disgrace or humiliation (p. 26). His analyses hit the mark in many respects, but they recognize only the power aspects of gift exchange. The people involved in such exchanges seldom have meaning for each other as individuals who have shared life's experiences. Their status and power is their meaning. Even the exchange of Valentine's Day gifts between two children is seen as a status competition between the children's parents. Again, I do not mean to deny the presence of this level of meaning or to doubt the validity of examining it, but it is not the sole meaning of gift exchange. W. Miller (1993) concludes his study as follows:

> What I want readers to come away with is a sense of the social and psychological complexity of the most innocuous of our daily encounters. I suggested that the reason such simple interactions are fraught with danger is that we still feel the demands of something like honor very keenly. This honor involves two basic ideas: (1) that we pay back what we owe, whether it be good or bad, and (2) that it matters deeply to us (more perhaps than we are willing to admit) that we acquit ourselves well with the people we encounter. At the most fundamental level our minimal desire is only that we do not lose esteem or undo the basis for maintaining self-esteem from the interaction. Most of our disposition with regard to honor is defensive rather than offensive, preserving rather than acquisitive [p. 204].

Miller's analysis of gifts has similarities to Mauss's (1990) study of the obligatory nature of giving and receiving across many cultures.

What is omitted from Miller's analysis of gift-giving? Among other things, it is the significance of the gift as a symbol of the personal feelings the giver holds for the intended receiver, which are especially important when the receiver is experienced as a particular, known individual and not just someone socially above or below one's rank. Thus, the fancy Valentine's gift that humiliates the receiving child's parents (who had bought no such gift for the giver) was important not only as an assertion of the giving family's power, but also as a statement of the giving child's more personal feelings for the receiving child, which might have included affection and admiration and a deep wish for the reciprocation of interest. The return of such loving feeling, but also the mere experiencing of it, contributes to an inner sense of fullness that generates a sense of well-being, sometimes of pride. Failure of reciprocity, or death of the inner experience of love, brings depletion and often shame. Earlier chapters have shown how these most natural of human responses sometimes are altered or obscured by neurotic need or conflict, so that, for example, the enthusiastic return of one's gift may bring anxiety and shame rather than joy and pride. Such deviations should be understood against the background of simpler, normative responses.

If we turn to Hyde's (1979) study of gifts, we find a set of emphases that differ strikingly from Miller's. Hyde is interested in gifts as expressions of bounty that move from person to person, connecting each to the other and to larger forces beyond the individual, forces that include creativity and generativity. According to Hyde, a gift is something that keeps moving within a community of individuals, creating a "gift circle." Hyde's notion of gifts is so remote from Miller's that his definition almost seems to refuse the status of gifts to the major material of Miller's study. For example, Hyde states:

> The moral is this: the gift is lost in self-consciousness. To count, measure, reckon value, or seek the cause of a thing, is to step outside the circle, to cease being "all of a piece" with the flow of gifts and become, instead, one part of the whole reflecting upon another part. We participate in the esemplastic power of a gift by way of a particular kind of unconsciousness, then: unanalytic, undialectical consciousness [p. 152].

In contrast, Miller's gifts are all about counting and reckoning.

Using Miller's analysis of gifts to look at America's donations of dollars or goods to poorer nations, we quickly imagine the humiliation and, thus, the hostility such offerings might generate, as they flaunt our wealth before those who cannot reciprocate. If we approach the picture with Hyde's concepts in mind, we may see America as the bountiful mother whose gifts nourish life and health and seed rich developments in the recipient. Such gifts will be received gratefully and passed along to another recipient and another in due time, making a gift circle. Both levels of analysis have merit and have relevance for the gift-exchange elements in psychotherapy.

SHAME ASPECTS OF GIVING AND RECEIVING IN PSYCHOANALYTIC THERAPY

The exchange of tangible gifts has only an occasional place in the psychoanalytic situation, but what of the multitude of stories, insights, and human responses that pass between patient and therapist? Can these be thought of as gift-exchange aspects of psychoanalytic therapy? Analogy between material and nonmaterial gifts appears to be valid in that the exchange of intangible gifts follows many of the rules of exchanging property. If we consider a friendship and the rules that govern the giving and receiving of personal time and attention, including attentive listening to a friend's concerns, we quickly see that rules of reciprocity and feelings of pride over generosity, shame over its absence, do obtain.

W. Miller (1993) summarily disposes of the question of shame and pride around psychoanalytic giving by classifying psychoanalysis among "certain ritualized degradations like confession" (p. 327). Though he does not elaborate on his comment, he presumably views psychoanalysis as a discrepant-power relationship in which any opportunity to bestow or withhold gifts belongs with the therapist and not with the pathetic patient who comes to display his deficiency of resources. The patient in such a schema is a shameful or dishonored emptiness that needs filling by the therapist's fullness.

There is no question that certain aspects of the usual psychoanalytic situation promote feelings that the patient is weaker, needier, less capable, and less authoritative than the analyst, a circumstance conducive to shame, as explored by Broucek (1991) and others. But such a construction is much affected by the therapist's management of the treatment setting and relationship, as well as by the patient's particular, analyzable needs with respect to feeling ashamed or feeling proud. Such factors influence the extent to which exchanges feel like competitions to determine who is more resourceful or like transmissions of riches that the receiver is free to disburse at will. To see humiliation of the patient as the inevitable result of psychoanalytic giving is based on a far too limited notion of the kinds of giving and receiving that can occur within the psychoanalytic situation. In fact, this situation offers various opportunities for largely nonexploitational exchange on the part of both participants and also provides contexts for the expression of conflict around giving and getting.

When therapist and patient are working well together, both participants have some sense of both giving and receiving what I will call "human gifts." The therapist may feel she gives her attention, insight, and compassion and she receives from her patient some degree of trust and openness and the sharing of interesting or poignant life experiences. She also gives time and receives money that has value for her. And she receives recognition of her skills and efforts, such recognition being conveyed by direct statements from the patient or by the patient's simple acceptance and use of what is offered. The patient will feel that she gives to the therapist the sharing of her inner experience, from which the therapist derives learning and a degree of personal enjoyment. She may also give the therapist her trust and patience and tolerance for the therapist's shortcomings, as well as payment for the therapist's time and service.

Both parties, at times, will have conflicts over either the giving or the receiving aspects of the relationship. A therapist anxious over her own generous impulses toward a patient may arbitrarily restrict giving or may give human gifts but then deny the giving when the patient responds with gratitude, with a wish to reciprocate, or with an impulse to pass on to a third party whatever gift the therapist has given her. An example comes from Juan, who experienced his usually sartorially conservative analyst as giving him a gift by allowing him to see her dressed in an especially festive, velvet skirt several times every Christmas season. Juan's experience of the skirt as a gift was revealed to the therapist through his associations to an erotic dream, which he shared with her. After the dream was related, the therapist never again wore the skirt. The patient felt wounded and chastized, as if the revelation that he had been receiving and enjoying the analyst's apparel as a gift had angered the analyst and caused her to withdraw it. More likely, the patient's incorporation of the gift into his own images of sexual pleasure and tactile comfort made the analyst anxious, as if she had been inappropriately seductive, which she had not. The patient was never able to share with the analyst his response to the disappearing skirt. He withdrew his gift of openness and nursed his wound. In this case, the gift that the analyst actually gave was her willingness to be herself in her choice of attire. The gift she could have given, but apparently withdrew, was an endorsement of the patient's freedom to respond to her according to his own history and feelings.

Another example of a therapist overly anxious about giving comes from the therapy of an emotionally reserved man who said to his therapist, "I feel like hugging you for those understanding words," and the therapist, who could not accept having given this gift to her patient and evoked such affection responded, "They were simple words; anyone could have given them." The comment humiliated the patient by devaluing the gift that brought him such joy and gratitude.

The true gift from therapist to patient is not always easy to discern. A late adolescent patient in the early months of treatment complained of my not answering an important question she had asked me ("Do you have a dog?") some weeks earlier. She was considering terminating our work because she found me unresponsive, compared with two previous therapists she had seen in early adolescence. I told her it had been a hard call for me to know whether to answer that question. On the one hand, it would have been enjoyable for both of us to share some feelings about our pets. But I wanted her to have the opportunity to explore her own thoughts about me and my relationship with animals, so I restrained myself with a bit of explanation about why I was doing so. What I didn't tell her was that, being a dog lover, I had had to make an effort at restraint, which I did because I thought my restraint would be the greater gift, but it was not, because she only felt humiliated by my failure to respond to her. Her strengths allowed her to bring her humiliated feeling into the treatment, which seemed to advance the work in a way it perhaps would not have advanced had I simply answered her question, but she discontinued treatment shortly thereafter.

Building on Winnicott's ideas about the paradoxical human needs both to give to others and to retreat to a state of privacy in which one remains "unfound," Pizer (1992) speaks to a core human anxiety that nonexploitational giving and receiving can evoke because of the universal need for a variety of independence Pizer describes as "a nonnegotiable retreat to relaxation within the subjective world of the inviolable self" (p. 220). Paired with this need for privacy is an equally profound investment in external reality, which includes the other to whom one may give and from whom one receives. Again following Winnicott, Pizer talks of maternal giving and "the mother's illusion that she continues to create her baby while she is merged with it by 'almost 100% adaptation' to its needs" (p. 222). He compares the mother's joy in providing to the occasional experience of the analyst who "is fortunate to experience a similar joy at being found and used" (p. 222). One of the therapist's deepest feelings of *receiving* occurs when the patient comfortably takes what the therapist has offered and experiences it as good.

The therapist's capacity to receive human gifts from her patient and to acknowledge such receipt is as important as the ability to give, but has been less attended. The therapist who cannot allow herself to receive from a patient will threaten the patient's self-regard within the relationship and beyond it, especially if the patient is someone whose early caregivers could not find pleasure in the patient's gifts of love or trust. Out of a need to deny human needs or wishes in relation to her patient, a therapist may deprive a patient of an essential sense of having positive human qualities to offer. Discussing what he calls the "masochistic-depressive syndrome," Markson (1993) says, "I believe these patients will not prosper unless the analyst is capable of enjoying them. Didactic interpretations of conflict and need will not suffice without the right 'music'" (p. 937).

When the therapist conveys that she has no gift-receiving needs or wishes of her own—a communication juxtaposed in many therapies with the patient's expression of *many* needs and wishes to receive human gifts—one message to the patient is: "You are mired in all the minutiae of earthly existence, I am at the other extreme, I am above being on this earth." This stance may represent an anxious therapist's effort to be free of shame, but as Broucek (1991) ably explicates, it often leads the therapist back to shame, since denying one's own personhood and making the self into a dispassionate thing can generate deep shame, as well as guilt over depriving the other person of a genuine relationship.

Always in therapy, it is necessary to take care to differentiate between those structures of the therapy that are designed to protect the process and those that are designed to protect the therapist from emotional strain. There may be times when we choose to maintain structures for our own comfort, but it is important to acknowledge the nature of such decisions. For example, if a therapist rejects a material gift from a patient, she should be clear about whether she refuses the gift out of a belief that verbal communications of feeling will be more helpful to the patient than communications through material items (and an associated notion that the latter may discourage the former) or out of anxiety about appearances of impropriety.

It is also essential to differentiate between any interference with productive giving and receiving that the therapist embeds within her therapy setting and those interferences that the patient establishes out of a need to re-create previous environments of stymied or dangerous give and take. A common example of the latter would be the patient who sees paying the therapist as humiliating, due to a belief that the therapist provides friend-ship or parenting that a more worthy person would be offered as a gift, either by the therapist or by others in her life. Patients who are fearful of receiving human gifts from others may insist that the therapist's requirement of payment means that the entire relationship lacks any quality of giving; it is nothing but cold, hard business. My patient, described above, picked out the one question I had not directly answered and complained it had humil-iated her enough for her to quit the therapy work; it was reasonable for me to wonder whether she had some preference to make of me an ungiving parent from whom she should flee, rather than move into a deeper relationship.

When a therapist utilizes a psychoanalytically disciplined ap-proach to listening and response, there is a danger of re-creating for the patient the shaming experience of being with the facially unresponsive caregiver, from whom one receives little and, of equal importance, to whom one can give little since nothing is wanted or needed. To mitigate this danger, both aspects of which can humiliate the patient and stymie the process, the therapist must provide the patient with a context for understanding the nature of the therapist's listening and response, and those responses the therapist does offer must demonstrate her ongoing involve-ment in the two-person exchange, even through long periods of silence or relative facial quiescence. If providing these things does not begin to build a sense of a listening mien rather than a shamingly removed one, the therapist should begin to wonder whether her patient may have an idiosyncratic need to feel shamed, which is worthy of analytic attention.

Simmel's (1950) consideration of "faithfulness" as a stance that supports ongoing interpersonal giving has relevance for psycho-analytic therapy as an institution. According to Simmel, faithfulness is the attitude through which one maintains a sociological connec-tion even when the initial feelings that supported the relationship do not, at the present moment, exist. Thus, one may maintain a marriage in the absence of passion, because one values the insti-tution. He states:

> [W]hat I mean is that faithfulness itself is a specific psychic state, which is directed toward the continuance of the relation as such, independently of any particular affective or volitional elements that sustain the content of this relation [p. 381].

If we alter Simmel's concept a bit to deemphasize the notion of sustaining a relationship when its *initial* motive disappears and to highlight instead the notion of preserving a relationship through *vicissitudes* of feeling, including wishes to part company or to behave destructively toward the other, the concept has applicability to therapy. In therapy, the "faithful" therapist continues to value the therapeutic endeavor and its principles despite complex crosscurrents of feeling that include hostility, indifference, countertransference love and other such emotions that, untempered by faithfulness to the institution, might profoundly disturb the therapy's course or continuation. Even during the most difficult passages, one attempts to continue one's therapeutic giving out of faithfulness. The patient, too, experiences faithfulness to the institution of the therapy, and thus she attempts to remain open, honest, hardworking, and the like, even when buffeted by emotions propagating destructive behavior. Faithfulness in either participant supports pride, whereas unfaithfulness generally sparks shame, though that most basic and widely distributed assignment of value may be complicated by secondary values born out of pathology or subcultural ethics, so that a person may feel at once that faithfulness is admirable and shameful. Simmel (1950) states:

> Faithfulness is that constitution of the soul (which is constantly moved and lives in a continuous flux), by means of which it fully incorporates into itself the stability of the super-individual form of relation and by means of which it admits to life, as the meaning and value of life, a content which, though created by the soul itself, is, in its form, nevertheless bound to contradict the rhythm or un-rhythm of life as actually lived [p. 387].

Simmel's words are particularly evocative when applied to psychoanalytic therapy because free association, which is the living process of such therapy, explores the "un-rhythm of life as actually lived," and thus the contrast between such "un-rhythm" and the constancy of the therapist's and patient's faithfulness to their endeavor is indeed a great one.

A patient's transferential distortion of the meaning of therapist gifts sometimes stirs anxiety in the therapist by portraying her gifts as if they were inappropriate, thus deserving of shame and guilt. Andrew often took a simple smile and turned it into a statement that I was fascinated by him or particularly delighted to see him that day. At times, he construed ordinary, attentive listening as intense pleasure fueled by erotic interest. It may be difficult for a therapist not to withdraw appropriate human gifts when they are made shameful by a patient's distortion of their meaning, especially if twisted readings of meaning are forced on the therapist abusively by the patient.

Those patients who have been "given too much" by parents who do not maintain generational boundaries or who force burdensome specialness on a child can quicken with anxiety in response to ordinary human giving since they fear the strings attached. Where there is a history of sexual abuse, any giving may lead the patient to dread a descent into overt seduction. Such patients may breed shame in the therapist by attributing all kinds of illicit motives to the therapist's simplest act of giving.

Also important to many therapies will be specific, transference-based fantasies of giving and receiving gifts. An example was one bulimic woman's structuring of the therapy interactions to mimic her bulimic symptom. Every idea or emotional response the therapist gave would be vomited up by the patient as unworthy of digestion, which led to humiliation and anger in the therapist and a need to consider this woman's relationship to giving and receiving as a central issue in the therapy. Early in the therapy, the therapist had privately noted her own countertransference interest in giving more than the previous therapist had, in order to persuade the woman of her value and of the possibility of a working relationship between the two of them, but that effort could soon be seen to be a losing battle, since the woman wanted the new therapist to be "just like the other therapist" who was ungiving or gave what was unworthy of receipt.

Within the community of professionals, referrals operate as gifts. An abundance of referrals (either received or given) brings feelings of pride like those associated with other acts of gift-giving and receiving. Referrals can be given out of appreciation for past gifts (e.g., of teaching, supervision, or therapy) or in anticipation of reciprocity. In treating referrals as gifts, one runs the risk of turning the patient into an object whose needs are not considered or are considered only after the needs of the gift giver and receiver. The acceptance of "bad referrals" also can operate as a gift, which may express appreciation or may create an obligation that the giver of the "bad referral" will send "good referrals" in the future.

CREATIVITY AS GIFTEDNESS: CREATIVITY AND THERAPY

A person brings to therapy a wounded self, which is a source of shame. Therapy seeks to return the person to her creative self and does so through a process that is itself creative. The self that is recovered is one that is not rule-bound and obsessional but is free to find the meaning in inner experience. That self is strengthened through an experience of interaction with a person who values honest exploratory and integrative activity. Both participants take pride in such a process and its products and feel diminished by its disruption.

The psychic material that is explored in psychoanalytic therapy can be seen as welling up from the fund of images and emotion within the self, which is the same source that feeds artistic creativity. Yet Hyde (1979) sees artistic creativity as something experienced as a gift from *outside* the self, as if from God or Nature. It is received by an individual and passed along to others, like any other gift that is borne around a gift circle. Hyde's image of the beggar's bowl conveys his understanding of creativity as a gift. The creative person is the beggar who holds out her bowl and finds it filled, for which bounty she is grateful. Hyde talks of the artist who kisses the ground after a work is completed. She kisses the ground in grateful and humble acknowledgment that the poem written or the drawing penned is a gift received from outside the self. The gift is a blessing.

Both the "inside" and the "outside" points of view are valid with respect to creativity, including the creativity that allows for psychoanalytic therapy. The creative person, whatever her medium, draws on an inner stock of images and emotions. She is aware that this life, which is within her, is a gift. Though it is about her and it is hers to exploit, it is not in any active or deliberate way created by her. What is inside her comes from the outside.

Inner life is a gift that is universal in its existence and universal in a portion of its content. It is also universal in aspects of its operation. The ways in which the elements of the individual's inner life offer themselves to awareness, filling the beggar's bowl, and the chemistry of their interactions, are like the grammar we all use in our speech: they are universal gifts that belong to the structure of the human mind. Though an individual may have no great intelligence, she still has the gift of grammar, in all its complexity, like she has the gifts of dreaming, imagining, and feeling, which may spawn artistic creativity.

The artist knows her work is about the self and about the moments in her life. But she knows as well that parts of the self are as mysterious to their owner and as far from her control as are forces in the natural world around her; she must find a way to receive these parts of the self, to let whatever orders the human mind deliver its images to consciousness, let them mingle, allow them to recombine. Her job is to monitor the many processes and pick and choose among their riches, like a fisherwoman standing attentive beside a teeming stream. Her talent lies in the harvesting. While we all have the gift of inner life, the special giftedness of the creative person is in her ability to receive, appreciate, and order her inner life, in both its universal and idiosyncratic aspects, and to do so in ways that communicate to others, so that others recognize their life in hers and pronounce her "gifted" in her capacities for expression.

Psychoanalytic therapy is a creative process conducted by two. In its beggar's bowl aspect, it differs from other therapies, which tend to impose structures seen as universally applicable without waiting for the individual's structure to reveal itself. How does the creative therapy relate to other creative enterprises? We can talk of creative products that are apart from the self, such as a painting or poem or garden. We can also talk of the "worked-on" self as a creative product. In either case, creativity heals personal woundedness in a number of ways (Broucek, 1991). The creative product (the song, story, essay, or self) is whole; it is not damaged. Even if it portrays damage or recalls damage, its own structure is sound, so it redeems the damaged aspects of self. A traumatized patient once told me she had asked a previous therapist if she ever would be normal. He told her "no" and described for her an image of a shattered vase and then a second image of a vase pieced together. In the second picture, the breakage marks still showed, yet the vase was whole: it was as formed and functional as any other vase might be. Thus, the self that emerges out of a successful therapy does not shed its history; nevertheless, it is sound.

As many have recognized, woundedness may spur creativity; it may cause us to develop that beggar's bowl capacity in ourselves out of a greater than usual need to know its riches. Through creativity, we link with others by way of what is universal both in our wounds and in our wounds' balms. We mend not only our private brokenness, but the brokenness of our bonds to the community.

Creative products such as music or visual art heal in part by presenting to the community the damaged self made whole, thus creating communion between self and other, with both the wounded self and the healed self (symbolized by the intact creative product) as the subject of the communion. Healing also occurs because the creative individual is enhanced by her recognition that her gifts enrich others. She who has much to give feels whole, not ashamed.

Also important to the creative individual is the fact that her gifts give voice to her indwelling self, both in its wounded and its joyful and intact aspects. Creativity speaks from a person's depth and her essence. If that creativity is celebrated by others, then the indwelling self has been celebrated, and it has been acknowledged as a voice that speaks to others and speaks for others; thus, the indwelling self is not isolated or extruded from the community. The interaction between the creative individual and the recipient of that creativity is what Broucek would call a subject–subject interaction, an I–thou connection through which one can heal wounds of objectification or rejection.

Creativity can be used to conceal the self as much as to reveal it. Andrew liked to offer his creative products (often, complex business proposals and plans) as gifts to others. At his first psychotherapy session, he offered the therapist such a gift, which he wished to have received and admired. Further discussion of his creative offerings extended over a long period of time and yielded a picture of his gifts as a distillation of self that occupied a Winnicottian transitional space between self and other. In this middle ground between self and not-self, they served to present only what was good, or even grand, about the self; thus, in Andrew's fantasy, they always commanded an admiring response. In displaying only the idealized facets of the self, the gifts both revealed and concealed, since they masked the imperfect aspects of self. Often, in therapy, Andrew would retreat from discussions of ordinary self-aspects into pleasurable musings about the astounding business ideas he envisioned displaying or offering to others.

Andrew regarded his gifts ambivalently, both as perfected versions of self and as masks or screens limiting contact between the fuller self and others. In the novel *Spring Snow* (Mishima, 1972), which portrays a Japanese society obsessed with social surfaces and ritual interactions, people, especially women, are presented as gifts. Though the gift of a beautiful woman is something splendid, which honors the giver and the receiver, the woman herself is degraded because she has become an object. She is fully objectified, in Broucek's (1991) meaning, because she is not known as a subject but is recognized only by her external features. A gift is a treasured object, as described by Mauss (1950), or it may be a beautiful part of the self offered to another (one's sexuality, one's warmth), but when the whole of a person is construed as a gift given to another by a third party, then the status of gift is that of object and is, therefore, a degradation. Thus, we have the young woman, Satoko, in *Spring Snow,* thinking as she is escorted to an introduction with her betrothed, "She disliked being given a special inspection today, as if she were a bolt of silk intended as a gift" (p. 153).

Though creative connection with others heals wounds of objectification by giving voice to the indwelling self, an objectifying attitude toward the self and its expressions often seems implicated in the production of art. It is said that an artist must subject herself and her work to cold self-scrutiny in order to produce fine art. Hyde (1979) quotes Flannery O'Connor, who described the writer's need to judge her own work without pity: "'The writer has to judge himself with a stranger's eye and a stranger's severity. . . . No art is sunk in the self, but rather, in art the self becomes self-forgetful in order to meet the demands of the thing seen and the thing being made'" (p. 150). At first reading, such a description of the operation of a writer's gifts sounds like self-objectification and also seems to contradict Hyde's notion that gifts are spoiled by objective analysis. Hyde states, for example:

> First, if we define use value as the value we sense in things as we use them and make them a part of our selves, and if exchange value is the value we assign to things as we compare them or alienate them from ourselves then there is something akin to ancient usury in the conversion of use values to exchange values. Second, there is a psychological parallel as well: something related to the spirit of usury lies in the removal of energy from the esemplastic powers and its reinvestment in the analytic or reflective powers [pp. 154–155].

The contradiction between Hyde and O'Connor may be more apparent than real, in that the objective spirit or "stranger's" eye that examines what has come into the artist's bowl is not a distantly analytic, "reckoning" eye, like the eye of the literary agent who may assess the work's "exchange value," but is one that understands the artist's terms and seeks the best way to make them known to others. The objectifying self that looks at its own work from a distance, and looks ruthlessly, is the self that says, "How would this story speak more clearly to others? What does this painting look like if I look with Mary's eye, or Fred's?" Thus, this "objectifying" eye helps the artist move beyond herself and beyond neurotic needs to impair her communication, so that her work can, indeed, be a gift receivable by others.

Another way to conceptualize the artist's relationship to her work is to say that, during moments of critiquing her work, the artist's needs fuse with those of the art itself, so that serving the integrity of the art is all that constitutes the artist's consciousness in that moment. Anything that enhances the art cannot diminish the artist. The artist's mind consists of the requirements of the art.

The self-consciousness that *destroys* gifts is more attentive to the self and its operation than to the work produced, and its consciousness of the self is a determinedly fault-finding one. In contrast, "the stranger's eye" with which the productive artist views her work is an eye that looks more at the work than at the self. Indeed, O'Connor says that the artist, while looking on his work with a stranger's eye, is "self-forgetful," not self-conscious or self-analytic. Thus, while the artist does objectify her work by looking at it as something to be known by others, her objectification aims at making the indwelling self audible to the other, not at muffling its voice.

Creativity fails if neurotic needs lead the artist to deform the structure of the work, rather than let an intact structure communicate about that which has been wounded. Similarly, in therapy, the two-person process at times is dysfunctional and mirrors damage in the participants, and at other times, the process is creative and models wholeness.

Interruption of the creative process can occur when a person cannot receive the gifts that are ready to be plucked from the stream of consciousness. This interference can occur for a variety of reasons. The preconceptual mind (Gendlin, 1962) may frighten its possessor, or she may need to destroy its gifts by devaluing them or by applying principles of organization or measurement that are inappropriate to creative work and destructive to it. Thus, Sidney, who thinks like a research scientist, can make no sense of therapy, which lacks defined goals and outcome measures for each session.

It is also the case that the artist, patient, or therapist may freely receive the gifts of the unconscious, yet remain unable to organize them for expression to self or others. To do the work of organization, to look upon her production with a stranger's eye, may threaten in various ways. The process may feel like an affront to omnipotence. The person feels that whatever wells up from her unconscious mind must be regarded as perfect. She is unable to criticize it without feeling rage or depression. She pretends it is flawless, or she discards it rather than continue the process of working. Reich (1960) gives an example of a talented writer, Daniel K, whose need for immediate acclaim for his creative work led to rushed, flawed work (pp. 217–218). Here, the person's genuine artistic gifts did not serve to heal narcissistic wounds but led only to work that mirrored them in its deficient structure. Another artist's work may suffer because the artist cannot complete it, which would signify sharing it with the community rather than retaining it as a fully private experience.

All artists presumably struggle with a degree of tension between the wish to find perfection in their product as it is and the effort to improve it, which means seeing perfection as a distant goal toward which to labor, not an immediate attribute of one's creative output. The artist who cannot desist from fine-tuning her work, though she has reached the limits of productive effort, may be as intolerant of imperfection as the artist who denies the need for labor.

In the earlier discussion of therapy and gift giving, I considered the giving of the "human gifts" of humor, warmth, or understanding between therapist and patient. Part of what any person has to offer another is her own "giftedness," that is, the use she makes of what talent has been given her, which is employed in the creative apprehension of her own or another's mind. That use and sharing of one's giftedness in relation to psychological material is a primary effort and exchange of a productive psychotherapy. Often, when a patient misses an absent therapist or fears termination, it is the creative interchange with another that is the focus of concern, because such an exchange allows the free flowering of the self and is experienced as loving appreciation of the self. Missing the therapist may be most acute when the person is not confident of her ability to maintain a creative stance in the world, by which I mean an experience of oneself in the world that allows for relatively full integration of one's feelings and ideas. Creative exchange can also be missed and mourned when a relationship continues, but is troubled. Either participant's withdrawal from a creative interaction may evoke strong anger in the other and shame over the disruption of relatedness. Some of the work of any treatment is the analysis of such disruptions.

My own writing about shame sprang from a research paper not on shame, but on disgust, undertaken years ago. I enjoyed the experience of delving into a particular emotion state in all its guises and wanted to stay with that effort in writing a doctoral dissertation. An adviser nudged me in the direction of an emotion less associated with the unpalatable and more integratable with the self-psychological theory much under discussion at that time and since.

Compared with disgust, shame has been harder to contemplate, because it occurs freely and in many configurations and is more linked with pain than is disgust, though it is important to recall as well shame's links with pleasure and excitement and with preservation of privacy and honor. Shame also protects links with community, both honorably, when the community is a moral one, and dishonorably, when shame over potential ostracism causes us to uphold what we ought to detest, a topic well-considered by the novelist Ishiguro (1989) and by Lynd (1958). Whenever the self must be made smaller, less steady, less significant, or less spontaneous, whenever a deficiency must be located within the self and not externally, shame will serve that purpose. Such needs may derive from our common evolutionary past, which connects us even with the canine who shows shamelike submission when attacked. And it may derive from our links, by way of the superego, to a particular community and its values, whether sound or corrupt, as well as from the idiosyncratic elements in our personal histories.

To write a book is always a personal quest, undertaken for personal reasons, which make one willing to labor at length over making sense of a complex area of thought. Writing this book has been an effort at distilling what has been given me, from experiences with patients, my own psychoanalytic therapy, and the writing of colleagues, for all of which I am much indebted. The distillation aims toward a shape of things that is my own, which I pass along by setting it into the stream of shared ideas.

References

Amery, J. (1995), Torture. In: *Art from the Ashes*, ed. L. Langer. New York: Oxford University Press.

Basch, M. (1988), *Understanding Psychotherapy*. New York: Basic Books.

Bell, M. (1985), *Waiting for the End of the World*. New York: Penguin Books.

Brodkey, H. (1994), Translating Brando. *The New Yorker*, October, p. 80.

Broucek, F. (1982), Shame and its relationship to early narcissistic developments. *Internat. J. Psycho-Anal.*, 63:369–378.

———(1991), *Shame and the Self*. New York: Guilford.

Doctorow, E. L. (1974), *Ragtime*. New York: Fawcett Crest.

Erikson, E. (1963), *Childhood and Society*. New York: Norton.

Esman, A. (1989), Psychoanalysis and general psychiatry: Obsessive-compulsive disorder as paradigm. *J. Amer. Psychoanal. Assn.*, 37:319–336.

Fenigstein, A., Scheier, M. & Buss, A. (1975), Public and private self-consciousness: Assessment and theory. *J. Consult. & Clin. Psychol.*, 43:522–527.

Freud, S. (1910), Five lectures on psycho-analysis. *Standard Edition*, 11:1–55. London: Hogarth Press, 1957.

Gedo, J. (1975), Forms of idealization in the analytic transference. *J. Amer. Psychoanal. Assn.*, 23:485–505.

Gendlin, E. (1962), *Experiencing and the Creation of Meaning*. New York: The Free Press of Glencoe.

Gill, M. (1994), *Psychoanalysis in Transition*. Hillsdale, NJ: The Analytic Press.

Goldberg, A. (1989), The shame of Hamlet and Oedipus. *Psychoanal. Rev.*, 76:581–603.

Grinker, R., Sr. (1955), Growth inertia and shame: Therapeutic implications and dangers. *Internat. J. Psycho-Anal.*, 36:242–253.

Hibbard, S. (1994), An empirical study of the differential roles of libidinous and aggressive shame components in normality and pathology. *Psychoanal. Psychol.*, 11:449–474.

Hyde, L. (1979), *The Gift: Imagination and the Erotic Life of Property*. New York: Vintage Books.

Ishiguro, K. (1989), *The Remains of the Day*. New York: Vintage International.

Izard, C. (1971), *The Face of Emotion*. New York: Appleton-Century-Crofts.

James, W. (1890), *The Principles of Psychology, Vol. 1*. New York: Holt.

Kaufman, G. (1989), *The Psychology of Shame*. New York: Springer.

Kernberg, O. (1975), *Borderline Conditions and Pathological Narcissism*. New York: Aronson.

Kincaid, J. (1994), Xuela. *The New Yorker*, May, pp. 82–92.

Kingston, M. (1977), *The Woman Warrior*. New York: Vintage Books.

Kinston, W. (1980), A theoretical and technical approach to narcissistic disturbance. *Internat. J. Psycho-Anal.*, 61:383–394.

———(1982), An intrapsychic developmental schema for narcissistic disturbance. *Internat. Rev. Psycho-Anal.*, 9:253–261.

————(1983), A theoretical context for shame. *Internat. J. Psycho-Anal.,* 64:213–226.

————(1987), The shame of narcissism. In: *The Many Faces of Shame,* ed. D. Nathanson. New York: Guilford.

Knapp, P. (1967), Purging and curbing: An inquiry into disgust, satiety, and shame. *J. Nerv. & Ment. Dis.,* 144:514–534.

Kohut, H. (1971), *The Analysis of the Self.* New York: International Universities Press.

————(1972), Thoughts on narcissism and narcissistic rage. *The Psychoanalytic Study of the Child,* 27:360–400. New Haven, CT: Yale University Press.

————(1984), *How Does Analysis Cure?* ed. A. Goldberg & P. Stepansky. Chicago: University of Chicago Press.

Lasch, C. (1992), For shame. *The New Republic,* August, p. 10.

Lee, H. (1960), *To Kill a Mockingbird.* New York: J. B. Lippincott Company.

Lewis, H. (1971), *Shame and Guilt in Neurosis.* New York: International Universities Press.

Lewis, M. (1992), *Shame, the Exposed Self.* New York: The Free Press.

Lynd, H. (1958), *On Shame and the Search for Identity.* New York: Harcourt, Brace.

Markson, E. (1993), Depression and moral masochism. *Internat. J. Psycho-Anal.,* 74:931–940.

Mauss, M. (1950), *The Gift,* trans. W. D. Halls. New York: Norton, 1990.

Mayman, M. (1974), The shame experience, the shame dynamic, and shame personalities in psychotherapy. Presented as the George Klein Memorial Address, American Psychological Association Annual Meeting.

Miller, S. (1985), *The Shame Experience.* Hillsdale, NJ: The Analytic Press.

————(1988), Humiliation and shame: Comparing two affect states as indicators of narcissistic stress. *Bull. Menn. Clin.,* 52:40–51.

————(1989), Shame as an impetus to the creation of conscience. *Internat. J. Psycho-Anal.,* 70:231–244.

————(1993), Disgust reactions: Their determinants and manifestations in treatment. *Contemp. Psychoanal.,* 29:711–735.

Miller, W. (1993), *Humiliation.* Ithaca, NY: Cornell University Press.

Mishima, Y. (1972), *Spring Snow.* New York: Vintage International, 1990.

Modell, A. (1968), *Object Love and Reality.* New York: International Universities Press.

Morrison, A. (1987), The eye turned inward: Shame and the self. In: *The Many Faces of Shame,* ed. D. Nathanson. New York: Guilford.

————(1989), *Shame: The Underside of Narcissism.* Hillsdale, NJ: The Analytic Press.

Nathanson, D., ed. (1987), *The Many Faces of Shame.* New York: Guilford.

————(1992), *Shame and Pride.* New York: Norton.

Novick, J. & Novick, K. (1991), Some comments on masochism and the delusion of omnipotence from a developmental perspective. *J. Amer. Psychoanal. Assn.,* 39:307–331.

Novick, K. & Novick, J. (1987), The essence of masochism. *The Psychoanalytic Study of the Child,* 42:353–384. New Haven, CT: Yale University Press.

Piers, G. & Singer, M. (1953), *Shame and Guilt.* Springfield, IL: Charles C. Thomas.

Pizer, S. (1992), The negotiation of paradox in the analytic process. *Psychoanal. Dial.,* 2:215–240.

Reich, A. (1960), Pathologic forms of self-esteem regulation. *The Psychoanalytic Study of the Child,* 15:215–232. New York: International Universities Press.

Salzman, L. (1980), *Treatment of the Obsessive Personality.* New York: Aronson.

Schafer, R. (1960), The loving and beloved superego in Freud's structural theory. *The Psychoanalytic Study of the Child,* 15:163–188. New York: International Universities Press.

———(1967), Ideals, the ego ideal, and the ideal self. In: *Motives and Thought,* ed. R. Holt. *Psychological Issues, 5,* No. 2–3. New York: International Universities Press, pp. 131–174.

Schneider, C. (1977), *Shame, Exposure and Privacy.* Boston: Beacon Press.

Schore, A. (1994), *Affect Regulation and the Origin of the Self.* Hillsdale, NJ: Lawrence Erlbaum Associates.

Shapiro, D. (1965), *Neurotic Styles.* New York: Basic Books.

———(1981), *Autonomy and Rigid Character.* New York: Basic Books.

Simmel, G. (1950), On faithfulness and gratitude. In: *The Sociology of Georg Simmel.* Glencoe, IL: The Free Press.

Socarides, D. & Stolorow, R. (1984/1985), Affects and selfobjects. *The Annual of Psychoanalysis,* 12/13:105–120. New York: International Universities Press.

Spero, M. (1984), Shame: An object-relational formulation. *The Psychoanalytic Study of the Child,* 39:259–282. New Haven, CT: Yale University Press.

Tomkins, S. (1963), *Affect/Imagery/Consciousness, Vol. 2.* New York: Springer.

White, G. M. & Kirkpatrick, J., eds. (1985), *Person, Self, and Experience.* Los Angeles: University of California Press.

Wilbur, R. (1988), Mind. In: *New and Collected Poems.* New York: Harcourt Brace Jovanovich.

Winnicott, D. (1965), *The Family and Individual Development.* New York: Basic Books.

Wurmser, L. (1981), *The Mask of Shame.* Baltimore: The Johns Hopkins University Press.

Zerbe, K. (1993), *The Body Betrayed.* Carlsbad, CA: Gurze Books.

Index

A

Abandonment, 178–179, 207–208
Abuse, effects of on groups, 184–185.
    see also Sexual abuse
Adoption, 112, 116, 124, 127
Affect, 15, 20, 100, 166, 181. *see also*
    Basic affects theory
  adult character stances and, 171
  anxiety and, 157–158
  narcissistic disturbances and,
    126–129
  need to disavow, 181
  shame and, 2, 24, 156–158, 208,
    213
  states, caregiver responsiveness
    and, 102–103
Aggression, 49, 74, 140, 193, 198,
    199, 210
  appropriate expressions of, 165
  conflict and, 47
  self and, 9–10
Alienation, 54, 65, 208
Amery, J., 169, *231*
Anxiety, 41, 45, 46, 47, 72, 102, 118,
    152, 178, 192, 209, 221
  affect and, 157–158
  developmental issues and, 156–158
Autonomy, 40, 104, 105
  obsessive-compulsive dynamics and,
    41, 80

B

Basch, M., 22, *231*
Basic affects theory, 30. *see also* Self-
    stopping theories
  "additive" theories of emotion and,
    15–16
  core affects and, 11–12, 14, 100,
    122
  guilt and, compared to shame,
    14–15
  Miller on, 13–14

Bell, M., 101, *231*
Brodkey, H., 196, *231*
Broucek, F., 3, 18, 20, 23, 26, 28, 31,
    50, 87, 90, 96, 98, 108, 156,
    160, 161, 186, 219, 224, 226,
    231
  objectification and, 7, 47–48, 74,
    175
  on objective self-awareness, 27–28,
    108
  on pathological narcissism, 122
  on the sense of self, 17, 76–77
  on types of narcissistic disturbance,
    113–114, 154
Buss, A., 209, *231*

C

Caregiver responsiveness, 28, 31, 153,
    166, 205. *see also* Infant;
    Infantile exhibitionism;
    Objectification; Objective self-
    awareness;
    Obsessive-compulsive dynamics
  caregiver deficiencies and, 49–50,
    70, 143, 161–163
  disgust and, 25, 186–187
  empathy and, 91, 102–103
  helplessness and, 205–206
  indwelling self and, 155–156
  narcissistic disturbances and, 107,
    158
  sense of self and, 20, 22
  still-face adult and, 22–23, 29, 155
Cognition, 15, 18, 161
Cognitive development, 101
Conscience. *see* Superego
Contempt, 21, 22
Creativity, 227
  indwelling self and, 225, 226
  psychoanalytic therapy and, 224,
    225–226, 228–229
  self and, 224–226, 229

235